Performance Programs Company
"The New Standard for Prelicense Preparation"

presents its

PowerPoint Presentation
to
Principles of Real Estate Practice in Georgia

2nd Edition by Mettling, Cusic, and Stanfill

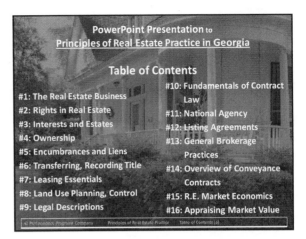

PowerPoint Presentation to
Principles of Real Estate Practice in Georgia

Table of Contents

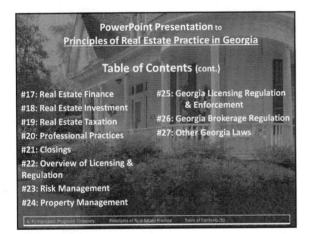

PowerPoint Presentation to
Principles of Real Estate Practice in Georgia

Table of Contents (cont.)

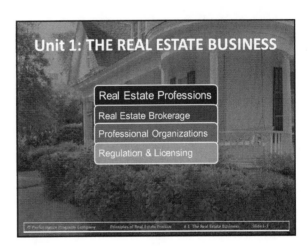

Unit 1: THE REAL ESTATE BUSINESS

Real Estate Professions

Real Estate Brokerage

Professional Organizations

Regulation & Licensing

 # 1:
The Real Estate Business

Real Estate Professions

Real Estate Brokerage

Professional Organizations

Regulation & Licensing

Real Estate Professions

Real estate activities

❑ Create
❑ Improve
❑ Manage
❑ Maintain
❑ Demolish
❑ Own
❑ Regulate
❑ Transfer

 # 1:
The Real Estate Business

Real Estate Professions

Real Estate Brokerage

Professional Organizations

Regulation & Licensing

Real Estate Professions

Property type specializations

❑ Residential
❑ Residential income
❑ Office
❑ Retail
❑ Industrial
❑ Farm and ranch
❑ Special purpose
❑ Land

 # 1:
The Real Estate Business

Real Estate Professions

Real Estate Brokerage

Professional Organizations

Regulation & Licensing

Real Estate Brokerage

❑ Procure a seller or landlord for a buyer or tenant, or a buyer or tenant for an owner or landlord

Forms of specialization

❑ By property type – residential, office, etc.
❑ geographical area – southern suburbs, etc.
❑ transaction type – lease,
❑ client type – multi-market users, small tenants, etc.
❑ business type – restaurants, relocations, etc.
❑ form of client relationship – brokerage, management, etc.

 # 1:
The Real Estate Business

Real Estate Professions

Real Estate Brokerage

Professional Organizations

Regulation & Licensing

Real Estate Brokerage

Skills and knowledge

❑ Market conditions
❑ Law
❑ Financing
❑ Marketing
❑ Ethics
❑ Selling
❑ Communications
❑ Computer / mobile device usage
❑ Social media
❑ Other skills

 # 1:
The Real Estate Business

Real Estate Professions

Real Estate Brokerage

Professional Organizations

Regulation & Licensing

Professional Organizations

Purpose: to promote interests of practitioners and enhance professional standing

Principal organizations:
❑ National Association of Realtors
  ▪ NAR-affiliated Institutes and Councils
❑ National Association of Home Builders
❑ American Society of Appraisers
❑ International Association of Assessing Officers
❑ Association of Real Estate License Law Officials
❑ Building Owners and Managers Association
❑ International Council of Shopping Centers
❑ Mortgage Bankers Association of America

 # 1:
The Real Estate Business

Real Estate Professions

Real Estate Brokerage

Professional Organizations

Regulation & Licensing

Regulation & Licensing

Regulation of business practices
❑ All facets are regulated by federal, state, local laws
❑ Practitioners must understand laws and adapt practices accordingly

Types of laws to understand
❑ License laws
❑ Agency and disclosure laws
❑ Contracts
❑ Environmental
❑ Fair housing
❑ Codes of ethics

 # 1:
The Real Estate Business

Real Estate Professions

Real Estate Brokerage

Professional Organizations

Regulation & Licensing

Regulation & Licensing

Real estate license laws

❑ Primary body of laws and regulations governing licensure and conduct of brokers and agents

❑ License laws administered and enforced under the jurisdiction of the state real estate commission or related governmental entity

---

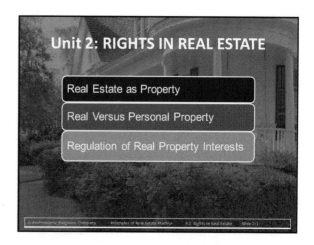

Unit 2: RIGHTS IN REAL ESTATE

Real Estate as Property

Real Versus Personal Property

Regulation of Real Property Interests

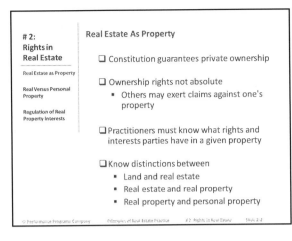

Real Estate As Property

2:
Rights in Real Estate

Real Estate as Property

Real Versus Personal Property

Regulation of Real Property Interests

❑ Constitution guarantees private ownership

❑ Ownership rights not absolute
  ▪ Others may exert claims against one's property

❑ Practitioners must know what rights and interests parties have in a given property

❑ Know distinctions between
  ▪ Land and real estate
  ▪ Real estate and real property
  ▪ Real property and personal property

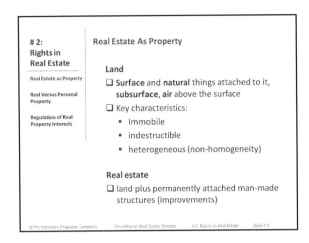

Real Estate As Property

2:
Rights in Real Estate

Real Estate as Property

Real Versus Personal Property

Regulation of Real Property Interests

Land
❑ **Surface** and **natural** things attached to it, **subsurface**, **air** above the surface
❑ Key characteristics:
  ▪ Immobile
  ▪ indestructible
  ▪ heterogeneous (non-homogeneity)

Real estate
❑ land plus permanently attached man-made structures (improvements)

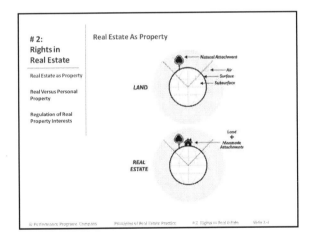

Real Estate As Property

2:
Rights in Real Estate

Real Estate as Property

Real Versus Personal Property

Regulation of Real Property Interests

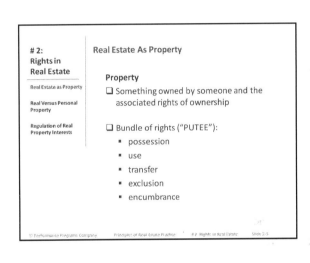

Real Estate As Property

2:
Rights in Real Estate

Real Estate as Property

Real Versus Personal Property

Regulation of Real Property Interests

Property
❑ Something owned by someone and the associated rights of ownership

❑ Bundle of rights ("PUTEE"):
  ▪ possession
  ▪ use
  ▪ transfer
  ▪ exclusion
  ▪ encumbrance

Real Estate As Property

2:
Rights in Real Estate

Real Estate as Property

Real Versus Personal Property

Regulation of Real Property Interests

THE BUNDLE OF RIGHTS

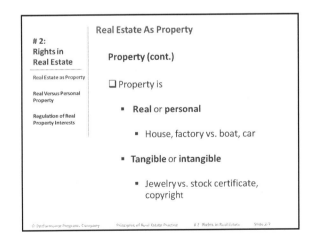

Real Estate As Property

2:
Rights in Real Estate

Real Estate as Property

Real Versus Personal Property

Regulation of Real Property Interests

Property (cont.)

❑ Property is
  ▪ **Real** or **personal**
    ▪ House, factory vs. boat, car
  ▪ **Tangible** or **intangible**
    ▪ Jewelry vs. stock certificate, copyright

 # 2:
Rights in
Real Estate

Real Estate as Property

Real Versus Personal Property

Regulation of Real Property Interests

Real Estate As Property

Real property rights

❑ Any of the **bundle of rights**: applied to

- Airspace = **air rights**
- Surface = **surface rights**
- Subsurface = **subsurface / mineral rights**

 # 2:
Rights in
Real Estate

Real Estate as Property

Real Versus Personal Property

Regulation of Real Property Interests

Real Estate As Property

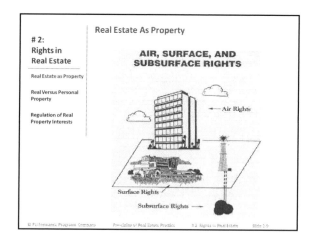

 # 2:
Rights in
Real Estate

Real Estate as Property

Real Versus Personal Property

Regulation of Real Property Interests

Real Estate As Property

Water rights

❑ Doctrine of Prior Appropriation

- State controls water usage

- Grants usage permits

 # 2:
Rights in
Real Estate

Real Estate as Property

Real Versus Personal Property

Regulation of Real Property Interests

Real Estate As Property

Water rights: littoral and riparian

❑ **Littoral rights**

- Applies to **seas & lakes**

- Abutting property owners **own land to high water mark** of shoreline

- State owns underlying land

 # 2:
Rights in
Real Estate

Real Estate as Property

Real Versus Personal Property

Regulation of Real Property Interests

Real Estate As Property

Water rights: littoral and riparian (cont.)

❑ **Riparian rights**
- Applies to **rivers & streams**

- If **navigable**:
  - abutting property owners own land to water's edge; state owns underlying land;

- If **non-navigable**,
  - owner owns land to midpoint of waterway

 # 2:
Rights in
Real Estate

Real Estate as Property

Real Versus Personal Property

Regulation of Real Property Interests

Real Estate As Property

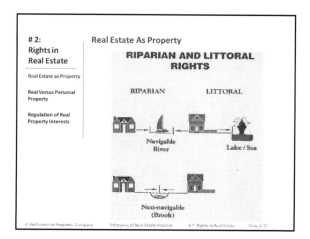

**# 2:
Rights in
Real Estate**

Real Estate as Property

Real Versus Personal
Property

Regulation of Real
Property Interests

Real Versus Personal Property

❑ Item is real or personal property depending on "attachment" criterion and other circumstances

Fixtures
❑ Personal property converted to real property by attachment

Differentiation criteria
❑ Intention
❑ Adaptation
❑ Functionality
❑ Relationship of parties
❑ Contract provisions

**# 2:
Rights in
Real Estate**

Real Estate as Property

Real Versus Personal
Property

Regulation of Real
Property Interests

Real Versus Personal Property

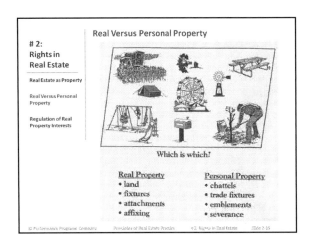

Which is which?

Real Property	Personal Property
• land	• chattels
• fixtures	• trade fixtures
• attachments	• emblements
• affixing	• severance

**# 2:
Rights in
Real Estate**

Real Estate as Property

Real Versus Personal
Property

Regulation of Real
Property Interests

Real Versus Personal Property

Trade fixtures

❑ **Personal property** temporarily attached to real estate to conduct business
❑ Item(s) to be removed at some point
❑ Example: grocery store refrigerators

Emblements

❑ Plants or crops considered **personal property** since human intervention is necessary for planting, harvesting

---

**# 2:
Rights in
Real Estate**

Real Estate as Property

Real Versus Personal
Property

Regulation of Real
Property Interests

Real Versus Personal Property

Factory-built housing

❑ Offsite, factory-built dwelling units transported, assembled on property site

 ▪ **Mobile home** – old name for units that can be moved from site to site

 ▪ **Manufactured home** – factory-built housing conforming to HUD standards

 ▪ Units are real or personal property

  ○ Real property if permanently affixed to ground; otherwise it is personal property

 ▪ Licensees should know local laws before marketing and selling

---

**# 2:
Rights in
Real Estate**

Real Estate as Property

Real Versus Personal
Property

Regulation of Real
Property Interests

Real Versus Personal Property

Conversion

❑ Transforming real property to personal property through **severance**

 ▪ Eg, cutting down a tree

❑ Transforming personal property to real property through **affixing**

 ▪ Eg, installing a pool filter

**# 2:
Rights in
Real Estate**

Real Estate as Property

Real Versus Personal
Property

Regulation of Real
Property Interests

Regulation of Real Property Interests

Federal regulation

❑ Grants rights of ownership
❑ Controls broad land usage standards
❑ Regulates anti-discrimination laws

 ▪ Examples: land grants; federal flood zones; fair housing laws; FHA; EPA

State regulation

❑ Governs real estate business
❑ Sets regional usage standards

 ▪ Examples: license laws; water rights; development regulation

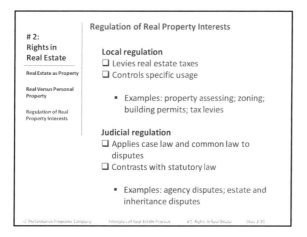

 # 2:
Rights in
Real Estate

Real Estate as Property

Real Versus Personal
Property

Regulation of Real
Property Interests

Regulation of Real Property Interests

Local regulation
- ❑ Levies real estate taxes
- ❑ Controls specific usage

  - ▪ Examples: property assessing; zoning; building permits; tax levies

Judicial regulation
- ❑ Applies case law and common law to disputes
- ❑ Contrasts with statutory law

  - ▪ Examples: agency disputes; estate and inheritance disputes

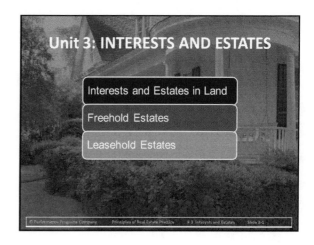

Unit 3: INTERESTS AND ESTATES

Interests and Estates in Land

Freehold Estates

Leasehold Estates

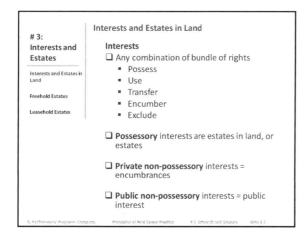

 # 3:
Interests and
Estates

Interests and Estates in
Land

Freehold Estates

Leasehold Estates

Interests and Estates in Land

Interests
- ❑ Any combination of bundle of rights
  - ▪ Possess
  - ▪ Use
  - ▪ Transfer
  - ▪ Encumber
  - ▪ Exclude

- ❑ **Possessory** interests are estates in land, or estates

- ❑ **Private non-possessory** interests = encumbrances

- ❑ **Public non-possessory** interests = public interest

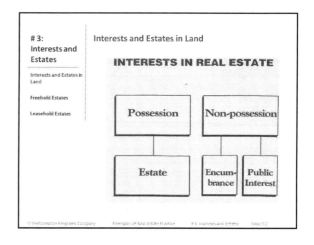

 # 3:
Interests and
Estates

Interests and Estates in
Land

Freehold Estates

Leasehold Estates

Interests and Estates in Land

INTERESTS IN REAL ESTATE

Possession — Estate

Non-possession — Encumbrance, Public Interest

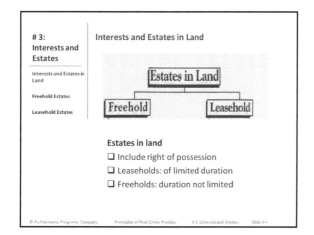

 # 3:
Interests and
Estates

Interests and Estates in
Land

Freehold Estates

Leasehold Estates

Interests and Estates in Land

Estates in Land — Freehold, Leasehold

Estates in land
- ❑ Include right of possession
- ❑ Leaseholds: of limited duration
- ❑ Freeholds: duration not limited

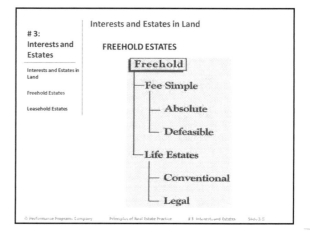

 # 3:
Interests and
Estates

Interests and Estates in
Land

Freehold Estates

Leasehold Estates

Interests and Estates in Land

FREEHOLD ESTATES

Freehold
- Fee Simple
  - Absolute
  - Defeasible
- Life Estates
  - Conventional
  - Legal

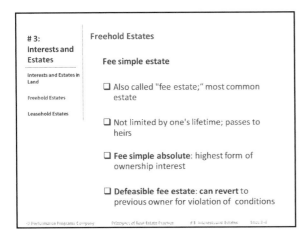

 # 3:
Interests and Estates

Interests and Estates in Land

Freehold Estates

Leasehold Estates

Freehold Estates

Fee simple estate

❑ Also called "fee estate;" most common estate

❑ Not limited by one's lifetime; passes to heirs

❑ **Fee simple absolute**: highest form of ownership interest

❑ **Defeasible fee estate**: can revert to previous owner for violation of conditions

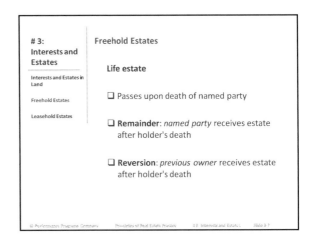

 # 3:
Interests and Estates

Interests and Estates in Land

Freehold Estates

Leasehold Estates

Freehold Estates

Life estate

❑ Passes upon death of named party

❑ **Remainder**: *named party* receives estate after holder's death

❑ **Reversion**: *previous owner* receives estate after holder's death

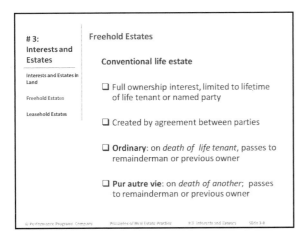

 # 3:
Interests and Estates

Interests and Estates in Land

Freehold Estates

Leasehold Estates

Freehold Estates

Conventional life estate

❑ Full ownership interest, limited to lifetime of life tenant or named party

❑ Created by agreement between parties

❑ **Ordinary**: on *death of life tenant*, passes to remainderman or previous owner

❑ **Pur autre vie**: on *death of another*; passes to remainderman or previous owner

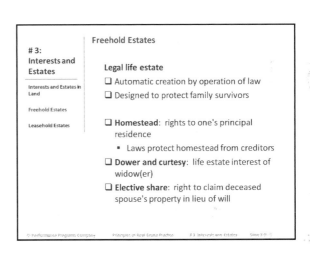

 # 3:
Interests and Estates

Interests and Estates in Land

Freehold Estates

Leasehold Estates

Freehold Estates

Legal life estate

❑ Automatic creation by operation of law

❑ Designed to protect family survivors

❑ **Homestead**: rights to one's principal residence
  ▪ Laws protect homestead from creditors

❑ **Dower and curtesy**: life estate interest of widow(er)

❑ **Elective share**: right to claim deceased spouse's property in lieu of will

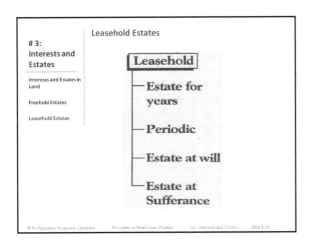

 # 3:
Interests and Estates

Interests and Estates in Land

Freehold Estates

Leasehold Estates

Leasehold Estates

Leasehold

— Estate for years

— Periodic

— Estate at will

— Estate at Sufferance

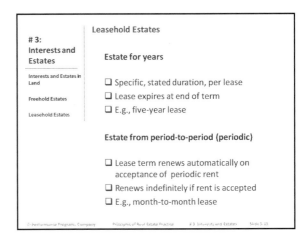

 # 3:
Interests and Estates

Interests and Estates in Land

Freehold Estates

Leasehold Estates

Leasehold Estates

Estate for years

❑ Specific, stated duration, per lease

❑ Lease expires at end of term

❑ E.g., five-year lease

Estate from period-to-period (periodic)

❑ Lease term renews automatically on acceptance of periodic rent

❑ Renews indefinitely if rent is accepted

❑ E.g., month-to-month lease

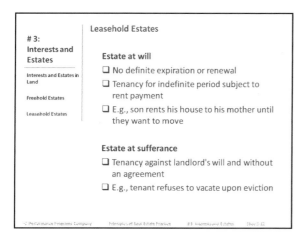

 # 3:
Interests and Estates

Interests and Estates in Land

Freehold Estates

Leasehold Estates

Leasehold Estates

Estate at will

❑ No definite expiration or renewal

❑ Tenancy for indefinite period subject to rent payment

❑ E.g., son rents his house to his mother until they want to move

Estate at sufferance

❑ Tenancy against landlord's will and without an agreement

❑ E.g., tenant refuses to vacate upon eviction

Unit 4: OWNERSHIP

Sole Ownership
Co-Ownership
Estates in Trust
Ownership by Business Entities
Condominiums
Cooperatives
Time-Shares

 # 4:
Ownership

Sole Ownership

Co-Ownership

Estates in Trust

Ownership by Business Entities

Condominiums

Cooperatives

Time-Shares

Sole Ownership

Sole ownership
❑ Tenancy in severalty

Co-ownership
❑ Tenancy in common

❑ Joint tenancy

❑ Tenancy by the entireties

❑ Community property

❑ Tenancy in partnership

 # 4:
Ownership

Sole Ownership

Co-Ownership

Estates in Trust

Ownership by Business Entities

Condominiums

Cooperatives

Time-Shares

Sole Ownership

Tenancy in severalty

❑ Sole ownership of a freehold estate

❑ Single-party ownership; passes to heirs

 # 4:
Ownership

Sole Ownership

Co-Ownership

Estates in Trust

Ownership by Business Entities

Condominiums

Cooperatives

Time-Shares

Co-Ownership

❑ Ownership by two or more owners

Tenancy in common
❑ Co-tenants enjoy individual, undivided interests

❑ Any ownership share possible

❑ No survivorship

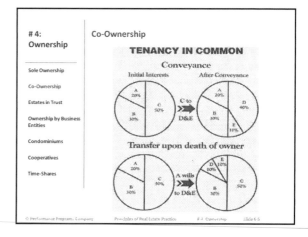

 # 4:
Ownership

Sole Ownership

Co-Ownership

Estates in Trust

Ownership by Business Entities

Condominiums

Cooperatives

Time-Shares

Co-Ownership

 # 4: Ownership

Sole Ownership

Co-Ownership

Estates in Trust

Ownership by Business Entities

Condominiums

Cooperatives

Time-Shares

Co-Ownership

Joint tenancy

❏ 2+ persons own collectively as if a single party

❏ Defining characteristics

- **Unity of ownership** – tenants hold a single title
- **Equal ownership** – each tenant owns equal shares
- **How to convey** -- may convey to outside party, but only as a tenant-in-common interest
- Possible **right of survivorship**– interests pass to surviving joint tenants; may be automatic, or depend on a state's laws

---

 # 4: Ownership

Sole Ownership

Co-Ownership

Estates in Trust

Ownership by Business Entities

Condominiums

Cooperatives

Time-Shares

Co-Ownership

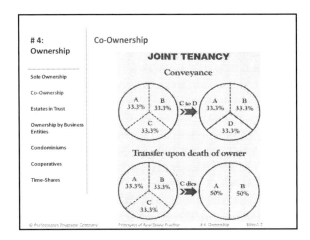

 # 4: Ownership

Sole Ownership

Co-Ownership

Estates in Trust

Ownership by Business Entities

Condominiums

Cooperatives

Time-Shares

Co-Ownership

Joint tenancy

❏ Creation of joint tenancy: the four unities

- **Unity of time** – all tenants must acquire interest at same time
- **Unity of title** – all tenants must acquire interest via one deed of conveyance
- **Unity of interest** – parties must receive equal, undivided interests
- **Unity of possession** – all parties must receive same rights of possession

---

 # 4: Ownership

Sole Ownership

Co-Ownership

Estates in Trust

Ownership by Business Entities

Condominiums

Cooperatives

Time-Shares

Co-Ownership

Tenancy by the entireties

❏ Equal, undivided interest jointly owned by **husband and wife**

❏ Estate passes automatically to spouse

❏ Terminated by

- divorce
- death
- mutual agreement
- joint debt judgments

❏ Still being determined in many states if this applies to same-sex spouses

---

 # 4: Ownership

Sole Ownership

Co-Ownership

Estates in Trust

Ownership by Business Entities

Condominiums

Cooperatives

Time-Shares

Co-Ownership

Community property

❏ Joint ownership of property by spouses as opposed to separate property

❏ Separate property:

- Property owned before marriage
- Property acquired by gift or inheritance
- Property acquired with separate-property funds
- Income from separate property

 # 4: Ownership

Sole Ownership

Co-Ownership

Estates in Trust

Ownership by Business Entities

Condominiums

Cooperatives

Time-Shares

Co-Ownership

Tenancy in partnership

❏ Ownership by business partners

❏ Grants equal rights to all partners

❏ Property must be used with business

❏ Individual rights not assignable

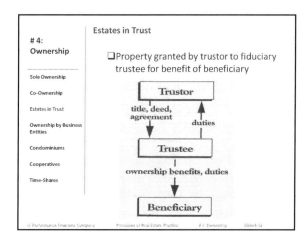

 # 4: Ownership

Sole Ownership
Co-Ownership
Estates in Trust
Ownership by Business Entities
Condominiums
Cooperatives
Time-Shares

Estates in Trust

❏ Property granted by trustor to fiduciary trustee for benefit of beneficiary

Trustor
title, deed, agreement → duties
Trustee
ownership benefits, duties
Beneficiary

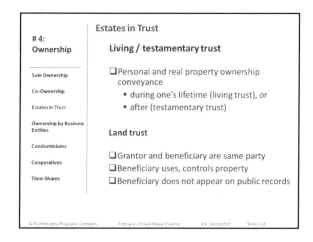

 # 4: Ownership

Sole Ownership
Co-Ownership
Estates in Trust
Ownership by Business Entities
Condominiums
Cooperatives
Time-Shares

Estates in Trust

Living / testamentary trust

❏ Personal and real property ownership conveyance
- during one's lifetime (living trust), or
- after (testamentary trust)

Land trust

❏ Grantor and beneficiary are same party
❏ Beneficiary uses, controls property
❏ Beneficiary does not appear on public records

 # 4: Ownership

Sole Ownership
Co-Ownership
Estates in Trust
Ownership by Business Entities
Condominiums
Cooperatives
Time-Shares

Ownership by Business Entities

❏ Corporation
- Legal entity owned by stockholders
- Officers liable for actions; stockholders only exposed to extent of holdings
- May own real estate in severalty or as tenant in common

❏ Partnership
- 2+ persons work together and share profits
- Not a distinct legal entity; general partners bear full responsibility for debts, obligations
- Both general and limited partnerships may own real estate

 # 4: Ownership

Sole Ownership
Co-Ownership
Estates in Trust
Ownership by Business Entities
Condominiums
Cooperatives
Time-Shares

Ownership by Business Entities

❏ Limited liability company (LLC)
- Income passes to members as individual income
- Members enjoy limited liability
- LLC may own real estate

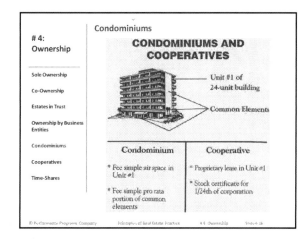

 # 4: Ownership

Sole Ownership
Co-Ownership
Estates in Trust
Ownership by Business Entities
Condominiums
Cooperatives
Time-Shares

Condominiums

CONDOMINIUMS AND COOPERATIVES

Unit #1 of 24-unit building
Common Elements

Condominium	Cooperative
* Fee simple air space in Unit #1	* Proprietary lease in Unit #1
* Fee simple pro rata portion of common elements	* Stock certificate for 1/24th of corporation

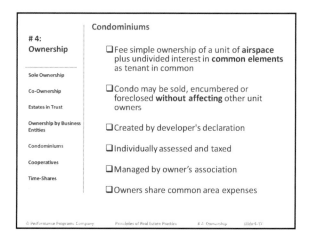

 # 4: Ownership

Sole Ownership
Co-Ownership
Estates in Trust
Ownership by Business Entities
Condominiums
Cooperatives
Time-Shares

Condominiums

❏ Fee simple ownership of a unit of **airspace** plus undivided interest in **common elements** as tenant in common

❏ Condo may be sold, encumbered or foreclosed **without affecting** other unit owners

❏ Created by developer's declaration

❏ Individually assessed and taxed

❏ Managed by owner's association

❏ Owners share common area expenses

 # 4:
Ownership

....

Sole Ownership

Co-Ownership

Estates in Trust

Ownership by Business Entities

Condominiums

Cooperatives

Time-Shares

Cooperatives

❑ Ownership of
- shares in corporation, plus
- proprietary lease in unit

❑ Corporation has sole, undivided ownership

❑ Owners potentially liable for expenses of entire co-op
- creditors may foreclose on entire property

 # 4:
Ownership

....

Sole Ownership

Co-Ownership

Estates in Trust

Ownership by Business Entities

Condominiums

Cooperatives

Time-Shares

Time-Shares

❑ Lease or ownership interest in a property for periodic use by owners or tenants on a scheduled basis

Time share lease

❑ Tenant leases property per lease's schedule

Time share freehold

❑ Tenants in common own undivided interests

❑ Expenses and usage rules set by separate agreement upon acquisition

---

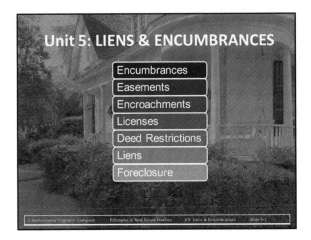

 # 5:
Liens &
Encumbrances

....

Encumbrances

Easements

Encroachments

Licenses

Deed Restrictions

Liens

Foreclosure

Encumbrances

❑ Non-possessory interests limiting the legal owner's rights

❑ Encumbrances do not include possession, thus is a lesser interest than freehold and not an estate

❑ Two overall types of encumbrance:
- Encumbrances that affect use
- Encumbrances that affect ownership, value & transfer

 # 5:
Liens &
Encumbrances

....

Encumbrances

Easements

Encroachments

Licenses

Deed Restrictions

Liens

Foreclosure

Encumbrances

Encumbrances affecting use

❑ Easements
❑ Encroachments
❑ Licenses
❑ Deed restrictions

Encumbrances affecting ownership, value, transfer

❑ Liens
❑ Deed conditions

 # 5:
Liens &
Encumbrances

....

Encumbrances

Easements

Encroachments

Licenses

Deed Restrictions

Liens

Foreclosure

Easements

Characteristics

❑ Rights to use portions of another's property

❑ Burdened party = giver of the easement
❑ Benefited party = receiver of the easement

❑ Cannot own easement over one's own property

❑ Affirmative easement = allow a use
❑ Negative easement = prohibit a use

 # 5:
Liens &
Encumbrances
....
Encumbrances

Easements

Encroachments

Licenses

Deed Restrictions

Liens

Foreclosure

Easements

Types of easements

❑ Easement **appurtenant**
  ▪ Easement by necessity
  ▪ Party wall

❑ Easement in **gross**
  ▪ Personal
  ▪ Commercial

 # 5:
Liens &
Encumbrances

Encumbrances

Easements

Encroachments

Licenses

Deed Restrictions

Liens

Foreclosure

Easements

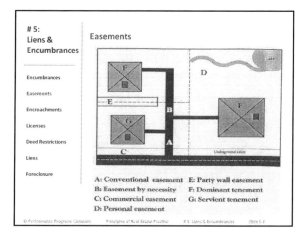

A: Conventional easement   E: Party wall easement
B: Easement by necessity   F: Dominant tenement
C: Commercial easement   G: Servient tenement
D: Personal easement

 # 5:
Liens &
Encumbrances

Encumbrances

Easements

Encroachments

Licenses

Deed Restrictions

Liens

Foreclosure

Easements

Easement appurtenant
❑ Gives right of one owner the right to use portions of adjoining property owned by another

❑ Property benefitting from easement is the **dominant tenement**

❑ Property containing easement is the **servient tenement**

 # 5:
Liens &
Encumbrances

Encumbrances

Easements

Encroachments

Licenses

Deed Restrictions

Liens

Foreclosure

Easements

Easement appurtenant (cont.)

❑ Appurtenant = attaches to the real property estate

❑ Rights and obligations of dominant and servient tenement transfer automatically with title conveyance of either property

❑ Easement use is not exclusive to the dominant tenement; both may use

---

 # 5:
Liens &
Encumbrances
....
Encumbrances

Easements

Encroachments

Licenses

Deed Restrictions

Liens

Foreclosure

Easements

Easement appurtenant (cont.)

❑ **Easement by necessity**: granted out of necessity, i.e., to **landlocked** owners
  ▪ Landlocked party is dominant tenement; property containing thoroughfare access is servient tenement

❑ **Party wall**: common wall shared by two separate owners along a property boundary

---

 # 5:
Liens &
Encumbrances

Encumbrances

Easements

Encroachments

Licenses

Deed Restrictions

Liens

Foreclosure

Easements

Easements in gross
❑ A right to use property; **does not attach to** the real estate
❑ Two types: **personal** and **commercial**

❑ **Personal**:
  ▪ **Not revocable** as with a license
  ▪ **Not transferrable**
  ▪ **Ends on death** of easement holder

  ▪ E.g., use of pathway to the beach

 # 5:
Liens &
Encumbrances

Encumbrances

Easements

Encroachments

Licenses

Deed Restrictions

Liens

Foreclosure

Easements

Easements in gross (cont.)

❑ **Commercial**
  ▪ granted to **businesses**
  ▪ duration is indeterminable
  ▪ easement right is transferrable, assignable

  ▪ E.g., utility lines across frontage of property

 # 5:
Liens &
Encumbrances

Encumbrances

Easements

Encroachments

Licenses

Deed Restrictions

Liens

Foreclosure

Easements

Easement creation

❑ Easements created by

  ▪ voluntary action

  ▪ court decree by necessity (landlocked)

  ▪ court order by prescription

  ▪ eminent domain & condemnation

 # 5:
Liens &
Encumbrances

Encumbrances

Easements

Encroachments

Licenses

Deed Restrictions

Liens

Foreclosure

Easements

Easement creation (cont.)
❑ Easements by prescription
  ▪ Property used **without permission** over a **statutory period** qualifies for easement creation **regardless of owner's wishes**

❑ Qualifies if use is
  ▪ Adverse and hostile (without permission)
  ▪ Open and notorious
  ▪ Continuous, uninterrupted

  ❑ Prescription period varies by state

 # 5:
Liens &
Encumbrances

Encumbrances

Easements

Encroachments

Licenses

Deed Restrictions

Liens

Foreclosure

Easements

Easement termination

❑ Easements terminated by:
  ▪ Express release by benefitting party
  ▪ Merger of properties
  ▪ Property abandoned by dominant party
  ▪ Condemnation via eminent domain
  ▪ Change/cessation of purpose for easement
  ▪ Destruction of an easement structure (party wall)
  ▪ Non-use of an easement by prescription

 # 5:
Liens &
Encumbrances

Encumbrances

Easements

Encroachments

Licenses

Deed Restrictions

Liens

Foreclosure

Encroachments

❑ Unauthorized intrusions of one owner's real property onto another's

❑ May require survey to detect

❑ May become prescriptive easements if not remedied over prescription period

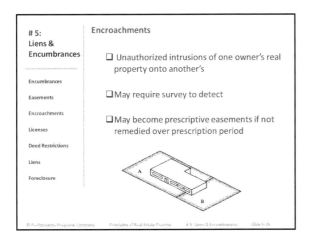

 # 5:
Liens &
Encumbrances

Encumbrances

Easements

Encroachments

Licenses

Deed Restrictions

Liens

Foreclosure

Licenses

❑ Personal rights to use / access a property
❑ Do not attach
❑ Non-transferrable
❑ Revocable
❑ Cease upon death of either party

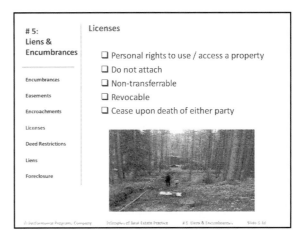

 # 5:
Liens &
Encumbrances

- Encumbrances
- Easements
- Encroachments
- Licenses
- Deed Restrictions
- Liens
- Foreclosure

Deed Restrictions

- ❑ Conditions and covenants imposed on a property by deed or subdivision plat
- ❑ Goes with the property upon transfer
- ❑ Established to control quality and standards of a property or subdivision
- ❑ Apply to land use, type of structure, setbacks, minimum house size, etc.

 # 5:
Liens &
Encumbrances

- Encumbrances
- Easements
- Encroachments
- Licenses
- Deed Restrictions
- Liens
- Foreclosure

Deed Restrictions

Conditions
- ❑ Created upon property transfer
- ❑ If violated, ownership may revert to previous owner

Covenants
- ❑ Created by mutual agreement
- ❑ Enforceable by injunction

 # 5:
Liens &
Encumbrances

- Encumbrances
- Easements
- Encroachments
- Licenses
- Deed Restrictions
- Liens
- Foreclosure

Liens

- ❑ Claims attaching to real and personal property as security for debt

Lien characteristics
- ❑ Recorded on title effectively reducing equity in the amount of the lien
- ❑ Does not convey ownership unless a mortgage in a title theory state
- ❑ Lien attaches to the property
- ❑ Property can be encumbered by multiple liens
- ❑ Lien terminates upon payment, recording satisfaction

 # 5:
Liens &
Encumbrances

- Encumbrances
- Easements
- Encroachments
- Licenses
- Deed Restrictions
- Liens
- Foreclosure

Liens

Lien characteristics (cont.)

- ❑ **Voluntary**
  - ▪ Owner borrows money

- ❑ **Involuntary**
  - ▪ **Statutory lien** (tax lien)
  - ▪ Court-imposed **equitable lien** (judgment lien)

 # 5:
Liens &
Encumbrances

- Encumbrances
- Easements
- Encroachments
- Licenses
- Deed Restrictions
- Liens
- Foreclosure

Liens

Lien characteristics (cont.)

- ❑ **General** vs. **specific** liens
  - ▪ General = lien placed against all property
  - ▪ Specific = lien placed on a specific property

- ❑ **Superior/senior** vs. **inferior/junior** lien
  - ▪ Establishes seniority ranking for order of payment in a foreclosure

---

 # 5:
Liens &
Encumbrances

- Encumbrances
- Easements
- Encroachments
- Licenses
- Deed Restrictions
- Liens
- Foreclosure

Liens
Lien priority

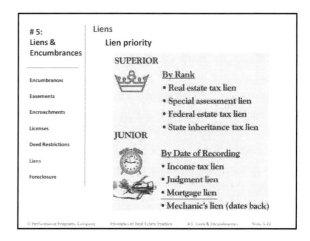

SUPERIOR

By Rank
- • Real estate tax lien
- • Special assessment lien
- • Federal estate tax lien
- • State inheritance tax lien

JUNIOR

By Date of Recording
- • Income tax lien
- • Judgment lien
- • Mortgage lien
- • Mechanic's lien (dates back)

Slide 1 (top left)

5:
Liens &
Encumbrances

Encumbrances
Easements
Encroachments
Licenses
Deed Restrictions
Liens
Foreclosure

Liens

Lien priority

❑ Rank order of claims

❑ Lien priority determines who gets paid first upon default

❑ Priority criterion:
- Categorization as superior vs junior
- Date of recordation

Slide 2 (top right)

5:
Liens &
Encumbrances

Encumbrances
Easements
Encroachments
Licenses
Deed Restrictions
Liens
Foreclosure

Liens

Superior liens

❑ Superior rank over junior liens
❑ **Not** ranked by recording date

❑ Superior real estate liens in rank order:
- Real estate tax liens
- Special assessment liens
- Federal estate tax liens

Slide 3 (middle left)

5:
Liens &
Encumbrances

Encumbrances
Easements
Encroachments
Licenses
Deed Restrictions
Liens
Foreclosure

Liens

Junior liens

❑ Rank by recording date:
- judgment
- mortgage
- vendor's
- utility
- mechanic's
- other tax liens

❑ Mechanic's lien priority "dates back" to when work or sale transpired

Slide 4 (middle right)

5:
Liens &
Encumbrances

Encumbrances
Easements
Encroachments
Licenses
Deed Restrictions
Liens
Foreclosure

Foreclosure

❑ Liquidation or transfer of collateral property by judicial, non-judicial, or strict foreclosure

Types of foreclosure

❑ Mortgage lien foreclosure

❑ Judicial foreclosure

❑ Non-judicial foreclosure

❑ Strict foreclosure

❑ Deed in lieu of foreclosure

Slide 5 (bottom left)

5:
Liens &
Encumbrances

Encumbrances
Easements
Encroachments
Licenses
Deed Restrictions
Liens
Foreclosure

Foreclosure

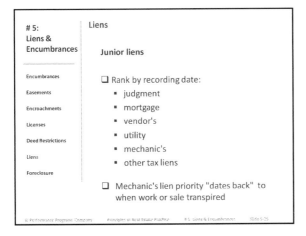

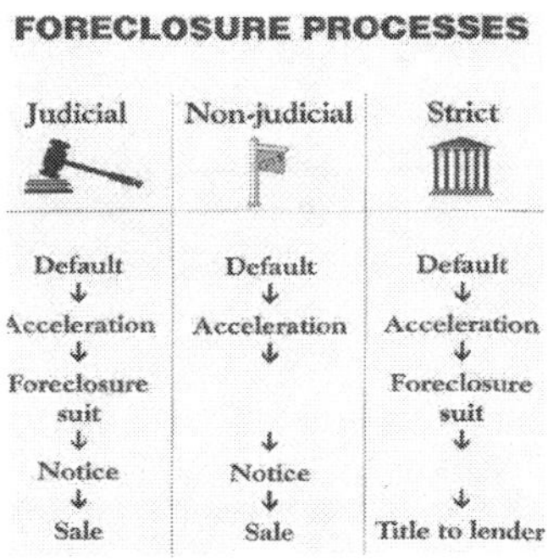

FORECLOSURE PROCESSES

Judicial	Non-judicial	Strict
Default	Default	Default
↓	↓	↓
Acceleration	Acceleration	Acceleration
↓	↓	↓
Foreclosure suit		Foreclosure suit
↓	↓	↓
Notice	Notice	
↓	↓	
Sale	Sale	Title to lender

Slide 6 (bottom right)

5:
Liens &
Encumbrances

Encumbrances
Easements
Encroachments
Licenses
Deed Restrictions
Liens
Foreclosure

Foreclosure

Mortgage lien foreclosure
❑ Foreclosed via judicial, non-judicial, or strict foreclosure

Judicial foreclosure
❑ Occurs when no 'power of sale' clause is in mortgage docs
❑ Lender files a foreclosure suit against defaulting borrower
❑ Court proceeding follows to enforce lien

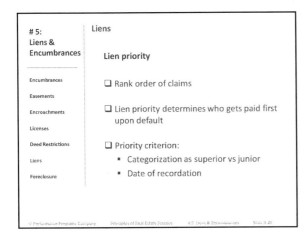
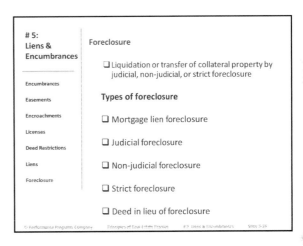

 # 5:
Liens &
Encumbrances

Encumbrances

Easements

Encroachments

Licenses

Deed Restrictions

Liens

Foreclosure

Foreclosure

Judicial foreclosure suit steps

1) Lender accelerates payment deadline to present; files suit
2) Court orders property to be publicly sold and the proceeds applied to the debt balance
3) Notice given to public (**lis pendens**) of impending action
4) Court issues **writ of execution** to seize and sell property
5) Property sold to highest bidder who gets clear and marketable title

---

 # 5:
Liens &
Encumbrances

Encumbrances

Easements

Encroachments

Licenses

Deed Restrictions

Liens

Foreclosure

Foreclosure

Judicial foreclosure: deficiency judgments

1) Following sale, taxes and liens are paid off

2) If shortfall, lender may ask for a deficiency judgment on other borrower property

3) If granted, lender can attach other assets for balance owed

---

 # 5:
Liens &
Encumbrances

Encumbrances

Easements

Encroachments

Licenses

Deed Restrictions

Liens

Foreclosure

Foreclosure

Judicial foreclosure: redemption

❑ Borrower's **right to reclaim** property before or after foreclosure sale
  ▪ Must repay all amounts owed creditors

❑ Most states allow redemption prior to sale

❑ Some states have statutory redemption periods following the foreclosure sale

---

 # 5:
Liens &
Encumbrances

Encumbrances

Easements

Encroachments

Licenses

Deed Restrictions

Liens

Foreclosure

Foreclosure

Non-judicial foreclosure

❑ 'Power of sale' clause can force public sale without court decree

❑ Lender delivers notice; conducts sale; pays off liens

❑ Title then delivered free and clear to buyer

❑ Lender must file separate deficiency suit

❑ Borrower may redeem prior to sale, but not afterwards

 # 5:
Liens &
Encumbrances

Encumbrances

Easements

Encroachments

Licenses

Deed Restrictions

Liens

Foreclosure

Foreclosure

Strict foreclosure
❑ Court proceeding that grants lender legal title directly, without public sale
❑ Defaulting borrower given a grace period to cure default prior to conveyance

Deed in lieu of foreclosure
❑ Defaulting borrower voluntarily deeds property to mortgagee to avoid foreclosure
❑ Action does not extinguish any liens

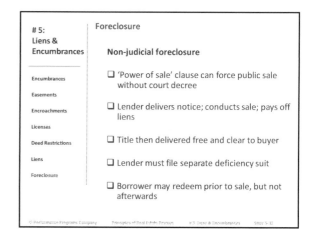

Unit 6: TRANSFERRING & RECORDING TITLE TO REAL ESTATE

Title to Real Estate

Deeds of Conveyance

Wills

Involuntary Title Transfer

Title Records

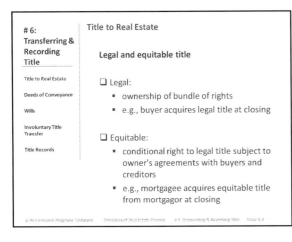

 # 6: Transferring & Recording Title

Title to Real Estate

Deeds of Conveyance

Wills

Involuntary Title Transfer

Title Records

Title to Real Estate

Legal and equitable title

❑ Legal:
  ▪ ownership of bundle of rights
  ▪ e.g., buyer acquires legal title at closing

❑ Equitable:
  ▪ conditional right to legal title subject to owner's agreements with buyers and creditors
  ▪ e.g., mortgagee acquires equitable title from mortgagor at closing

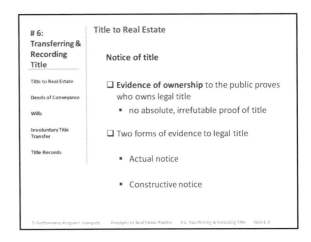

 # 6: Transferring & Recording Title

Title to Real Estate

Deeds of Conveyance

Wills

Involuntary Title Transfer

Title Records

Title to Real Estate

Notice of title

❑ **Evidence of ownership** to the public proves who owns legal title
  ▪ no absolute, irrefutable proof of title

❑ Two forms of evidence to legal title

  ▪ Actual notice

  ▪ Constructive notice

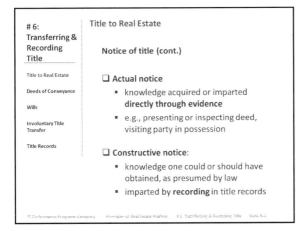

 # 6: Transferring & Recording Title

Title to Real Estate

Deeds of Conveyance

Wills

Involuntary Title Transfer

Title Records

Title to Real Estate

Notice of title (cont.)

❑ **Actual notice**
  ▪ knowledge acquired or imparted **directly through evidence**
  ▪ e.g., presenting or inspecting deed, visiting party in possession

❑ **Constructive notice**:
  ▪ knowledge one could or should have obtained, as presumed by law
  ▪ imparted by **recording** in title records

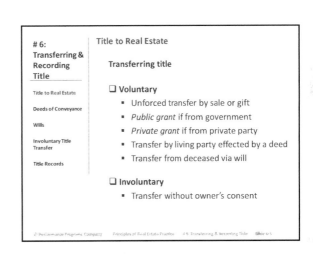

 # 6: Transferring & Recording Title

Title to Real Estate

Deeds of Conveyance

Wills

Involuntary Title Transfer

Title Records

Title to Real Estate

Transferring title

❑ **Voluntary**
  ▪ Unforced transfer by sale or gift
  ▪ *Public grant* if from government
  ▪ *Private grant* if from private party
  ▪ Transfer by living party effected by a deed
  ▪ Transfer from deceased via will

❑ **Involuntary**
  ▪ Transfer without owner's consent

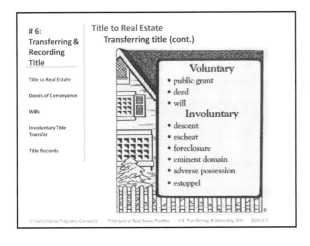

 # 6: Transferring & Recording Title

Title to Real Estate

Deeds of Conveyance

Wills

Involuntary Title Transfer

Title Records

Title to Real Estate
Transferring title (cont.)

Voluntary
• public grant
• deed
• will

Involuntary
• descent
• escheat
• foreclosure
• eminent domain
• adverse possession
• estoppel

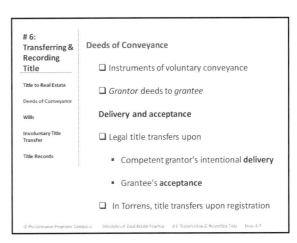

 # 6: Transferring & Recording Title

Title to Real Estate

Deeds of Conveyance

Wills

Involuntary Title Transfer

Title Records

Deeds of Conveyance

❑ Instruments of voluntary conveyance

❑ *Grantor* deeds to *grantee*

Delivery and acceptance

❑ Legal title transfers upon

  ▪ Competent grantor's intentional **delivery**

  ▪ Grantee's **acceptance**

❑ In Torrens, title transfers upon registration

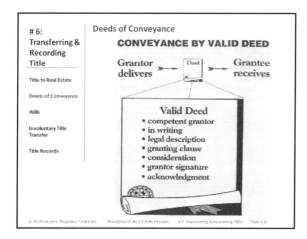

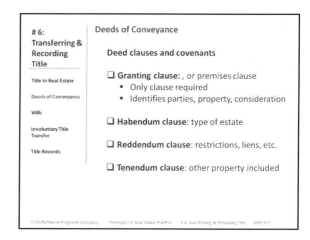

Deed clauses and covenants

- ❑ **Granting clause:** , or premises clause
  - Only clause required
  - Identifies parties, property, consideration

- ❑ **Habendum clause:** type of estate

- ❑ **Reddendum clause:** restrictions, liens, etc.

- ❑ **Tenendum clause:** other property included

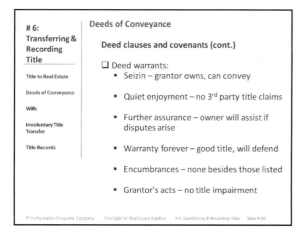

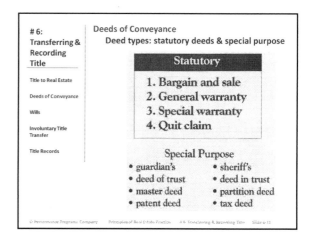

6: Transferring & Recording Title

Title to Real Estate

Deeds of Conveyance

Wills

Involuntary Title Transfer

Title Records

Deeds of Conveyance

Deed types: statutory deeds

- ❑ Bargain and sale: "I own, won't defend"

- ❑ General warranty: "I own, will defend"

- ❑ Special warranty: "I own, warrant myself only"

- ❑ Quitclaim: "I may or may not own, won't defend"

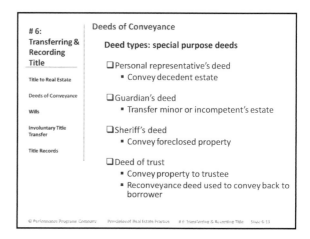

Slide 1

 # 6: Transferring & Recording Title

Title to Real Estate

Deeds of Conveyance

Wills

Involuntary Title Transfer

Title Records

Deeds of Conveyance

Deed types: special purpose deeds (cont.)

❑ Deed *in* trust
- Convey to a land trust

❑ Master deed
- Convey land to condo developer

❑ Partition deed
- Convey partitioned property

❑ Patent deed
- Convey government property to private owner

❑ Tax deed
- Convey property sold at tax sale

Slide 2

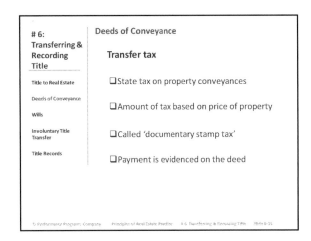

 # 6: Transferring & Recording Title

Title to Real Estate

Deeds of Conveyance

Wills

Involuntary Title Transfer

Title Records

Deeds of Conveyance

Transfer tax

❑ State tax on property conveyances

❑ Amount of tax based on price of property

❑ Called 'documentary stamp tax'

❑ Payment is evidenced on the deed

Slide 3

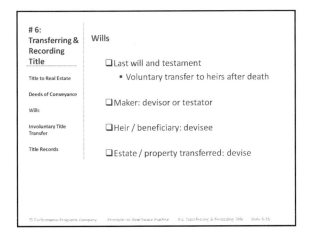

 # 6: Transferring & Recording Title

Title to Real Estate

Deeds of Conveyance

Wills

Involuntary Title Transfer

Title Records

Wills

❑ Last will and testament
- Voluntary transfer to heirs after death

❑ Maker: devisor or testator

❑ Heir / beneficiary: devisee

❑ Estate / property transferred: devise

Slide 4

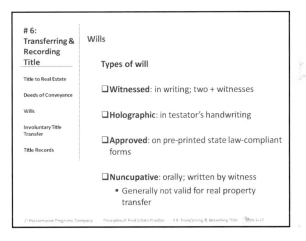

 # 6: Transferring & Recording Title

Title to Real Estate

Deeds of Conveyance

Wills

Involuntary Title Transfer

Title Records

Wills

Types of will

❑ **Witnessed**: in writing; two + witnesses

❑ **Holographic**: in testator's handwriting

❑ **Approved**: on pre-printed state law-compliant forms

❑ **Nuncupative**: orally; written by witness
- Generally not valid for real property transfer

Slide 5

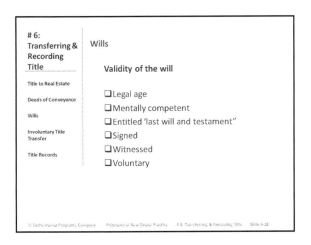

 # 6: Transferring & Recording Title

Title to Real Estate

Deeds of Conveyance

Wills

Involuntary Title Transfer

Title Records

Wills

Validity of the will

❑ Legal age

❑ Mentally competent

❑ Entitled 'last will and testament"

❑ Signed

❑ Witnessed

❑ Voluntary

Slide 6

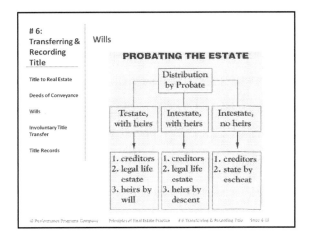

 # 6: Transferring & Recording Title

Title to Real Estate

Deeds of Conveyance

Wills

Involuntary Title Transfer

Title Records

Wills

PROBATING THE ESTATE

Distribution by Probate

Testate, with heirs	Intestate, with heirs	Intestate, no heirs
1. creditors 2. legal life estate 3. heirs by will	1. creditors 2. legal life estate 3. heirs by descent	1. creditors 2. state by escheat

 # 6:
Transferring & Recording Title

Title to Real Estate

Deeds of Conveyance

Wills

Involuntary Title Transfer

Title Records

Wills

Probate process

❑ Validate will

❑ Validate and settle claims

❑ Pay debts against estate

❑ Distribute remaining estate to heirs

 # 6:
Transferring & Recording Title

Title to Real Estate

Deeds of Conveyance

Wills

Involuntary Title Transfer

Title Records

Involuntary Title Transfer

Types of involuntary transfer

❑ Via laws of descent:
- Prescribes who gets what in absence of will
- If a will; identifies heirs
- If no will, property escheats to state/county

❑ Abandonment: escheats if unused for statutory period

❑ Foreclosure: lose title by forfeiture

 # 6:
Transferring & Recording Title

Title to Real Estate

Deeds of Conveyance

Wills

Involuntary Title Transfer

Title Records

Involuntary Title Transfer

Types of involuntary transfer (cont.)

❑ Eminent domain
- lose title to public for the "greater good"
- owner receives just compensation

❑ Estoppel
- barred by prior acts or claims from claiming a right or interest in a property
- can prevent an owner from re-claiming a property transferred under false pretenses

---

 # 6:
Transferring & Recording Title

Title to Real Estate

Deeds of Conveyance

Wills

Involuntary Title Transfer

Title Records

Involuntary Title Transfer

Involuntary transfer: adverse possession

❑ Adverse possession
- "Unwanted owner" may claim, obtain ownership

❑ Adverse possession criteria
- show **claim of right** as reason
- **notorious possession**: unconcealed occupation
- **hostile possession**: claim ownership
- **continuous** occupation for statutory period
- may require payment of taxes

 # 6:
Transferring & Recording Title

Title to Real Estate

Deeds of Conveyance

Wills

Involuntary Title Transfer

Title Records

Title Records

❑ Instruments affecting title must be recorded

❑ Purposes for recordation / title records

- Gives public constructive notice of title condition, ownership, claims

- Determines property marketability; protects buyers

- Protects lienholders; establishes priority

 # 6:
Transferring & Recording Title

Title to Real Estate

Deeds of Conveyance

Wills

Involuntary Title Transfer

Title Records

Title Records

Chain of title

❑ **Chain of title**: successive property owners from original grant to present owner

❑ **Cloud on title** – unrecorded claims

❑ **Suit to quiet title** – lawsuit to settle claims

❑ **Abstract of title**: written chronology of recorded owners, transfers, encumbrances

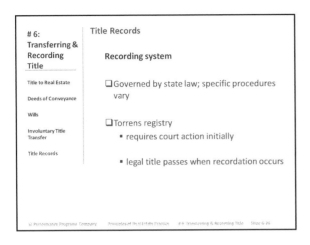

 # 6: Transferring & Recording Title

Title to Real Estate

Deeds of Conveyance

Wills

Involuntary Title Transfer

Title Records

Title Records

Recording system

❑ Governed by state law; specific procedures vary

❑ Torrens registry
  ▪ requires court action initially
  ▪ legal title passes when recordation occurs

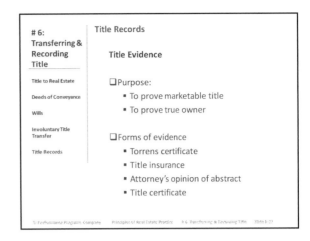

 # 6: Transferring & Recording Title

Title to Real Estate

Deeds of Conveyance

Wills

Involuntary Title Transfer

Title Records

Title Records

Title Evidence

❑ Purpose:
  ▪ To prove marketable title
  ▪ To prove true owner

❑ Forms of evidence
  ▪ Torrens certificate
  ▪ Title insurance
  ▪ Attorney's opinion of abstract
  ▪ Title certificate

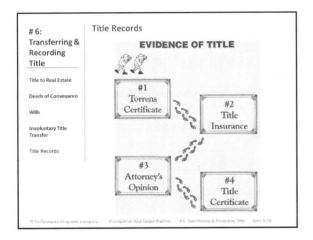

 # 6: Transferring & Recording Title

Title to Real Estate

Deeds of Conveyance

Wills

Involuntary Title Transfer

Title Records

Title Records

EVIDENCE OF TITLE

#1 Torrens Certificate

#2 Title Insurance

#3 Attorney's Opinion

#4 Title Certificate

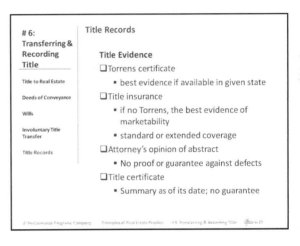

 # 6: Transferring & Recording Title

Title to Real Estate

Deeds of Conveyance

Wills

Involuntary Title Transfer

Title Records

Title Records

Title Evidence

❑ Torrens certificate
  ▪ best evidence if available in given state

❑ Title insurance
  ▪ if no Torrens, the best evidence of marketability
  ▪ standard or extended coverage

❑ Attorney's opinion of abstract
  ▪ No proof or guarantee against defects

❑ Title certificate
  ▪ Summary as of its date; no guarantee

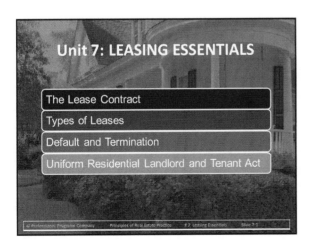

Unit 7: LEASING ESSENTIALS

The Lease Contract

Types of Leases

Default and Termination

Uniform Residential Landlord and Tenant Act

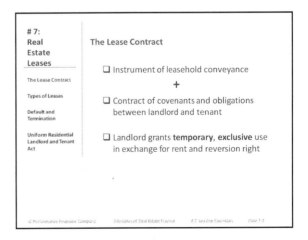

 # 7: Real Estate Leases

The Lease Contract

Types of Leases

Default and Termination

Uniform Residential Landlord and Tenant Act

The Lease Contract

❑ Instrument of leasehold conveyance

    +

❑ Contract of covenants and obligations between landlord and tenant

❑ Landlord grants **temporary, exclusive** use in exchange for rent and reversion right

**# 7:
Real
Estate
Leases**

The Lease Contract

Types of Leases

Default and
Termination

Uniform Residential
Landlord and Tenant
Act

The Lease Contract

Forms of leasehold estate

For years   2017 ➡ 2037

Periodic   2017 ➡ 2018 ➡ 2019

At will   2017 ➡   ?

At sufferance

**# 7:
Real
Estate
Leases**

The Lease Contract

Types of Leases

Default and
Termination

Uniform Residential
Landlord and Tenant
Act

The Lease Contract

Leasehold rights and obligations: tenants

❑ **Tenant rights**
  - exclusive use and possession
  - quiet enjoyment
  - profits

❑ **Tenant obligations**
  - pay rent
  - maintain premises
  - follow rules

**# 7:
Real
Estate
Leases**

The Lease Contract

Types of Leases

Default and
Termination

Uniform Residential
Landlord and Tenant
Act

The Lease Contract

Leasehold rights and obligations: landlords

❑ **Landlord rights**
  - receive rent
  - repossess at lease expiration
  - monitor tenant's compliance

❑ **Landlord obligations**
  - building support and services
  - maintain property condition

❑ Leasehold rights survive death,
  conveyancing and encumbrances

**# 7:
Real
Estate
Leases**

The Lease Contract

Types of Leases

Default and
Termination

Uniform Residential
Landlord and Tenant
Act

The Lease Contract

Lease contract validity requirements

❑ **Parties** – legally competent

❑ **Legal description** – or locally acceptable
  description

❑ **Exclusive possession** – must be granted

❑ **Legal and permitted use**

❑ **Consideration** – paid by tenant for lease

**# 7:
Real
Estate
Leases**

The Lease Contract

Types of Leases

Default and
Termination

Uniform Residential
Landlord and Tenant
Act

The Lease Contract

Lease contract validity requirements (cont.)

❑ **Offer and acceptance** – acceptance must
  be communicated to other party

❑ **Signatures** – by landlord; tenants signing
  are jointly and severally liable

❑ **Written** -- if term exceeds one year, in
  order to be enforceable
  - Oral leases terminate upon death of
    landlord

**# 7:
Real
Estate
Leases**

The Lease Contract

Types of Lease

Default and
Termination

Uniform Residential
Landlord and Tenant
Act

The Lease Contract

Lease clauses

❑ **Rent** – how paid, deadlines, penalties

❑ **Deposit** – how forfeited; escrowed

❑ **Term** – tenancy at will if no lease term

❑ **Repairs and maintenance** – defines who is
  responsible for what

❑ **Subletting and assignment** – must be
  approved; tenant remains liable

 # 7: Real Estate Leases

The Lease Contract
Types of Lease
Default and Termination
Uniform Residential Landlord and Tenant Act

The Lease Contract

Lease clauses (cont.)

❑ **Rules and regulations** – tenant must comply

❑ **Improvements, alterations** – must be approved; define who owns

❑ **Options** – to renew; purchase; expand; downsize

❑ **Damage / destruction** – defines rights & obligations if premises is damaged / destroyed

---

 # 7: Real Estate Leases

The Lease Contract
Types of Lease
Default and Termination
Uniform Residential Landlord and Tenant Act

Types of Lease

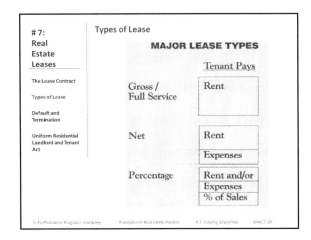

MAJOR LEASE TYPES

	Tenant Pays
Gross / Full Service	Rent
Net	Rent
	Expenses
Percentage	Rent and/or Expenses
	% of Sales

 # 7: Real Estate Leases

The Lease Contract
Types of Lease
Default and Termination
Uniform Residential Landlord and Tenant Act

Types of Lease

Gross lease
❑ Landlord pays expenses
❑ Tenant pays higher rent

Net lease
❑ Tenant pays some or all operating expenses
❑ Rent is reduced

Percentage lease
❑ Tenant pays landlord a percent of gross sales
❑ May or may not pay a base minimum rent

 # 7: Real Estate Leases

The Lease Contract
Types of Lease
Default and Termination
Uniform Residential Landlord and Tenant Act

Types of Lease

Residential lease
❑ Shorter terms
❑ Gross – landlord pays most expenses
❑ Standard clauses
❑ Must comply with landlord-tenant relations laws
❑ Clauses generally not negotiable

Commercial lease
❑ Net, gross or percentage
❑ Complex legal documents
❑ Longer term, typically 5-10 years
❑ All clauses negotiable

 # 7: Real Estate Leases

The Lease Contract
Types of Lease
Default and Termination
Uniform Residential Landlord and Tenant Act

Types of Lease

Ground lease
❑ Landlord owns and leases ground but does not own improvements

Proprietary lease
❑ For cooperative unit owners; indefinite term; assigned to new unit owner on sale

Leasing of rights
❑ Leasehold transfer of rights for limited use
  ▪ examples: air, mineral, water rights

 # 7: Real Estate Leases

The Lease Contract
Types of Lease
Default and Termination
Uniform Residential Landlord and Tenant Act

Default and Termination

Remedies for default
❑ Sue for *damages*, *lease cancellation*, and/or *specific performance*

Default by tenant
❑ Cancellation; damages; suit for possession; must give proper notice

Default by landlord
❑ Suit for constructive eviction; must vacate premises to uphold

Slide 1

 # 7: Real Estate Leases

The Lease Contract

Types of Lease

Default and Termination

Uniform Residential Landlord and Tenant Act

Default and Termination

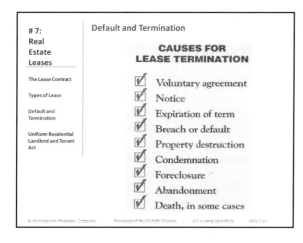

CAUSES FOR LEASE TERMINATION

☑ Voluntary agreement
☑ Notice
☑ Expiration of term
☑ Breach or default
☑ Property destruction
☑ Condemnation
☑ Foreclosure
☑ Abandonment
☑ Death, in some cases

Slide 2

 # 7: Real Estate Leases

The Lease Contract

Types of Lease

Default and Termination

Uniform Residential Landlord and Tenant Act

Default and Termination

Causes for lease termination (cont.)

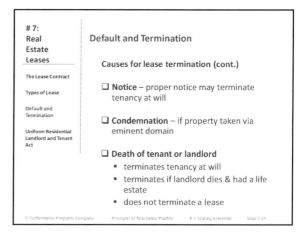

❑ **Notice** – proper notice may terminate tenancy at will

❑ **Condemnation** – if property taken via eminent domain

❑ **Death of tenant or landlord**
- terminates tenancy at will
- terminates if landlord dies & had a life estate
- does not terminate a lease

Slide 3

 # 7: Real Estate Leases

The Lease Contract

Types of Lease

Default and Termination

Uniform Residential Landlord and Tenant Act

Uniform Residential Landlord and Tenant Act

Purposes of URLTA

❑ Balance landlord and tenant rights

❑ Standardize leases

❑ Have uniform eviction procedures

❑ Protect tenants

❑ Serve as model for state-level legislation

Slide 4

 # 7: Real Estate Leases

The Lease Contract

Types of Lease

Default and Termination

Uniform Residential Landlord and Tenant Act

Uniform Residential Landlord and Tenant Act

Areas of regulation – leases, deposits

❑ Lease agreements
- Vague lease becomes periodic tenancy
- Rent must be fair market or court-rendered
- Cannot waive certain rights

❑ Deposits, advances
- Sets maximum deposit amounts
- Tenant may earn interest
- Cannot co-mingle deposit / advance funds
- Deadline, criteria for returning deposit

Slide 5

 # 7: Real Estate Leases

The Lease Contract

Types of Lease

Default and Termination

Uniform Residential Landlord and Tenant Act

Uniform Residential Landlord and Tenant Act

Areas of regulation - landlord

❑ Landlord obligations

- Bargain in good faith

- Provide required maintenance, repairs

- Comply with building codes

- Maintain access & safety services

- Follow rule for giving notice

Slide 6

 # 7: Real Estate Leases

The Lease Contract

Types of Lease

Default and Termination

Uniform Residential Landlord and Tenant Act

Uniform Residential Landlord and Tenant Act

Areas of regulation - tenant

❑ Tenant obligations

- Bargain in good faith

- Maintain condition of premises

- Comply with building rules

- Limit usages to approved uses

- Avoid undue disturbance of tenants

# 7: Real Estate Leases	Uniform Residential Landlord and Tenant Act
The Lease Contract	**Areas of regulation (cont.)**
Types of Lease	**Landlord access**
Default and Termination	❑ Balance access right with tenant's quiet enjoyment
Uniform Residential Landlord and Tenant Act	❑ Give sufficient notice
	❑ Have justification for entry
	❑ Tenant cannot deny access for emergencies

# 7: Real Estate Leases	Uniform Residential Landlord and Tenant Act
The Lease Contract	**Areas of regulation (cont.)**
Types of Lease	**Default and eviction**
Default and Termination	❑ Tenant may sue for damages; terminate; or negotiate rent abatement
Uniform Residential Landlord and Tenant Act	▪ Tenant remains liable for rent during dispute
	❑ Landlord may terminate and evict
	▪ Must give proper notice; follow procedures
	▪ Action must be justified

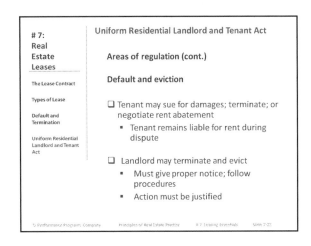

Unit 8: LAND USE PLANNING & CONTROL

- Real Estate Planning
- Public Land Use Control
- Private Land Use Control
- Environmental Controls

# 8: Land Use Planning and Control	Real Estate Planning
Real Estate Planning	**Goals of land use control**
Public Land Use Control	❑ Preserve property values
Private Land Use Control	❑ Promote highest & best use
Environmental Controls	❑ Safeguard public health, safety, welfare
	❑ Control growth
	❑ Incorporate community consensus

# 8: Land Use Planning and Control	Real Estate Planning
Real Estate Planning	**The planning process**
Public Land Use Control	❑ Develop the master land use plan
Private Land Use Control	❑ Establish corresponding administration
Environmental Controls	❑ Implement authorized controls

# 8: Land Use Planning and Control	Real Estate Planning
Real Estate Planning	**The planning process**
Public Land Use Control	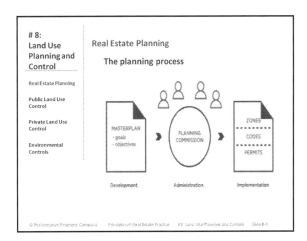
Private Land Use Control	
Environmental Controls	

25

Slide 1

8:
Land Use Planning and Control

Real Estate Planning

Public Land Use Control

Private Land Use Control

Environmental Controls

Real Estate Planning

The master plan

❑ Long term growth & usage strategies

❑ Local plans combine
  ▪ municipal goals and needs
  ▪ state and regional laws

❑ Plans become guideline for zones, codes & development requirements

Slide 2

8:
Land Use Planning and Control

Real Estate Planning

Public Land Use Control

Private Land Use Control

Environmental Controls

Real Estate Planning

Planning objectives

❑ control growth rates and patterns

❑ accommodate demand for services and infrastructure

Slide 3

8:
Land Use Planning and Control

Real Estate Planning

Public Land Use Control

Private Land Use Control

Environmental Controls

Real Estate Planning

Growth considerations

❑ extent of permitted uses

❑ availability of sanitation facilities

❑ adequacy of drainage, waste collection, and potable water systems

❑ adequacy of utilities companies

Slide 4

8:
Land Use Planning and Control

Real Estate Planning

Public Land Use Control

Private Land Use Control

Environmental Controls

Real Estate Planning

Growth considerations (cont.)

❑ adequacy and patterns of thoroughfares

❑ housing availability

❑ conservation of natural resources

❑ adequacy of recreational facilities

❑ new taxes, bond issues, and assessments

Slide 5

8:
Land Use Planning and Control

Real Estate Planning

Public Land Use Control

Private Land Use Control

Environmental Controls

Real Estate Planning

Demand, infrastructure considerations

❑ Government facilities requirements

❑ Construction for streets, schools, and social services

❑ Construction for power, water and sewer services

Slide 6

8:
Land Use Planning and Control

Real Estate Planning

Public Land Use Control

Private Land Use Control

Environmental Controls

Real Estate Planning

Plan development

❑ Research trends and conditions
❑ Blend objectives into master plan

❑ Analyze
  ▪ population and demographic trends
  ▪ economic trends
  ▪ existing land use
  ▪ existing support facilities
  ▪ traffic patterns

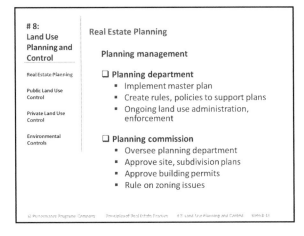

 # 8:
Land Use Planning and Control

Real Estate Planning

Public Land Use Control

Private Land Use Control

Environmental Controls

Real Estate Planning

Planning management

❑ **Planning department**
- Implement master plan
- Create rules, policies to support plans
- Ongoing land use administration, enforcement

❑ **Planning commission**
- Oversee planning department
- Approve site, subdivision plans
- Approve building permits
- Rule on zoning issues

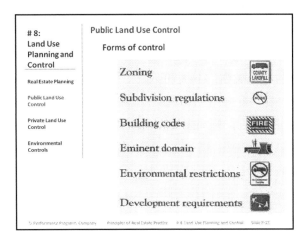

 # 8:
Land Use Planning and Control

Real Estate Planning

Public Land Use Control

Private Land Use Control

Environmental Controls

Public Land Use Control

Forms of control

Zoning

Subdivision regulations

Building codes

Eminent domain

Environmental restrictions

Development requirements

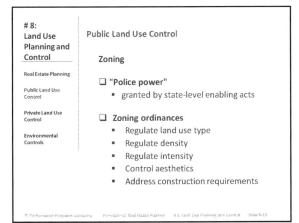

 # 8:
Land Use Planning and Control

Real Estate Planning

Public Land Use Control

Private Land Use Control

Environmental Controls

Public Land Use Control

Zoning

❑ **"Police power"**
- granted by state-level enabling acts

❑ **Zoning ordinances**
- Regulate land use type
- Regulate density
- Regulate intensity
- Control aesthetics
- Address construction requirements

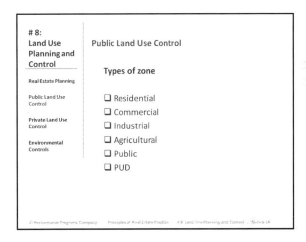

 # 8:
Land Use Planning and Control

Real Estate Planning

Public Land Use Control

Private Land Use Control

Environmental Controls

Public Land Use Control

Types of zone

❑ Residential
❑ Commercial
❑ Industrial
❑ Agricultural
❑ Public
❑ PUD

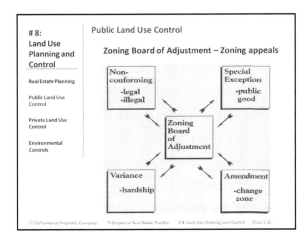

 # 8:
Land Use Planning and Control

Real Estate Planning

Public Land Use Control

Private Land Use Control

Environmental Controls

Public Land Use Control

Zoning Board of Adjustment – Zoning appeals

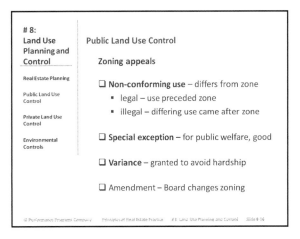

 # 8:
Land Use Planning and Control

Real Estate Planning

Public Land Use Control

Private Land Use Control

Environmental Controls

Public Land Use Control

Zoning appeals

❑ **Non-conforming use** – differs from zone
- legal – use preceded zone
- illegal – differing use came after zone

❑ **Special exception** – for public welfare, good

❑ **Variance** – granted to avoid hardship

❑ Amendment – Board changes zoning

Slide 1

8:
Land Use Planning and Control

Real Estate Planning

Public Land Use Control

Private Land Use Control

Environmental Controls

Public Land Use Control

Subdivision regulation

❑ Plat of subdivision and relevant requirements must be met

❑ Must comply with zoning, building codes

❑ Must meet FHA requirements for insured financing

© Performance Programs Company   Principles of Real Estate Practice   # 8 Land Use Planning and Control   Slide 8-17

Slide 2

8:
Land Use Planning and Control

Real Estate Planning

Public Land Use Control

Private Land Use Control

Environmental Controls

Public Land Use Control

Building codes

❑ **Codes** address onsite & offsite construction standards
- architectural, engineering standards
- construction materials
- building support systems

❑ **Certificate of occupancy**
- certifies compliance with code, enables occupancy

© Performance Programs Company   Principles of Real Estate Practice   # 8 Land Use Planning and Control   Slide 8-18

Slide 3

8:
Land Use Planning and Control

Real Estate Planning

Public Land Use Control

Private Land Use Control

Environmental Controls

Public Land Use Control

Public acquisition and ownership

❑ **Eminent domain**
- Allows a government entity to acquire a fee, leasehold, or easement interest in a privately owned property

- Must pay owner 'just compensation'

- Justified by "public good"

- Effected by condemnation suit

© Performance Programs Company   Principles of Real Estate Practice   # 8 Land Use Planning and Control   Slide 8-19

Slide 4

8:
Land Use Planning and Control

Real Estate Planning

Public Land Use Control

Private Land Use Control

Environmental Controls

Public Land Use Control

Environmental restrictions

❑ **Purposes**
- Limit damage to environment
- Establish pollution-related standards for land use

© Performance Programs Company   Principles of Real Estate Practice   # 8 Land Use Planning and Control   Slide 8-20

Slide 5

8:
Land Use Planning and Control

Real Estate Planning

Public Land Use Control

Private Land Use Control

Environmental Controls

Private Land Use Control

Deed restrictions

❑ Single-property use restriction stipulated in a deed

❑ May not be discriminatory

❑ Also called 'covenants, conditions, and restrictions', or "CCRs"

❑ Examples
- minimum living area of house
- setback requirements
- prohibit out-buildings

© Performance Programs Company   Principles of Real Estate Practice   # 8 Land Use Planning and Control   Slide 8-21

Slide 6

8:
Land Use Planning and Control

Real Estate Planning

Public Land Use Control

Private Land Use Control

Environmental Controls

Private Land Use Control

Declaration restriction

❑ Use restriction in multiple-property declarations

❑ Enforced by court injunction

❑ Examples: PUD, condominium, industrial park private use restrictions

Deed condition

❑ Usage restriction that can trigger repossession by a previous owner if violated

© Performance Programs Company   Principles of Real Estate Practice   # 8 Land Use Planning and Control   Slide 8-22

 # 8:
Land Use Planning and Control

Real Estate Planning

Public Land Use Control

Private Land Use Control

Environmental Controls

Environmental Controls

Areas of concern
- ❑ Air
- ❑ Soil
- ❑ Water quality
- ❑ Ambient health hazards
- ❑ Natural hazards

Major legislation
- ❑ To limit damage to environment
- ❑ Establish standards for air, land, water, materials use

 # 8:
Land Use Planning and Control

Real Estate Planning

Public Land Use Control

Private Land Use Control

Environmental Controls

Environmental Controls

Air quality issues

- ❑ Asbestos
- ❑ Carbon monoxide
- ❑ Formaldehyde
- ❑ Lead
- ❑ Mold
- ❑ Radon

 # 8:
Land Use Planning and Control

Real Estate Planning

Public Land Use Control

Private Land Use Control

Environmental Controls

Environmental Controls

Soil and water issues

- ❑ Dioxins
- ❑ Lead and mercury
- ❑ Methyl tertiary butyl ether, or MTBE
- ❑ Polychlorinated biphenyl, or PCB
- ❑ Underground storage tanks
- ❑ Wetlands

 # 8:
Land Use Planning and Control

Real Estate Planning

Public Land Use Control

Private Land Use Control

Environmental Controls

Environmental Controls

Other environmental conditions to control

- ❑ Electromagnetic fields
- ❑ Noise pollution
- ❑ Earthquake and flood hazards that impact insurance, lending, construction practices

---

 # 8:
Land Use Planning and Control

Real Estate Planning

Public Land Use Control

Private Land Use Control

Environmental Controls

Environmental Controls

Major environmental legislation

Laws addressing air and water quality:

- ❑ National Environmental Policy Act (1969)
- ❑ Clean Air Amendment (1970)
- ❑ Water Quality Improvement Act (1970)
- ❑ Water Pollution Control Act Amendment (1972)

 # 8:
Land Use Planning and Control

Real Estate Planning

Public Land Use Control

Private Land Use Control

Environmental Controls

Environmental Controls

Major environmental legislation (cont.)

Legislation addressing solid, toxic waste:

- ❑ Resource Recovery Act
- ❑ Resource Conservation and Recovery Act (1976)
- ❑ Comprehensive Environmental Response, Compensation and Liability Act (Superfund) (1980)
- ❑ Superfund Amendment and Reauthorization Act (1986)

8:
Land Use
Planning and
Control

Real Estate Planning

Public Land Use
Control

Private Land Use
Control

Environmental
Controls

Environmental Controls

Major environmental legislation (cont.)

Laws addressing lead and lead-based paint:

❏ Lead-based paint ban (1978)

❏ Residential Lead-based Paint Hazard
Reduction Act (1992, 1996)

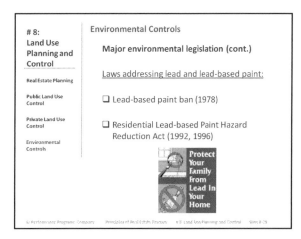

8:
Land Use
Planning and
Control

Real Estate Planning

Public Land Use
Control

Private Land Use
Control

Environmental
Controls

Environmental Controls

Responsibilities & liabilities

❏ Sellers
- disclose lead paint-related problems in
  pre-1978 properties
- may be liable for environmental violations
  under CERCLA

❏ Licensees' guidelines
- be aware of potential hazards
- disclose known material facts
- distribute the HUD booklet
- know where to seek professional help

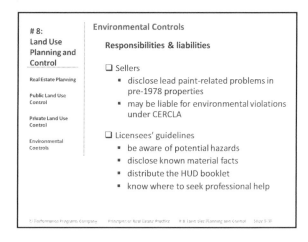

Unit 9: LEGAL DESCRIPTIONS

- Methods of Legal Description
- Metes and Bounds
- The Rectangular Survey System
- Recorded Plat Method
- Describing Elevation

9:
Legal
Descriptions

Methods of Legal
Description

Metes and Bounds

The Rectangular
Survey System

Recorded Plat Method

Describing Elevation

Methods of legal description

Purpose and applications

❏ To accurately locate / identify boundaries
  of a property acceptable to local courts

❏ Application / where required
- Public recording
- Creating a valid deed or lease
- Completing mortgage documents
- Executing, recording other legal
  documents

9:
Legal
Descriptions

Methods of Legal
Description

Metes and Bounds

The Rectangular
Survey System

Recorded Plat Method

Describing Elevation

Methods of legal description

Three description methods

❏ Metes and bounds

❏ Rectangular survey system / government
  survey

❏ Recorded plat / lot and block

9:
Legal
Descriptions

Methods of Legal
Description

Metes and Bounds

The Rectangular
Survey System

Recorded Plat Method

Describing Elevation

Metes and Bounds

❏ Describes property perimeter by
  **landmarks & monuments, distances,
  angles**

❏ **Metes** = distance, direction

❏ **Bounds** = fixed reference points

❏ *Always* identifies an **enclosed area**

Slide 1

 # 9:

Legal Descriptions

Methods of Legal Description

Metes and Bounds

The Rectangular Survey System

Recorded Plat Method

Describing Elevation

Metes and Bounds

Methodology

☐ Begins with ID of city, county, state

☐ Then, from **point of beginning** (POB), describes perimeter and returns to POB

☐ Details distance and direction from each monument in description

☐ usable within rectangular survey system

Slide 2

 # 9:

Legal Descriptions

Methods of Legal Description

Metes and Bounds

The Rectangular Survey System

Recorded Plat Method

Describing Elevation

Metes and Bounds

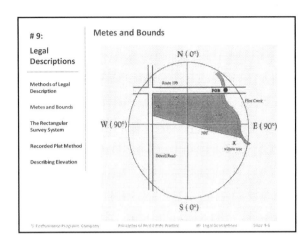

Slide 3

 # 9:

Legal Descriptions

Methods of Legal Description

Metes and Bounds

The Rectangular Survey System

Recorded Plat Method

Describing Elevation

Metes and Bounds

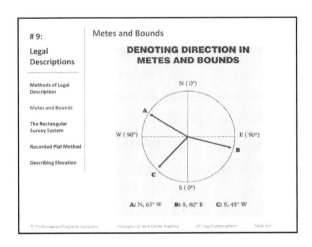

DENOTING DIRECTION IN METES AND BOUNDS

A: N, 65° W   B: S, 80° E   C: S, 45° W

Slide 4

 # 9:

Legal Descriptions

Methods of Legal Description

Metes and Bounds

The Rectangular Survey System

Recorded Plat Method

Describing Elevation

Metes and Bounds

Description of metes and bounds illustration

A parcel of land located in Bucks County, Pennsylvania, having the following description: commencing at the intersection of the south line of Route 199 and the middle of Flint Creek, thence southeasterly along the center thread of Flint Creek 410 feet, more or less, to the willow tree landmark, thence north 65 degrees west 500 feet, more or less to the east line of Dowell Road, thence north 2 degrees east 200 feet, more or less, along the east line of Dowell Road to the south line of Route 199, thence north 90 degrees east 325 feet, more or less, along the south line of Route 199 to the point of beginning

Slide 5

 # 9:

Legal Descriptions

Methods of Legal Description

Metes and Bounds

The Rectangular Survey System

Recorded Plat Method

Describing Elevation

The Rectangular Survey System

☐ Simplify and standardize property descriptions

☐ Facilitate the transfer of large quantities of government-owned western lands to private parties

☐ All land in system surveyed using longitude and latitude lines

☐ Lines created uniform grids of squares called townships

Slide 6

 # 9:

Legal Descriptions

Methods of Legal Description

Metes and Bounds

The Rectangular Survey System

Recorded Plat Method

Describing Elevation

The Rectangular Survey System

Terminology

☐ **Meridians**: north-south, longitudinal lines on the survey grid

☐ **Parallels**: east-west, latitudinal lines

☐ **Range**: **north-south area** between consecutive meridians

☐ **Tier, or township strip**: **east-west area** between two parallels

☐ **Township**: the area enclosed by the intersection of two consecutive meridians and two consecutive parallels

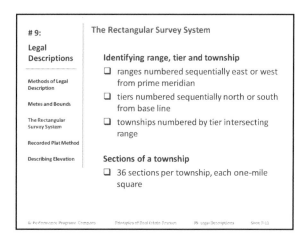

9:

Legal Descriptions

Methods of Legal Description

Metes and Bounds

The Rectangular Survey System

Recorded Plat Method

Describing Elevation

The Rectangular Survey System

Identifying range, tier and township

❑ ranges numbered sequentially east or west from prime meridian

❑ tiers numbered sequentially north or south from base line

❑ townships numbered by tier intersecting range

Sections of a township

❑ 36 sections per township, each one-mile square

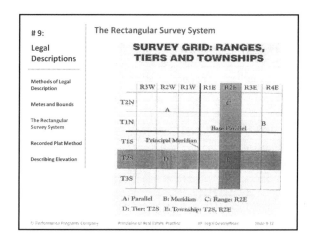

9:

Legal Descriptions

Methods of Legal Description

Metes and Bounds

The Rectangular Survey System

Recorded Plat Method

Describing Elevation

The Rectangular Survey System

SURVEY GRID: RANGES, TIERS AND TOWNSHIPS

A: Parallel   B: Meridian   C: Range: R2E
D: Tier: T2S   E: Township: T2S, R2E

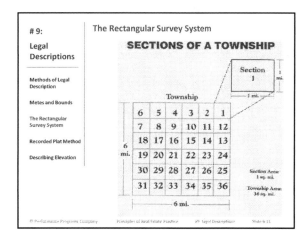

9:

Legal Descriptions

Methods of Legal Description

Metes and Bounds

The Rectangular Survey System

Recorded Plat Method

Describing Elevation

The Rectangular Survey System

SECTIONS OF A TOWNSHIP

Section Area: 1 sq. mi.
Township Area: 36 sq. mi.

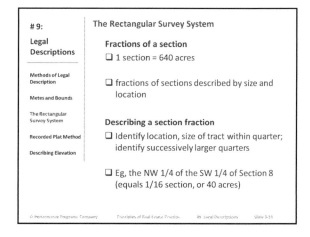

9:

Legal Descriptions

Methods of Legal Description

Metes and Bounds

The Rectangular Survey System

Recorded Plat Method

Describing Elevation

The Rectangular Survey System

Fractions of a section

❑ 1 section = 640 acres

❑ fractions of sections described by size and location

Describing a section fraction

❑ Identify location, size of tract within quarter; identify successively larger quarters

❑ Eg, the NW 1/4 of the SW 1/4 of Section 8 (equals 1/16 section, or 40 acres)

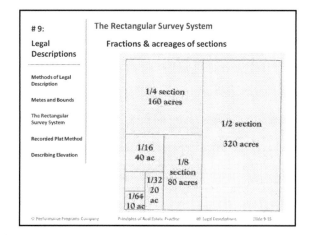

9:

Legal Descriptions

Methods of Legal Description

Metes and Bounds

The Rectangular Survey System

Recorded Plat Method

Describing Elevation

The Rectangular Survey System

Fractions & acreages of sections

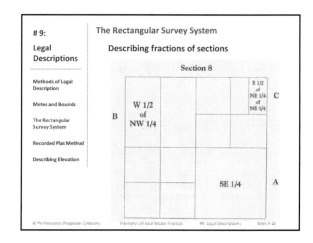

9:

Legal Descriptions

Methods of Legal Description

Metes and Bounds

The Rectangular Survey System

Recorded Plat Method

Describing Elevation

The Rectangular Survey System

Describing fractions of sections

Recorded Plat Method

Subdivision plat map

❑ Recorded plat method / lot and block system used to describe properties in subdivisions

❑ Tracts of land are subdivided into lots

❑ Lots may be grouped together into blocks

❑ Survey data built into a **plat of survey**, or **subdivision plat map**
  ▪ must comply with standards and ordinances

Recorded Plat Method

Subdivision plat map

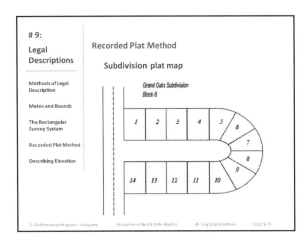

Describing Elevation

Datums

❑ Standard elevation reference points

❑ Surveyor uses a **datum** as an elevation point to describe height or depth of a property

❑ **Benchmark** – reference elevations for nearby properties to simplify surveying

---

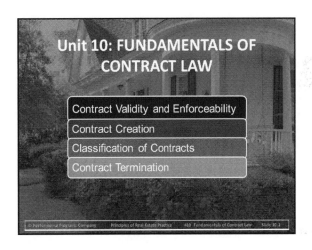

Unit 10: FUNDAMENTALS OF CONTRACT LAW

Contract Validity and Enforceability

Contract Creation

Classification of Contracts

Contract Termination

Contract Validity and Enforceability

Contracts defined

❑ Mutual promises based on a "meeting of the minds" to do (or refrain from doing) something

❑ Potentially enforceable if created validly

❑ Validity = complies with legal validity criteria

Contract Validity and Enforceability

Legal status of contracts

❑ **Valid**: meets all validity criteria

❑ **Void**: does not meet criteria; is not a contract

❑ **Voidable**: invalid if disaffirmed; enforceable if not disaffirmed

❑ **Valid yet unenforceable**: certain oral contracts, e.g., real property conveyance

Slide 1

 # 10:

Real Estate Contract Law

Contract Validity and Enforceability

Contract Creation

Classification of Contracts

Contract Termination

Contract Validity and Enforceability

CONTRACT VALIDITY REQUIREMENTS

Slide 2

 # 10:

Real Estate Contract Law

Contract Validity and Enforceability

Contract Creation

Classification of Contracts

Contract Termination

Contract Validity and Enforceability

Validity Criteria

❑ **Competent parties**
  - legal age
  - mentally capable
  - has legal authority to contract

❑ **Mutual consent**
  - offer and acceptance / meeting of minds
  - must be unequivocal, unqualified

❑ **Valuable consideration**
  - Two-way exchange of something valuable

Slide 3

 # 10:

Real Estate Contract Law

Contract Validity and Enforceability

Contract Creation

Classification of Contracts

Contract Termination

Contract Validity and Enforceability

Validity Criteria (cont.)

❑ **Legal purpose**
  - Illegal acts are not contractible, i.e., are void

❑ **Voluntary, good faith**
  - No duress, coercion, fraud or misrepresentation by either party
  - Violation creates right of rescission

Slide 4

 # 10:

Real Estate Contract Law

Contract Validity and Enforceability

Contract Creation

Classification of Contracts

Contract Termination

Contract Validity and Enforceability

Validity of a conveyance contract

❑ To convey an interest in real property, the contract
  - Must be in writing
  - Must contain a legal description
  - Must be signed by one or more parties

❑ Exception: leases for one year or less may be verbal and still enforceable

Slide 5

 # 10:

Real Estate Contract Law

Contract Validity and Enforceability

Contract Creation

Classification of Contracts

Contract Termination

Contract Validity and Enforceability

Contract enforcement limitations

❑ Statute of frauds: must be written to be enforceable

❑ Statute of limitations: injured party must act within time frame

Electronic contracting

❑ E-contracting facilitates, expedites completion of transactions, file storage, doc sharing

❑ E-docs legally enforceable due to Uniform Electronic Signatures Act & Electronic Signatures in Global, National Commerce Act

Slide 6

 # 10:

Real Estate Contract Law

Contract Validity and Enforceability

Contract Creation

Classification of Contracts

Contract Termination

Contract Creation

Offer and acceptance

❑ **Offeror** makes offer to **offeree**

❑ Valid offer and valid acceptance creates contract
  - Offeree **cannot alter** offer if accepting

❑ Offeree has 'reasonable time' to accept

❑ Offer becomes contract **on communication of acceptance** by offeree to offeror
  - if mailed, acceptance is complete when mailed

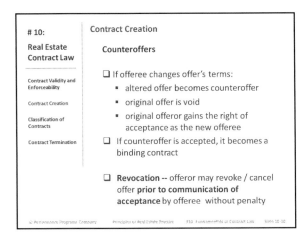

 # 10:

Real Estate Contract Law

Contract Validity and Enforceability

Contract Creation

Classification of Contracts

Contract Termination

Contract Creation

Counteroffers

❑ If offeree changes offer's terms:
- altered offer becomes counteroffer
- original offer is void
- original offeror gains the right of acceptance as the new offeree

❑ If counteroffer is accepted, it becomes a binding contract

❑ **Revocation** -- offeror may revoke / cancel offer **prior to communication of acceptance** by offeree without penalty

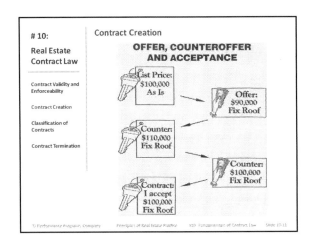

 # 10:

Real Estate Contract Law

Contract Validity and Enforceability

Contract Creation

Classification of Contracts

Contract Termination

Contract Creation

OFFER, COUNTEROFFER AND ACCEPTANCE

List Price: $100,000 As Is

Offer: $90,000 Fix Roof

Counter: $110,000 Fix Roof

Counter: $100,000 Fix Roof

Contract: I accept $100,000 Fix Roof

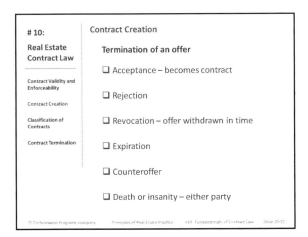

 # 10:

Real Estate Contract Law

Contract Validity and Enforceability

Contract Creation

Classification of Contracts

Contract Termination

Contract Creation

Termination of an offer

❑ Acceptance – becomes contract

❑ Rejection

❑ Revocation – offer withdrawn in time

❑ Expiration

❑ Counteroffer

❑ Death or insanity – either party

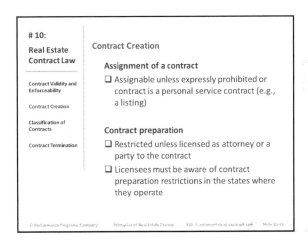

 # 10:

Real Estate Contract Law

Contract Validity and Enforceability

Contract Creation

Classification of Contracts

Contract Termination

Contract Creation

Assignment of a contract
❑ Assignable unless expressly prohibited or contract is a personal service contract (e.g., a listing)

Contract preparation
❑ Restricted unless licensed as attorney or a party to the contract
❑ Licensees must be aware of contract preparation restrictions in the states where they operate

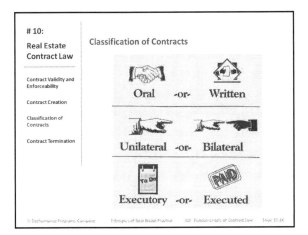

 # 10:

Real Estate Contract Law

Contract Validity and Enforceability

Contract Creation

Classification of Contracts

Contract Termination

Classification of Contracts

Oral -or- Written

Unilateral -or- Bilateral

Executory -or- Executed

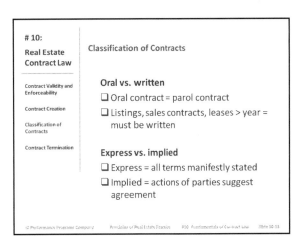

 # 10:

Real Estate Contract Law

Contract Validity and Enforceability

Contract Creation

Classification of Contracts

Contract Termination

Classification of Contracts

Oral vs. written
❑ Oral contract = parol contract
❑ Listings, sales contracts, leases > year = must be written

Express vs. implied
❑ Express = all terms manifestly stated
❑ Implied = actions of parties suggest agreement

10:

Real Estate Contract Law

Contract Validity and Enforceability

Contract Creation

Classification of Contracts

Contract Termination

Classification of Contracts

Unilateral vs. bilateral

❑ **Unilateral**: one party promises to perform if other party acts – but other party does not have to act
  ▪ e.g., option-to-sell where seller must sell if buyer opts to buy

❑ **Bilateral**: both parties promise to perform in exchange for performance by other party
  ▪ e.g., listing where broker finds buyer, seller sells property and compensates broker

---

10:

Real Estate Contract Law

Contract Validity and Enforceability

Contract Creation

Classification of Contracts

Contract Termination

Classification of Contracts

Executed vs. executory

❑ **Executed**: contract is fully performed
  ▪ e.g., expired lease

❑ **Executory**: performance is yet to be completed
  ▪ e.g., sales contract prior to closing

10:

Real Estate Contract Law

Contract Validity and Enforceability

Contract Creation

Classification of Contracts

Contract Termination

Contract Termination

Forms of contract termination

❑ **Performance** – contract is fulfilled

❑ **Infeasibility** – impossible to perform

❑ **Mutual agreement** – parties agree to alternate form of action

❑ **Rescission** – cooling period nullification

10:

Real Estate Contract Law

Contract Validity and Enforceability

Contract Creation

Classification of Contracts

Contract Termination

Contract Termination

Forms of contract termination (cont.)

❑ **Revocation** – one party cancels without consent of the other party
  ▪ Revoker may or may not incur liability
❑ **Abandonment** – failure to perform
  ▪ E.g., listing agent abandons overpriced listing
❑ **Lapse** – contract expires on its deadline
❑ **Invalidity** – if void, need not be terminated
❑ **Breach** – one party defaults

10:

Real Estate Contract Law

Contract Validity and Enforceability

Contract Creation

Classification of Contracts

Contract Termination

Contract Termination

Breach of contract

❑ Default of contract for failure to perform terms

❑ Gives other party right to legal recourse

❑ Legal remedies
  ▪ Rescission
  ▪ Forfeiture
  ▪ Suit for damages
  ▪ Specific performance

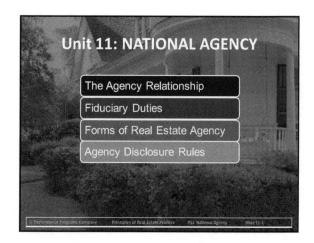

Unit 11: NATIONAL AGENCY

The Agency Relationship

Fiduciary Duties

Forms of Real Estate Agency

Agency Disclosure Rules

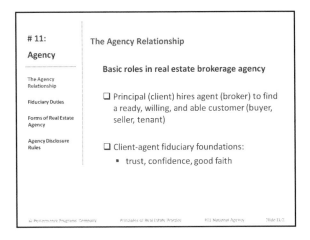

 # 11:

Agency

The Agency Relationship

Fiduciary Duties

Forms of Real Estate Agency

Agency Disclosure Rules

The Agency Relationship

Basic roles in real estate brokerage agency

❑ Principal (client) hires agent (broker) to find a ready, willing, and able customer (buyer, seller, tenant)

❑ Client-agent fiduciary foundations:
   ▪ trust, confidence, good faith

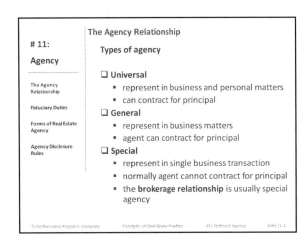

 # 11:

Agency

The Agency Relationship

Fiduciary Duties

Forms of Real Estate Agency

Agency Disclosure Rules

The Agency Relationship

Types of agency

❑ **Universal**
   ▪ represent in business and personal matters
   ▪ can contract for principal
❑ **General**
   ▪ represent in business matters
   ▪ agent can contract for principal
❑ **Special**
   ▪ represent in single business transaction
   ▪ normally agent cannot contract for principal
   ▪ the **brokerage relationship** is usually special agency

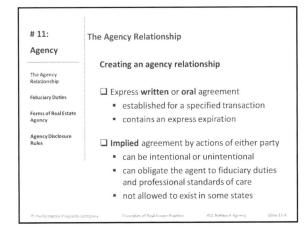

 # 11:

Agency

The Agency Relationship

Fiduciary Duties

Forms of Real Estate Agency

Agency Disclosure Rules

The Agency Relationship

Creating an agency relationship

❑ Express **written** or **oral** agreement
   ▪ established for a specified transaction
   ▪ contains an express expiration

❑ **Implied** agreement by actions of either party
   ▪ can be intentional or unintentional
   ▪ can obligate the agent to fiduciary duties and professional standards of care
   ▪ not allowed to exist in some states

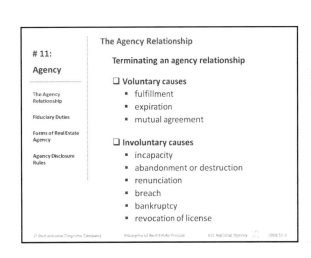

 # 11:

Agency

The Agency Relationship

Fiduciary Duties

Forms of Real Estate Agency

Agency Disclosure Rules

The Agency Relationship

Terminating an agency relationship

❑ **Voluntary causes**
   ▪ fulfillment
   ▪ expiration
   ▪ mutual agreement

❑ **Involuntary causes**
   ▪ incapacity
   ▪ abandonment or destruction
   ▪ renunciation
   ▪ breach
   ▪ bankruptcy
   ▪ revocation of license

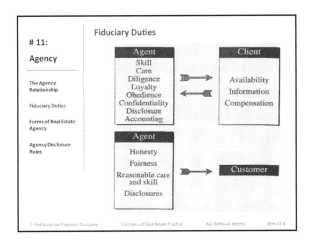

 # 11:

Agency

The Agency Relationship

Fiduciary Duties

Forms of Real Estate Agency

Agency Disclosure Rules

Fiduciary Duties

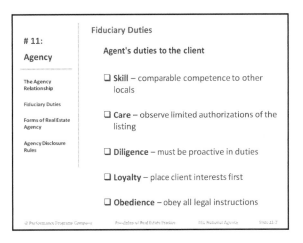

 # 11:

Agency

The Agency Relationship

Fiduciary Duties

Forms of Real Estate Agency

Agency Disclosure Rules

Fiduciary Duties

Agent's duties to the client

❑ **Skill** – comparable competence to other locals

❑ **Care** – observe limited authorizations of the listing

❑ **Diligence** – must be proactive in duties

❑ **Loyalty** – place client interests first

❑ **Obedience** – obey all legal instructions

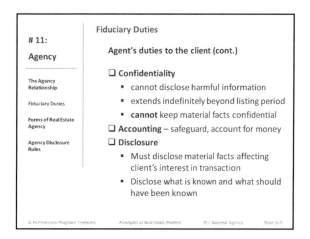

11:

Agency

The Agency Relationship

Fiduciary Duties

Forms of Real Estate Agency

Agency Disclosure Rules

Fiduciary Duties

Agent's duties to the client (cont.)

❑ **Confidentiality**
  - cannot disclose harmful information
  - extends indefinitely beyond listing period
  - **cannot** keep material facts confidential
❑ **Accounting** – safeguard, account for money
❑ **Disclosure**
  - Must disclose material facts affecting client's interest in transaction
  - Disclose what is known and what should have been known

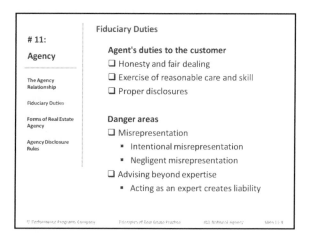

11:

Agency

The Agency Relationship

Fiduciary Duties

Forms of Real Estate Agency

Agency Disclosure Rules

Fiduciary Duties

Agent's duties to the customer
❑ Honesty and fair dealing
❑ Exercise of reasonable care and skill
❑ Proper disclosures

Danger areas
❑ Misrepresentation
  - Intentional misrepresentation
  - Negligent misrepresentation
❑ Advising beyond expertise
  - Acting as an expert creates liability

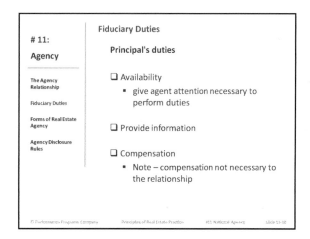

11:

Agency

The Agency Relationship

Fiduciary Duties

Forms of Real Estate Agency

Agency Disclosure Rules

Fiduciary Duties

Principal's duties

❑ Availability
  - give agent attention necessary to perform duties

❑ Provide information

❑ Compensation
  - Note – compensation not necessary to the relationship

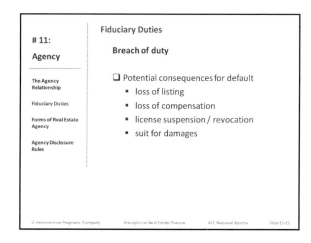

11:

Agency

The Agency Relationship

Fiduciary Duties

Forms of Real Estate Agency

Agency Disclosure Rules

Fiduciary Duties

Breach of duty

❑ Potential consequences for default
  - loss of listing
  - loss of compensation
  - license suspension / revocation
  - suit for damages

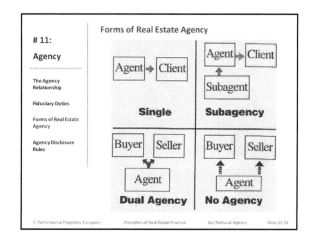

11:

Agency

The Agency Relationship

Fiduciary Duties

Forms of Real Estate Agency

Agency Disclosure Rules

Forms of Real Estate Agency

11:

Agency

The Agency Relationship

Fiduciary Duties

Forms of Real Estate Agency

Agency Disclosure Rules

Forms of Real Estate Agency

Single agency
❑ seller agency – agent represents seller
❑ buyer agency – agent represents buyer
❑ tenant representation – agent represents tenants

Subagency
❑ outside brokers and agents who help listing agent
❑ listing broker's own agents

Forms of Real Estate Agency

11:

Agency

The Agency Relationship

Fiduciary Duties

Forms of Real Estate Agency

Agency Disclosure Rules

Dual agency
- ❑ Representing both sides of transaction
- ❑ Potential conflict of interest
- ❑ Must disclose, obtain written consent

Types of dual agency
- ❑ Voluntary by consent
- ❑ Involuntary by actions of parties (implied agency)

Duties: all but full disclosure and loyalty

Forms of Real Estate Agency

11:

Agency

The Agency Relationship

Fiduciary Duties

Forms of Real Estate Agency

Agency Disclosure Rules

Dual agency duties

- ❑ Disclose to both parties, get written consent

- ❑ Owes certain fiduciary duties: skill, care, diligence, obedience, confidentiality, accounting

- ❑ **Does not owe** full disclosure, undivided loyalty, exclusive representation of client interest

---

Forms of Real Estate Agency

11:

Agency

The Agency Relationship

Fiduciary Duties

Forms of Real Estate Agency

Agency Disclosure Rules

No agency

- ❑ "Facilitator" or "transaction broker"

- ❑ Representing neither party in the transaction

- ❑ Duties to both parties:
  - accounting
  - skill, care and diligence
  - honesty and fair dealing
  - disclosures affecting property value

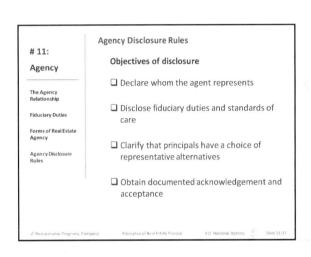

Agency Disclosure Rules

11:

Agency

The Agency Relationship

Fiduciary Duties

Forms of Real Estate Agency

Agency Disclosure Rules

Objectives of disclosure

- ❑ Declare whom the agent represents

- ❑ Disclose fiduciary duties and standards of care

- ❑ Clarify that principals have a choice of representative alternatives

- ❑ Obtain documented acknowledgement and acceptance

Agency Disclosure Rules

11:

Agency

The Agency Relationship

Fiduciary Duties

Forms of Real Estate Agency

Agency Disclosure Rules

Seller agent disclosures

- ❑ To client
  - in writing on or before listing is executed

- ❑ To customer
  - before or upon first substantive contact
  - Substantive = showing, eliciting material information, or completing an offer

- ❑ Oral disclosure
  - permitted but must have written follow-up

Agency Disclosure Rules

11:

Agency

The Agency Relationship

Fiduciary Duties

Forms of Real Estate Agency

Agency Disclosure Rules

Buyer agent disclosures
- ❑ in writing
- ❑ upon first contact with listing agent or seller

Dual agent disclosures
- ❑ "informed, written consent"
- ❑ may not disclose without authorization
  - Price, financing positions, motivations

Facilitator disclosures
- ❑ on becoming transaction broker, or upon substantive contact, whichever is first

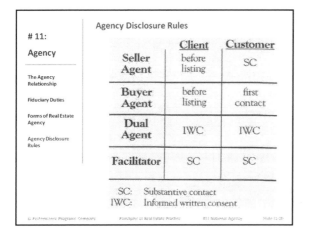

 # 11:

Agency

The Agency Relationship

Fiduciary Duties

Forms of Real Estate Agency

Agency Disclosure Rules

Agency Disclosure Rules

	Client	Customer
Seller Agent	before listing	SC
Buyer Agent	before listing	first contact
Dual Agent	IWC	IWC
Facilitator	SC	SC

SC: Substantive contact
IWC: Informed written consent

Unit 12: LISTING AGREEMENTS: AN OVERVIEW

- Review of Legal Foundations
- Types of Listing Agreement
- Fulfillment and Termination
- Agreement Clauses

 # 12:

Listing Agreements

Review of Legal Foundations

Types of Listing Agreement

Fulfillment and Termination

Agreement Clauses

Review of Legal Foundations

Listings – key characteristics

- ❑ Broker's **enforceable contract** of employment
- ❑ Establishes **special agency** relationship
- ❑ Defines **roles** of parties
- ❑ Creates **fiduciary duties** for the agent
- ❑ Describes agent's **scope of authority**

 # 12:

Listing Agreements

Review of Legal Foundations

Types of Listing Agreement

Fulfillment and Termination

Agreement Clauses

Review of Legal Foundations

Agency law

- ❑ **Parties:** listing broker and client
- ❑ **Fiduciary duties:** loyalty; obedience; disclosure; care; diligence; accounting

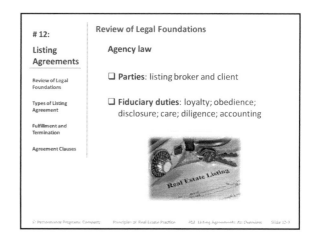

 # 12:

Listing Agreements

Review of Legal Foundations

Types of Listing Agreement

Fulfillment and Termination

Agreement Clauses

Review of Legal Foundations

Agency law (cont.)

- ❑ **Scope of authority**
  - **special or limited agency,** not general agency
  - broker may not contract for client unless authorized
  - client liable only for broker's acts within scope of authority

---

 # 12:

Listing Agreements

Review of Legal Foundations

Types of Listing Agreement

Fulfillment and Termination

Agreement Clauses

Review of Legal Foundations

Contract law and listings

- ❑ **Validity** - listing must be valid contract to be enforceable
- ❑ **Termination** - performance, infeasibility, mutual agreement, rescission, revocation, abandonment, lapse of time, invalidity, and breach
- ❑ **Legal form** - oral or written
  - Oral listings may be valid but can limit enforceability
  - Exclusive right-to-sell must be written to be enforceable
- ❑ **Assignment** - are not assignable since they are personal service contracts

 # 12:

Listing Agreements

Review of Legal Foundations

Types of Listing Agreement

Fulfillment and Termination

Agreement Clauses

Types of Listing Agreement

Owner listings
- ❑ Exclusive right-to-sell
- ❑ Exclusive agency
- ❑ Open listing
- ❑ Net listing

Buyer/tenant listings
- ❑ Exclusive right to represent
- ❑ Other types may be used

 # 12:

Listing Agreements

Review of Legal Foundations

Types of Listing Agreement

Fulfillment and Termination

Agreement Clauses

Types of Listing Agreement

Exclusive right-to-sell (or lease)

- ❑ Most prevalent in residential brokerage
- ❑ Given to one broker
- ❑ Must be written
- ❑ Must expire
- ❑ **Broker gets commission if property transfers** during listing period, regardless

---

 # 12:

Listing Agreements

Review of Legal Foundations

Types of Listing Agreement

Fulfillment and Termination

Agreement Clauses

Types of Listing Agreement

Exclusive agency

- ❑ Exclusive excepting owner
- ❑ Oral or written
- ❑ Must expire
- ❑ **Broker gets commission unless owner sells**

 # 12:

Listing Agreements

Review of Legal Foundations

Types of Listing Agreement

Fulfillment and Termination

Agreement Clauses

Types of Listing Agreement

Open listing

- ❑ Non-exclusive
- ❑ Oral or written
- ❑ No stated expiration
- ❑ **Party with procuring cause gets commission**
- ❑ **No commission if client or other agent** procures customer

---

 # 12:

Listing Agreements

Review of Legal Foundations

Types of Listing Agreement

Fulfillment and Termination

Agreement Clauses

Types of Listing Agreement

Net listing
- ❑ All sale proceeds above a seller's minimum price go to the broker
- ❑ Discouraged practice; illegal in some states

- ❑ Example
  - ▪ Seller wants to net $200,000 after sale
  - ▪ Broker lists, sells for $400,000
  - ▪ Net proceeds after costs, mortgage = $250,000
  - ▪ Broker pays seller $200,000, pockets $50,000

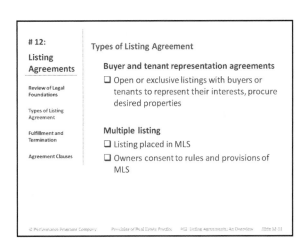

 # 12:

Listing Agreements

Review of Legal Foundations

Types of Listing Agreement

Fulfillment and Termination

Agreement Clauses

Types of Listing Agreement

Buyer and tenant representation agreements
- ❑ Open or exclusive listings with buyers or tenants to represent their interests, procure desired properties

Multiple listing
- ❑ Listing placed in MLS
- ❑ Owners consent to rules and provisions of MLS

12:

Listing Agreements

Review of Legal Foundations

Types of Listing Agreement

Fulfillment and Termination

Agreement Clauses

Types of Listing Agreement

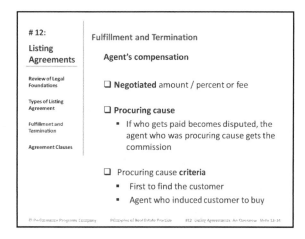

Listing	Commission Terms
Exclusive	$ if anybody procures
Exclusive Agency	$ unless client procures
Open	$ only if agent procures
Net	$ = (sale price - listing price)

12:

Listing Agreements

Review of Legal Foundations

Types of Listing Agreement

Fulfillment and Termination

Agreement Clauses

Fulfillment and Termination

Agent's performance

❑ Based on results

❑ Find ready willing and able customer, or effect a sale

❑ May perform only authorized tasks to achieve result

❑ Must verify owner and property data

❑ May delegate duties to salespeople and other brokers

12:

Listing Agreements

Review of Legal Foundations

Types of Listing Agreement

Fulfillment and Termination

Agreement Clauses

Fulfillment and Termination

Agent's compensation

❑ **Negotiated** amount / percent or fee

❑ **Procuring cause**
- If who gets paid becomes disputed, the agent who was procuring cause gets the commission

❑ Procuring cause **criteria**
- First to find the customer
- Agent who induced customer to buy

12:

Listing Agreements

Review of Legal Foundations

Types of Listing Agreement

Fulfillment and Termination

Agreement Clauses

Fulfillment and Termination

Causes for listing termination

❑ **Performance** – listing is fulfilled

❑ **Infeasibility** – impossible to perform

❑ **Mutual agreement** – voluntary cancel

❑ **Revocation** – one party cancels, whether right or wrong

❑ **Abandonment** – agent drops the listing

12:

Listing Agreements

Review of Legal Foundations

Types of Listing Agreement

Fulfillment and Termination

Agreement Clauses

Fulfillment and Termination

Causes for listing termination (cont.)

❑ **Breach** – one or both parties default

❑ **Expiration** - listing terminates on given date

❑ **Invalidity** – failed contract validity criteria

❑ **Incapacitation or death** – due to listings being personal service contracts

❑ **Involuntary transfer** – condemnation, bankruptcy, foreclosure

❑ **Destruction** of property

12:

Listing Agreements

Review of Legal Foundations

Types of Listing Agreement

Fulfillment and Termination

Agreement Clauses

Fulfillment and Termination

Revoking a listing

❑ Clients always have power to revoke during period
- may incur liability for commission or damages
- must pay commission if buyer was procured
- If no buyer procured, client may have to re-pay broker's expenses

❑ If broker revokes listing
- Client may sue for damages

Slide 1

12:

Listing Agreements

Review of Legal Foundations

Types of Listing Agreement

Fulfillment and Termination

Agreement Clauses

Agreement Clauses

Exclusives (minimal requirements)

- ❑ Broker's and owners' names
- ❑ Address or legal description
- ❑ Listing price
- ❑ Time period
- ❑ Commission terms
- ❑ Authority granted

Slide 2

12:

Listing Agreements

Review of Legal Foundations

Types of Listing Agreement

Fulfillment and Termination

Agreement Clauses

Agreement Clauses

Common clauses - exclusive listings

- ❑ **Parties and authorization**
  - all owners must sign
  - What type of listing it is
- ❑ **Real property**
  - Address / legal description
  - What fixtures, personal property is included
- ❑ **Price**
  - Price, purchase terms, financing permitted
  - What closing costs seller will pay

Slide 3

12:

Listing Agreements

Review of Legal Foundations

Types of Listing Agreement

Fulfillment and Termination

Agreement Clauses

Agreement Clauses

Common clauses - exclusive listings (cont.)

- ❑ **Listing term**
  - Must have beginning and ending dates
  - No automatic renewals allowed
- ❑ **Agent's duties**
  - Marketing activities
  - What agent may not do
- ❑ **Compensation**
  - Fee or percent amount
  - Conditions for earning compensation
  - Agent's remedies if seller defaults

Slide 4

12:

Listing Agreements

Review of Legal Foundations

Types of Listing Agreement

Fulfillment and Termination

Agreement Clauses

Agreement Clauses

Common clauses - exclusive listings (cont.)

- ❑ **Protection period**
  - Seller is liable for a period beyond expiration if property sells to a procured customer
- ❑ **Multiple listing**
  - Seller must consent to participate
- ❑ **Cooperation**
  - Must get approval to work & pay subagents
- ❑ **Non-discrimination**
  - Must comply with state and federal laws

Slide 5

12:

Listing Agreements

Review of Legal Foundations

Types of Listing Agreement

Fulfillment and Termination

Agreement Clauses

Agreement Clauses

Common clauses - exclusive listings (cont.)

- ❑ **Dual agency**
  - Obtains sellers consent or refusal to engage in dual agency
- ❑ **Seller's representations**
  - Owner will deliver marketable title
  - Will not lease during listing period w/o approval
  - Will provide information
  - Will refer prospects to broker
  - Has reviewed sale contract
  - Will make property presentable for showings

Slide 6

12:

Listing Agreements

Review of Legal Foundations

Types of Listing Agreement

Fulfillment and Termination

Agreement Clauses

Agreement Clauses

Common clauses - exclusive listings (cont.)

- ❑ **Seller's property condition disclosure**
  - Will provide, comply with disclosures
- ❑ **Seller's title, deed**
  - Will provide clear title, title insurance, what type of deed to be used
- ❑ **Flood, hazard insurance**
  - Disclose whether required
- ❑ **Signatures** – all owners & broker

# 12:	Agreement Clauses
Listing Agreements	**Common clauses - exclusive buyer agency**
Review of Legal Foundations	❑ Differences from seller's exclusive
Types of Listing Agreement	▪ Buyer is the principal
Fulfillment and Termination	▪ Agent's objectives
Agreement Clauses	▪ How agent is paid

# 12:	Agreement Clauses
Listing Agreements	**Common clauses – transaction brokerage**
Review of Legal Foundations	❑ Differences from seller's / buyer's exclusive
Types of Listing Agreement	▪ Non-agency declaration; no fiduciary
Fulfillment and Termination	▪ Agent's duties – to assist, facilitate as opposed to 'represent'
Agreement Clauses	

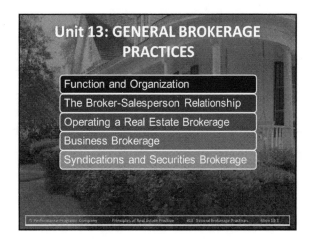

Unit 13: GENERAL BROKERAGE PRACTICES

- Function and Organization
- The Broker-Salesperson Relationship
- Operating a Real Estate Brokerage
- Business Brokerage
- Syndications and Securities Brokerage

# 13:	Function and Organization
The Brokerage Business	**The core activity of brokerage**
Function and Organization	❑ Procuring buyer, seller, tenant, or leased property for a client
The Broker-Salesperson Relationship	▪ commonly involves other brokers and multiple listing service(s)
Operating a Real Estate Brokerage	❑ Skills: listing, marketing, facilitating, managing information
Business Brokerage	
Syndications and Securities Brokerage	❑ Multiple listing service: network of brokers who share listings

# 13:	Function and Organization
The Brokerage Business	**Brokerage specializations**
Function and Organization	❑ By transaction type
The Broker-Salesperson Relationship	▪ sales; rentals; exchanges; subleases; options
Operating a Real Estate Brokerage	❑ By property type
Business Brokerage	▪ residential; retail; office; industrial; land; special purpose
Syndications and Securities Brokerage	❑ By geography
	▪ local; regional; national; global

# 13:	Function and Organization
The Brokerage Business	**Who may legally broker real estate?**
Function and Organization	❑ May broker
	▪ sole proprietorship
The Broker-Salesperson Relationship	▪ for-profit corporation
	▪ general or limited partnership
Operating a Real Estate Brokerage	▪ joint venture
Business Brokerage	❑ May not broker
Syndications and Securities Brokerage	▪ non-profit corporation
	▪ business trust
	▪ cooperative association

 # 13:
The Brokerage Business

Function and Organization

The Broker-Salesperson Relationship

Operating a Real Estate Brokerage

Business Brokerage

Syndications and Securities Brokerage

Function and Organization

Types of brokerage organization

❑ Independents

❑ Franchises

❑ Real estate agencies by
  ▪ property type
  ▪ transaction type
  ▪ client type
  ▪ form of service rendered

❑ Limited and full service agencies

 # 13:
The Brokerage Business

Function and Organization

The Broker-Salesperson Relationship

Operating a Real Estate Brokerage

Business Brokerage

Syndications and Securities Brokerage

The Broker-Salesperson Relationship

Legal relationships

❑ Salesperson is
  ▪ agent, fiduciary of broker
  ▪ acts in broker's name
  ▪ subagent of client

❑ Salesperson may not
  ▪ have two employers
  ▪ be paid by other parties
  ▪ bind clients contractually

 # 13:
The Brokerage Business

Function and Organization

The Broker-Salesperson Relationship

Operating a Real Estate Brokerage

Business Brokerage

Syndications and Securities Brokerage

The Broker-Salesperson Relationship

Salesperson's employment status

❑ May be employee or independent contractor (IC) – typically is a contractor
  ▪ IC works own hours
  ▪ IC responsible for taxes
  ▪ IC does not get benefits

❑ Relationship, respective responsibilities, compensation defined by agreement

❑ Unlicensed, licensed assistants
  ▪ If unlicensed, must limit activities to administrative tasks
  ▪ Licensed assistants may perform licensed activities and must be paid by employing broker

---

 # 13:
The Brokerage Business

Function and Organization

The Broker-Salesperson Relationship

Operating a Real Estate Brokerage

Business Brokerage

Syndications and Securities Brokerage

The Broker-Salesperson Relationship

Agent obligations and responsibilities

❑ Obtain & sell listings

❑ Follow policies and employment provisions

❑ Fulfill fiduciary duties

❑ Promote ethics and broker's reputation

 # 13:
The Brokerage Business

Function and Organization

The Broker-Salesperson Relationship

Operating a Real Estate Brokerage

Business Brokerage

Syndications and Securities Brokerage

The Broker-Salesperson Relationship

Broker obligations and responsibilities to agent

❑ Make listings, market data available

❑ Provide office support, training

❑ Fulfill compensation, other covenants of employment agreement

❑ Uphold brokerage ethics

 # 13:
The Brokerage Business

Function and Organization

The Broker-Salesperson Relationship

Operating a Real Estate Brokerage

Business Brokerage

Syndications and Securities Brokerage

The Broker-Salesperson Relationship

Agent compensation

❑ Commissions payable per schedule after splits with cooperating brokers
  ▪ commission portion for broker
  ▪ commission portion for co-op broker
  ▪ commission portion for listing the property
  ▪ commission portion for selling the property

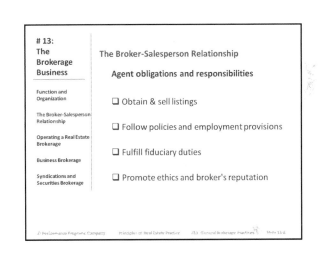

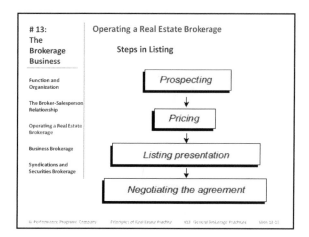

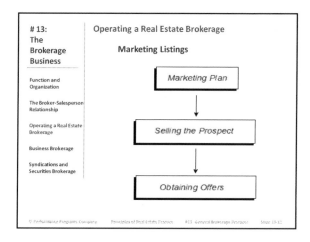

 # 13:
The
Brokerage
Business

Function and
Organization

The Broker-Salesperson
Relationship

Operating a Real Estate
Brokerage

Business Brokerage

Syndications and
Securities Brokerage

Operating a Real Estate Brokerage

Pre-closing activities

❑ Facilitate fulfillment of contract contingencies
and provisions
- Buyer's financing
- Seller's title work
- Property repairs
- Inspectors, appraisers, attorneys
- Handle documents, communications

❑ No commingling or conversion of escrow
funds

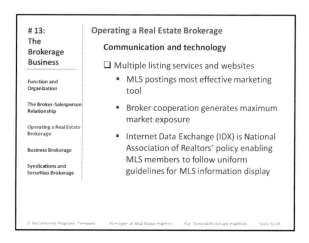

 # 13:
The
Brokerage
Business

Function and
Organization

The Broker-Salesperson
Relationship

Operating a Real Estate
Brokerage

Business Brokerage

Syndications and
Securities Brokerage

Operating a Real Estate Brokerage

Communication and technology

❑ Email and texting
- Enables instantaneous communications
- Considered advertising, thus licensees
must obey advertising regulations and
avoid deceptive messaging, solicitation
rules

❑ Social media – also subject to state
advertising regulations

❑ Smart phones – facilitates email, texting,
social media, internet access, document
review, photo sharing, storage, video
conferencing, mobile officing

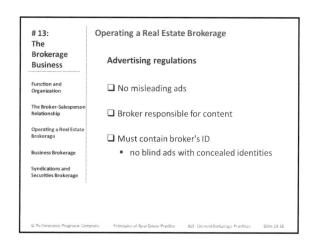

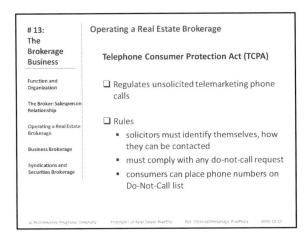

13:
The
Brokerage
Business

Function and Organization

The Broker-Salesperson Relationship

Operating a Real Estate Brokerage

Business Brokerage

Syndications and Securities Brokerage

Operating a Real Estate Brokerage

Telephone Consumer Protection Act (TCPA)

❑ Regulates unsolicited telemarketing phone calls

❑ Rules
- solicitors must identify themselves, how they can be contacted
- must comply with any do-not-call request
- consumers can place phone numbers on Do-Not-Call list

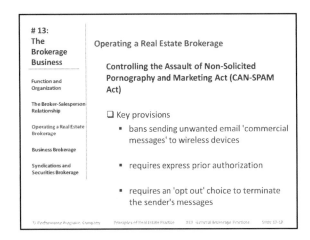

13:
The
Brokerage
Business

Function and Organization

The Broker-Salesperson Relationship

Operating a Real Estate Brokerage

Business Brokerage

Syndications and Securities Brokerage

Operating a Real Estate Brokerage

Controlling the Assault of Non-Solicited Pornography and Marketing Act (CAN-SPAM Act)

❑ Key provisions
- bans sending unwanted email 'commercial messages' to wireless devices
- requires express prior authorization
- requires an 'opt out' choice to terminate the sender's messages

13:
The
Brokerage
Business

Function and Organization

The Broker-Salesperson Relationship

Operating a Real Estate Brokerage

Business Brokerage

Syndications and Securities Brokerage

Operating a Real Estate Brokerage

Anti-trust laws

❑ Purpose is to prevent unfair trade practices

❑ Sherman, Clayton anti-trust laws
- No restraint of trade
- No monopolistic practices
- No predatory pricing, price-fixing
- No exclusive dealing

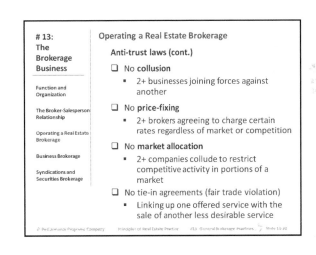

13:
The
Brokerage
Business

Function and Organization

The Broker-Salesperson Relationship

Operating a Real Estate Brokerage

Business Brokerage

Syndications and Securities Brokerage

Operating a Real Estate Brokerage

Anti-trust laws (cont.)

❑ No **collusion**
- 2+ businesses joining forces against another

❑ No **price-fixing**
- 2+ brokers agreeing to charge certain rates regardless of market or competition

❑ No **market allocation**
- 2+ companies collude to restrict competitive activity in portions of a market

❑ No tie-in agreements (fair trade violation)
- Linking up one offered service with the sale of another less desirable service

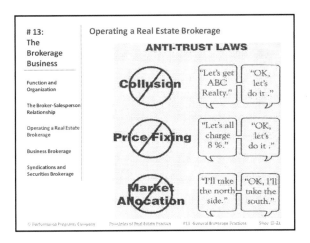

13:
The
Brokerage
Business

Function and Organization

The Broker-Salesperson Relationship

Operating a Real Estate Brokerage

Business Brokerage

Syndications and Securities Brokerage

Operating a Real Estate Brokerage

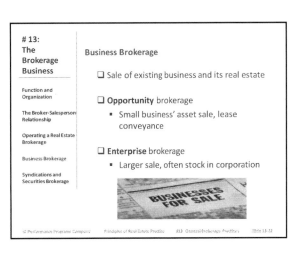

13:
The
Brokerage
Business

Function and Organization

The Broker-Salesperson Relationship

Operating a Real Estate Brokerage

Business Brokerage

Syndications and Securities Brokerage

Business Brokerage

❑ Sale of existing business and its real estate

❑ **Opportunity** brokerage
- Small business' asset sale, lease conveyance

❑ **Enterprise** brokerage
- Larger sale, often stock in corporation

 # 13:
The Brokerage Business

Function and Organization

The Broker-Salesperson Relationship

Operating a Real Estate Brokerage

Business Brokerage

Syndications and Securities Brokerage

Business Brokerage

Business brokerage regulation

❑ Generally, must have **active real estate license**
❑ **Uniform Commercial Code (UCC)**
 ▪ regulates the sale of personal property
 ▪ forms the basis for standardized sale documents (promissory notes, security agreements, bills of sale)
❑ **Bulk Sales Act**
 ▪ protects creditors against loss through undisclosed sale of business's inventory

---

 # 13:
The Brokerage Business

Function and Organization

The Broker-Salesperson Relationship

Operating a Real Estate Brokerage

Business Brokerage

Syndications and Securities Brokerage

Syndications and Securities Brokerage

Syndicating real estate

❑ Pooling capital and expertise to acquire, manage, sell, and profit from property investment

❑ Syndicator organizes syndication; procures investors

❑ Syndication is a security; investor may profit without management

---

 # 13:
The Brokerage Business

Function and Organization

The Broker-Salesperson Relationship

Operating a Real Estate Brokerage

Business Brokerage

Syndications and Securities Brokerage

Syndications and Securities Brokerage

Syndicating real estate (cont.)

❑ Securities licensing
 ▪ must obtain securities license to sell syndications to investors

❑ Securities registration
 ▪ must register certain syndications with SEC

Unit 14: OVERVIEW OF CONVEYANCE CONTRACTS

Contract for Sale

Sale Contract Provisions

Option-to-Buy Contract

Contract for Deed

 # 14:
Contracts for the Sale of Real Estate

Contract for Sale

Sale Contract Provisions

Option-to-Buy Contract

Contract for Deed

Contract for Sale

❑ General characteristics

 ▪ binding, enforceable contract to buy and sell parcel of real property

 ▪ 3 stages of property conveyance
  o offering, negotiating phase
  o execution and pre-closing phase
  o closing, contract extinguishment

 ▪ aka, agreement of sale, earnest money contract

 # 14:
Contracts for the Sale of Real Estate

Contract for Sale

Sale Contract Provisions

Option-to-Buy Contract

Contract for Deed

Contract for Sale

❑ Legal characteristics

 ▪ **executory contract** – signed contract has yet to be performed, fulfilled

 ▪ **signatures** – all owners must sign, including spouses

 ▪ **enforceability** – must fulfill all requirements of contract validity

 ▪ **written vs. oral** – must be in writing to be enforceable

 ▪ **assignment** – fully assignable

 # 14:
Contracts
for the Sale
of Real Estate

Contract for Sale

Sale Contract Provisions

Option-to-Buy Contract

Contract for Deed

Contract for Sale

❑ Legal characteristics

- **who may complete**
  - broker may assist buyer or seller
  - cannot charge separate fee for assisting
  - advisable or required to use standard forms
  - broker must avoid practicing law; follow state guidelines for completion

---

 # 14:
Contracts
for the Sale
of Real Estate

Contract for Sale

Sale Contract Provisions

Option-to-Buy Contract

Contract for Deed

Contract for Sale

❑ Contract creation

- offer and acceptance
  - offer cannot be changed to be accepted; any change nullifies previous offer
  - offeror may revoke offer prior to acceptance without penalty
- equitable title
  - buyer can obtain *legal* title upon seller default via specific performance

---

 # 14:
Contracts
for the Sale
of Real Estate

Contract for Sale

Sale Contract Provisions

Option-to-Buy Contract

Contract for Deed

Contract for Sale

❑ Earnest money escrow

- secures contract validity and buyer's equitable interest
- varies in amount; governed by custom
- deposit controlled by **escrow instructions and escrow agent**
  - escrow agent is fiduciary to buyer, seller
  - must act according to escrow instructions, state laws

 # 14:
Contracts
for the Sale
of Real Estate

Contract for Sale

Sale Contract Provisions

Option-to-Buy Contract

Contract for Deed

Contract for Sale

❑ Contract contingencies

- conditions that must be met for the contract to be enforceable
- contingencies should
  - be explicit, clear
  - have an expiration date
  - require that diligence be expended to fulfill the requirement

---

 # 14:
Contracts
for the Sale
of Real Estate

Contract for Sale

Sale Contract Provisions

Option-to-Buy Contract

Contract for Deed

Contract for Sale

❑ Default

- buyer default
  - seller can cancel and claim liquidated damages or sue for specific performance
  - liquidated damages = buyer's deposit
- seller default
  - buyer can cancel or sue for damages and/or specific performance

---

 # 14:
Contracts
for the Sale
of Real Estate

Contract for Sale

Sale Contract Provisions

Option-to-Buy Contract

Contract for Deed

Sale Contract Provisions

❑ Primary provisions

- **parties, consideration, and property's legal description**
  - must identify principals, price and property's legal description
  - must be two parties
  - parties must be able to contract
  - contract must include all personal property and fixtures included
- **price and terms**
  - deposit amount
  - final terms; downpayment amount
  - seller financing terms if applicable

Slide 1

 # 14:
Contracts for the Sale of Real Estate

Contract for Sale

Sale Contract Provisions

Option-to-Buy Contract

Contract for Deed

Sale Contract Provisions

❑ Primary provisions

- **loan approval**
  - financing contingency details
- **earnest money, escrow**
  - exact payment amount, terms
  - seller's acknowledgement in contract
  - how funds will be escrowed, paid out
- **closing and possession dates**
  - what must take place at closing (deed, clear title, all funds)
  - failure to deliver is grounds for default

Slide 2

 # 14:
Contracts for the Sale of Real Estate

Contract for Sale

Sale Contract Provisions

Option-to-Buy Contract

Contract for Deed

Sale Contract Provisions

❑ Primary provisions

- **conveyed interest, type of deed**
  - type of estate (fee simple, commonly)
  - type of deed (general warranty)
  - deed conditions
- **title evidence** – title insurance
- **closing costs** – who will pay what
- **damage and destruction**
  - respective duties, obligations if damage or destruction occurs

Slide 3

 # 14:
Contracts for the Sale of Real Estate

Contract for Sale

Sale Contract Provisions

Option-to-Buy Contract

Contract for Deed

Sale Contract Provisions

❑ Primary provisions (cont.)

- **default**
  - identifies remedies
  - damages; specific performance; cancellation
- **broker's representation, commission**
  - relationship disclosure
  - commission arrangement
- **seller's representations**
  - warrant of clear title upon closing
  - all representations are true

Slide 4

 # 14:
Contracts for the Sale of Real Estate

Contract for Sale

Sale Contract Provisions

Option-to-Buy Contract

Contract for Deed

Sale Contract Provisions

❑ Secondary provisions

- **inspections** – undertake, agree on remedial actions
- **owner's association disclosure** – agree on obligations
- **survey** – to satisfy lender requirements
- **environmental hazards** - disclosures
- **compliance with laws** – no undisclosed code or zoning violations
- **seller financing disclosure** – make required disclosures
- **rental property tenant's rights**

Slide 5

 # 14:
Contracts for the Sale of Real Estate

Contract for Sale

Sale Contract Provisions

Option-to-Buy Contract

Contract for Deed

Sale Contract Provisions

❑ Secondary provisions

- **FHA or VA financing conditions** – cancel option if price exceeds VA or FHA value
- **flood insurance** – may require if in flood plain
- **condominium assessments** - disclosure
- **foreign seller withholding** – 15% of price if seller is alien
- **dispute resolution** – parties agree to arbitrate disputes versus litigate

Slide 6

 # 14:
Contracts for the Sale of Real Estate

Contract for Sale

Sale Contract Provisions

Option-to-Buy Contract

Contract for Deed

Sale Contract Provisions

❑ Secondary provisions

- **C.L.U.E. Report**
  - stands for Comprehensive Loss Underwriting Exchange
  - insurance database used for underwriting insurance policies
  - used in closings to disclose any prior claims or losses on property
  - no recent claims helps to assure marketability of title
- **addenda** – binding, special-topic agreements added to sale contract

 # 14:
Contracts for the Sale of Real Estate

Contract for Sale

Sale Contract Provisions

Option-to-Buy Contract

Contract for Deed

Option-to-Buy Contract

❑ Contract requirements
  ▪ optionor = grantor; optionee = grantee
  ▪ option conveys right to buy at a given time for a given price and terms
  ▪ optionee must pay an amount for option
  ▪ unilateral contract:
    ○ optionee does not have to buy, but if s/he does, optionor must sell
  ▪ lease option
    ○ landlord allows portion of rent to be applied to purchase during the option period

---

 # 14:
Contracts for the Sale of Real Estate

Contract for Sale

Sale Contract Provisions

Option-to-Buy Contract

Contract for Deed

Option-to-Buy Contract

❑ Option contract requirements

  ▪ non-refundable consideration for the option right
  ▪ unchangeable price and terms of the sale
  ▪ expiration date
  ▪ legal description
  ▪ must be in writing
  ▪ must meet contract validity requirements

 # 14:
Contracts for the Sale of Real Estate

Contract for Sale

Sale Contract Provisions

Option-to-Buy Contract

Contract for Deed

Option-to-Buy Contract

❑ Common clause provisions
  ▪ how to exercise option
  ▪ forfeiture terms
  ▪ property, good title warranties
  ▪ how option money will be applied to purchase price

❑ Legal aspects

  ▪ **equitable interest**: optionee has right to obtain title
  ▪ option should be recorded
  ▪ options are assignable

 # 14:
Contracts for the Sale of Real Estate

Contract for Sale

Sale Contract Provisions

Option-to-Buy Contract

Contract for Deed

Contract For Deed

❑ General characteristics, mechanics
  ▪ also called **land contract, conditional sales contract, installment sale**
  ▪ vendor (seller) sells to vendee (buyer)
  ▪ seller retains legal title; buyer gets equitable title and possession
  ▪ vendor allows vendee to make periodic payments of price and interest over time
  ▪ at end of period, vendee refinances, pays seller remaining purchase price, gets legal title

---

 # 14:
Contracts for the Sale of Real Estate

Contract for Sale

Sale Contract Provisions

Option-to-Buy Contract

Contract for Deed

Contract For Deed

❑ Interests and rights
  ▪ seller may
    ○ encumber or assign interest
    ○ sell or assign interest
    ○ incur judgments
  ▪ seller remains liable for underlying mortgage; must convey title at end of term
  ▪ buyer must
    ○ make payments
    ○ maintain the property
    ○ purchase at end of term

 # 14:
Contracts for the Sale of Real Estate

Contract for Sale

Sale Contract Provisions

Option-to-Buy Contract

Contract for Deed

Contract For Deed

❑ Default and recourse
  ▪ If seller defaults
    ○ buyer may sue for cancellation and damages, or specific performance
  ▪ If buyer defaults
    ○ may sue for specific performance or damages
    ○ may need to foreclose
    ○ if breach of contract, may cancel contract

 # 14:
Contracts for the Sale of Real Estate

Contract for Sale

Sale Contract Provisions

Option-to-Buy Contract

Contract for Deed

Contract For Deed

❑ Usage guidelines

- contracts not standardized

  o must obtain competent counsel on both sides

- buyer without significant equity may cause damage, vacate

- seller may have undue power upon breach by buyer

  o may be able to cancel contract, retain moneys, avoid redemption rights

---

 # 14:
Contracts for the Sale of Real Estate

Contract for Sale

Sale Contract Provisions

Option-to-Buy Contract

Contract for Deed

Contract For Deed

❑ Usage guidelines – to minimize risk:

- use attorneys to draft agreement; use standardized forms

- be clear about how contract is to be enforced

- utilize professional escrow, title services

- record properly

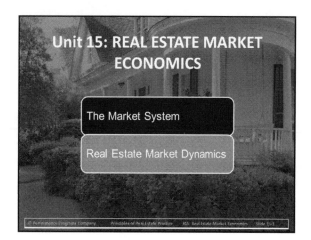

 # 15:
Real Estate Market Economics

The Market System

Real Estate Market Dynamics

The Market System

Why understand real estate market dynamics?

❑ Recognize effects of economic trends on real estate transaction volume, prices

❑ Forecast future conditions, trends

❑ Apply economics to a particular property or site

 # 15:
Real Estate Market Economics

The Market System

Real Estate Market Dynamics

The Market System

Supply and demand

❑ **Supply**

- goods or services available for sale, lease, or trade at any given time

❑ **Demand**

- goods or services desired for purchase, lease, or trade at any given time

❑ **Economic activity**

- production, distribution, sale of goods and services to meet demand

---

 # 15:
Real Estate Market Economics

The Market System

Real Estate Market Dynamics

The Market System

Price and value

❑ **Price mechanism**

- quantified value of an exchange

- Asking, bidding prices – amounts of value used to negotiate final price

- final price – the ending amount of value following bidding

 # 15:
Real Estate Market Economics

The Market System

Real Estate Market Dynamics

The Market System

Components of value

❑ **Desire**
  ▪ How bad do you want it?

❑ **Utility**
  ▪ How well can the item do the job?

❑ **Scarcity**
  ▪ How available is the item in relation to demand?

❑ **Purchasing power**
  ▪ How affordable is it?

 # 15:
Real Estate Market Economics

The Market System

Real Estate Market Dynamics

The Market System

Productivity and costs

❑ Essential production costs
  ▪ capital; materials; supplies; labor; management; overhead

❑ Must maximize efficiency to minimize costs

❑ Cost plus profit equals minimum price
  ▪ May conflict with desire, utility scarcity variables
  ▪ If cannot profit after costs, cannot produce

 # 15:
Real Estate Market Economics

The Market System

Real Estate Market Dynamics

The Market System

Market interaction

❑ The market
  ▪ transaction arena where suppliers and demanders define value through the price mechanism

❑ Supply and demand movements
  ▪ if supply increases relative to demand, price decreases

  ▪ if demand increases relative to supply, price increases

 # 15:
Real Estate Market Economics

The Market System

Real Estate Market Dynamics

The Market System

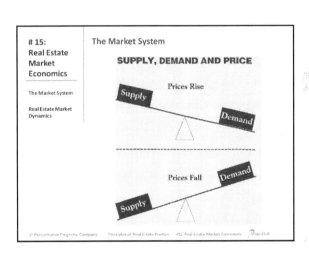

SUPPLY, DEMAND AND PRICE

 # 15:
Real Estate Market Economics

The Market System

Real Estate Market Dynamics

The Market System

Market equilibrium

❑ Supply and demand tend toward balance

❑ Market equilibrium
  ▪ price, cost, value theoretically the same

  ▪ market imbalances caused by changes in supply or demand

 # 15:
Real Estate Market Economics

The Market System

Real Estate Market Dynamics

Real Estate Market Dynamics

Economic characteristics of real estate

❑ Governed by
  ▪ supply
  ▪ demand
  ▪ price
  ▪ costs
  ▪ value components
  ▪ government influence

 # 15: Real Estate Market Economics

The Market System

Real Estate Market Dynamics

Real Estate Market Dynamics

Distinguishing features of real estate

❏ Inherent value
  ▪ real estate is scarce and a factor of production

❏ Unique appeal – no two parcels alike

❏ Immovable supply
  ▪ Demand must come to the supply!

 # 15: Real Estate Market Economics

The Market System

Real Estate Market Dynamics

Real Estate Market Dynamics

Distinguishing features of real estate (cont.)

❏ Illiquid
  ▪ cannot readily be sold for cash; takes time

❏ Slow response to cycles
  ▪ construction of new supply takes time

❏ Decentralized market
  ▪ Susceptible to local market swings

 # 15: Real Estate Market Economics

The Market System

Real Estate Market Dynamics

Real Estate Market Dynamics

Real estate supply

❏ Property available for sale or lease

❏ Measured in dwelling units, square feet, acres

❏ Influenced by
  ▪ costs
  ▪ finance
  ▪ returns
  ▪ government regulation

 # 15: Real Estate Market Economics

The Market System

Real Estate Market Dynamics

Real Estate Market Dynamics

Real estate demand

❏ Property buyers and tenants **wish to acquire**

❏ Residential demand measured in number of **households**

❏ Commercial demand measured in **square feet**

❏ Undeveloped land demand measured in **acres**

 # 15: Real Estate Market Economics

The Market System

Real Estate Market Dynamics

Real Estate Market Dynamics

Influences on real estate demand

❏ **Residential**-- quality, amenities, price convenience

❏ **Retail**-- trade area, sales, competition, site access, visibility; growth patterns

❏ **Office**-- efficiency, costs, functionality

❏ **Industrial**-- functionality, regulatory compliance, access to labor, supplies, distribution channels

---

 # 15: Real Estate Market Economics

The Market System

Real Estate Market Dynamics

Real Estate Market Dynamics

BASIS OF REAL ESTATE DEMAND

Base employment → Total employment → Population → Industrial Demand, Retail Demand, Residential Demand

15:
Real Estate
Market
Economics

The Market System

Real Estate Market Dynamics

Real Estate Market Dynamics

Effects of employment, population on real estate demand

❑ If employment and population increase, demand and prices increase

❑ If employment and population decrease, the opposite occurs

❑ Example: gold is mined out of the mine → boom town becomes ghost town

---

15:
Real Estate
Market
Economics

The Market System

Real Estate Market Dynamics

Real Estate Market Dynamics

Supply-demand indicators

❑ **Price, vacancy, absorption** indicate demand-supply trends

❑ **Vacancy** is existing, unoccupied supply

❑ **Absorption** is the "filling up" of vacancy

❑ **Occupancy rate** is reciprocal of vacancy rate

15:
Real Estate
Market
Economics

The Market System

Real Estate Market Dynamics

Real Estate Market Dynamics

THE REAL ESTATE SUPPLY AND DEMAND CYCLE

15:
Real Estate
Market
Economics

The Market System

Real Estate Market Dynamics

Real Estate Market Dynamics

Real estate supply-demand cycle

❑ Cycle starts at undersupply > accelerated construction adds supply >

❑ Cycle reaches equilibrium > construction continues however

❑ Cycle reaches oversupply > construction stops

❑ Cycle reaches equilibrium > demand absorbs supply

❑ Demand continues > cycle returns to undersupply

15:
Real Estate
Market
Economics

The Market System

Real Estate Market Dynamics

Real Estate Market Dynamics

Market influences on supply and demand

❑ Local economic factors
  * employment conditions
  * population trends
  * planning department factors

❑ National economic trends
  * money supply
  * interest rates
  * inflation
  * government regulation at all levels

Unit 16: APPRAISING & ESTIMATING MARKET VALUE

Real Estate Value

Appraising Market Value

The Sales Comparison Approach

The Cost Approach

The Income Capitalization Approach

Regulation of Appraisal Practice

 # 16:
Appraising & Estimating Market Value

Real Estate Value

Appraising Market Value

The Sales Comparison Approach

The Cost Approach

The Income Capitalization Approach

Regulation of Appraisal Practice

Real Estate Value

❑ Present monetary worth of benefits from ownership, including

- income
- appreciation
- use
- tax benefits

 # 16:
Appraising & Estimating Market Value

Real Estate Value

Appraising Market Value

The Sales Comparison Approach

The Cost Approach

The Income Capitalization Approach

Regulation of Appraisal Practice

Real Estate Value

Foundations of real estate value

❑ **Supply and demand**
- Values decrease when supply outstrips demand
- Values increase when demand outstrips supply

❑ **Utility**
- The degree of usefulness affects the level of value
- E.g., air conditioners in the tropics vs. the Arctic

❑ **Transferability**
- The easier the transfer, the greater the value
- E.g., clear title; no liens; no repairs

 # 16:
Appraising & Estimating Market Value

Real Estate Value

Appraising Market Value

The Sales Comparison Approach

The Cost Approach

The Income Capitalization Approach

Regulation of Appraisal Practice

Real Estate Value

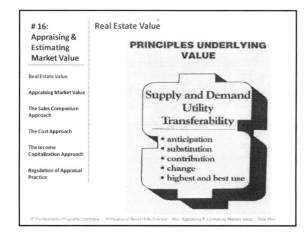

 # 16:
Appraising & Estimating Market Value

Real Estate Value

Appraising Market Value

The Sales Comparison Approach

The Cost Approach

The Income Capitalization Approach

Regulation of Appraisal Practice

Real Estate Value

Foundations of real estate value (cont.)

❑ **Anticipation**
- What the investor expects to benefit from a property over a holding period determines value

❑ **Substitution**
- All things being equal, buyers will buy the cheaper property
- E.g., a $500,000 house will not sell if a very similar house is priced at $350,000

❑ **Contribution**
- How much a component of a property contributes to the overall value

---

 # 16:
Appraising & Estimating Market Value

Real Estate Value

Appraising Market Value

The Sales Comparison Approach

The Cost Approach

The Income Capitalization Approach

Regulation of Appraisal Practice

Real Estate Value

Foundations of real estate value (cont.)

❑ **Change**
- Changing conditions change property value
- E.g., deteriorating neighborhood lowers value

❑ **Highest and best use**
- A property's use will gravitate toward the use that has the greatest economic return

❑ **Conformity**
- Maximum value accrues from a use conforming to the surroundings

---

 # 16:
Appraising & Estimating Market Value

Real Estate Value

Appraising Market Value

The Sales Comparison Approach

The Cost Approach

The Income Capitalization Approach

Regulation of Appraisal Practice

Real Estate Value

Foundations of real estate value (cont.)

❑ **Progression and regression**
- Values are affected by surrounding properties
- If they are higher, the subject's value is higher
- If they are lower, the subject's value is lower

❑ **Assemblage**
- Conjoining of properties can raise (or lower) values

❑ **Subdivision**
- Dividing a parcel into smaller pieces can increase total value

 # 16:
Appraising & Estimating Market Value

Real Estate Value
Appraising Market Value
The Sales Comparison Approach
The Cost Approach
The Income Capitalization Approach
Regulation of Appraisal Practice

Real Estate Value

Types of value

❑ **Market** - estimate of selling value; most common in real estate brokerage

❑ **Reproduction** – value based on constructing a precise duplicate

❑ **Replacement** – value based on constructing a functional equivalent

❑ **Salvage** – value at end of economic life

 # 16:
Appraising & Estimating Market Value

Real Estate Value
Appraising Market Value
The Sales Comparison Approach
The Cost Approach
The Income Capitalization Approach
Regulation of Appraisal Practice

Real Estate Value

Types of value (cont.)

❑ **Plottage** – additional value resulting from combining properties

❑ **Assessed** – value by tax assessor for ad valorem taxation

❑ **Condemned** – value resulting from condemnation suit

❑ **Depreciated** – price paid minus accumulated depreciation

---

 # 16:
Appraising & Estimating Market Value

Real Estate Value
Appraising Market Value
The Sales Comparison Approach
The Cost Approach
The Income Capitalization Approach
Regulation of Appraisal Practice

Real Estate Value

Types of value (cont.)

❑ **Appraised** - appraiser's opinion of value; typically market value

❑ **Insured** – amount an insurer will pay on a policyholder's policy

❑ **Book** – the value on a business' books, typically cost plus capital improvements minus depreciation

❑ **Mortgage** – value of the property as collateral for a loan

---

 # 16:
Appraising & Estimating Market Value

Real Estate Value
Appraising Market Value
The Sales Comparison Approach
The Cost Approach
The Income Capitalization Approach
Regulation of Appraisal Practice

Appraising Market Value

Market value

❑ Price a willing buyer and seller would agree to, given:
- cash transaction
- reasonable exposure to market
- principals are reasonably informed
- no pressure to transact
- arm's length – no relatives
- marketable title
- no hidden influences – undisclosed discounts, etc.

 # 16:
Appraising & Estimating Market Value

Real Estate Value
Appraising Market Value
The Sales Comparison Approach
The Cost Approach
The Income Capitalization Approach
Regulation of Appraisal Practice

Appraising Market Value

The appraisal and its uses

❑ Appraisal is a professional's opinion of value
- supported by data
- regulated
- following professional standards

❑ Broker's opinion of value
- not performed by disinterested third party
- not subject to regulation
- not subject to professional standards

 # 16:
Appraising & Estimating Market Value

Real Estate Value
Appraising Market Value
The Sales Comparison Approach
The Cost Approach
The Income Capitalization Approach
Regulation of Appraisal Practice

Appraising Market Value

STEPS IN THE APPRAISAL PROCESS

* Identify purpose
* Assimilate data
* Assess highest and best use
* Estimate value of land
* Apply three approaches to value
* Reconcile values

 # 16:
Appraising &
Estimating
Market Value

Real Estate Value

Appraising Market Value

The Sales Comparison
Approach

The Cost Approach

The Income
Capitalization Approach

Regulation of Appraisal
Practice

The Sales Comparison Approach

❑ Relies on principles of substitution and contribution

Steps in the approach

1) Identify comparable sales

2) Compare comparables to subject

3) Adjust comparables

4) Weigh adjusted values; reconcile final estimate

 # 16:
Appraising &
Estimating
Market Value

Real Estate Value

Appraising Market Value

The Sales Comparison
Approach

The Cost Approach

The Income
Capitalization Approach

Regulation of Appraisal
Practice

The Sales Comparison Approach

STEPS IN THE SALES COMPARISION APPROACH

1. Identify comps   2. Adjust comps   3. Weight comp values for subject value estimate

---

 # 16:
Appraising &
Estimating
Market Value

Real Estate Value

Appraising Market Value

The Sales Comparison
Approach

The Cost Approach

The Income
Capitalization Approach

Regulation of Appraisal
Practice

The Sales Comparison Approach

Guidelines

❑ Identifying comparable sales
  - physically similar
  - in the vicinity
  - recently sold in arm's length sale

❑ Adjusting comparables
  - deduct comp if better than subject
  - increase comp if worse than subject

❑ Weighting adjustments
  - best indicator is comp with least adjustments

 # 16:
Appraising &
Estimating
Market Value

Real Estate Value

Appraising Market Value

The Sales Comparison
Approach

The Cost Approach

The Income
Capitalization Approach

Regulation of Appraisal
Practice

The Cost Approach

❑ For recently built properties, special-purpose buildings

❑ Accurate for newer properties

❑ Depreciation difficult to estimate

Types of cost appraised
❑ Reproduction – precise replica
❑ Replacement – functional equivalent

 # 16:
Appraising &
Estimating
Market Value

Real Estate Value

Appraising Market Value

The Sales Comparison
Approach

The Cost Approach

The Income
Capitalization Approach

Regulation of Appraisal
Practice

The Cost Approach

Depreciation
❑ loss in value of an improvement over time from **deterioration** or **obsolescence**

❑Physical deterioration
  - Loss from use, decay, wear
  - Curable – resulting value greater than cost to fix
  - Incurable – resulting value less than cost to fix

❑ Functional obsolescence
  - Outmoded physical or design features
  - Curable or incurable

 # 16:
Appraising &
Estimating
Market Value

Real Estate Value

Appraising Market Value

The Sales Comparison
Approach

The Cost Approach

The Income
Capitalization Approach

Regulation of Appraisal
Practice

The Cost Approach

Depreciation (cont.)

❑ Economic obsolescence
  - Also, **external** obsolescence

  - Loss due to adverse changes in environment

  - Always incurable: **cannot fix**

  - E.g., large employer goes bankrupt

16: Appraising & Estimating Market Value

Real Estate Value

Appraising Market Value

The Sales Comparison Approach

The Cost Approach

The Income Capitalization Approach

Regulation of Appraisal Practice

The Cost Approach

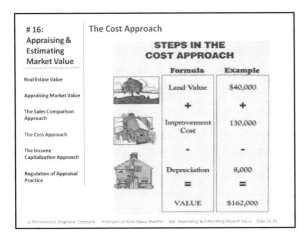

STEPS IN THE COST APPROACH

	Formula	Example
	Land Value	$40,000
	+	+
	Improvement Cost	130,000
	−	−
	Depreciation	8,000
	=	=
	VALUE	$162,000

16: Appraising & Estimating Market Value

Real Estate Value

Appraising Market Value

The Sales Comparison Approach

The Cost Approach

The Income Capitalization Approach

Regulation of Appraisal Practice

The Cost Approach

Steps in the approach (cont.)

❑ **Estimate land value**
- Cannot depreciate land
- Assume land is vacant
- Use sales comparison method

❑ **Estimate replacement cost**
- Unit comparison method
- Unit-in-place method
- Quantity survey method

16: Appraising & Estimating Market Value

Real Estate Value

Appraising Market Value

The Sales Comparison Approach

The Cost Approach

The Income Capitalization Approach

Regulation of Appraisal Practice

The Cost Approach

Steps in the approach (cont.)

❑ **Estimate accrued depreciation**
- Economic age-life method

❑ **Subtract depreciation from replacement cost; add land value = value estimate**

16: Appraising & Estimating Market Value

Real Estate Value

Appraising Market Value

The Sales Comparison Approach

The Cost Approach

The Income Capitalization Approach

Regulation of Appraisal Practice

The Income Capitalization Approach

❑ Used to appraise income properties

❑ Based on value principle of anticipation:
- what is the expected future return

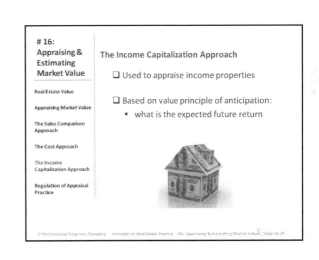

16: Appraising & Estimating Market Value

Real Estate Value

Appraising Market Value

The Sales Comparison Approach

The Cost Approach

The Income Capitalization Approach

Regulation of Appraisal Practice

The Income Capitalization Approach

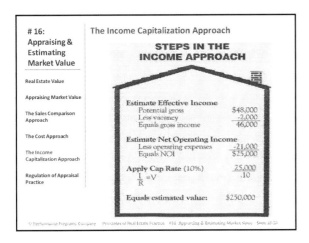

STEPS IN THE INCOME APPROACH

Estimate Effective Income	
Potential gross	$48,000
Less vacancy	-2,000
Equals gross income	46,000
Estimate Net Operating Income	
Less operating expenses	-21,000
Equals NOI	$25,000
Apply Cap Rate (10%)	25,000
$\frac{I}{R} = V$	.10
Equals estimated value:	$250,000

16: Appraising & Estimating Market Value

Real Estate Value

Appraising Market Value

The Sales Comparison Approach

The Cost Approach

The Income Capitalization Approach

Regulation of Appraisal Practice

The Income Capitalization Approach

Income approach - guidelines

❑ **Income − expenses ÷ cap rate = value**

- Potential income is fully-occupied rent + other income
- Take out projected vacancy and credit losses (rent defaults) to estimate effective income
- Subtract operating expenses to derive pre-tax net income (NOI)
- Apply cap rate to NOI to derive value estimate

Slide 1

# 16: Appraising & Estimating Market Value	The Income Capitalization Approach
Real Estate Value	**Gross Rent Multiplier (GRM) & Gross Income Multiplier (GIM)**
Appraising Market Value	❑ GRM derives a value from **monthly rent**
The Sales Comparison Approach	❑ GIM derives a value from **annual rent**
The Cost Approach	❑ GRM and GIM are simplistic methods used for very rough value estimates
The Income Capitalization Approach	
Regulation of Appraisal Practice	❑ Primarily used with multi-unit residential dwellings, e.g., duplexes

Slide 2

# 16: Appraising & Estimating Market Value	The Income Capitalization Approach
	(GRM) & (GIM) Formulas
Real Estate Value	
Appraising Market Value	GRM
	$\dfrac{Price}{Mo.\ Rent} = GRM \qquad \dfrac{\$100,000}{\$1,000} = 100$
The Sales Comparison Approach	**GRM x Mo. Rent = Value**
The Cost Approach	100 x $1,000 = $100,000
The Income Capitalization Approach	GIM
Regulation of Appraisal Practice	$\dfrac{Price}{Gross\ Annual\ Income} = GRM \qquad \dfrac{\$100,000}{\$10,000} = 10$
	GIM x Gross Annual Income = Value
	10 x $10,000 = $100,000

Slide 3

# 16: Appraising & Estimating Market Value	Regulation of Appraisal Practice
	Licensure
Real Estate Value	
Appraising Market Value	❑ Financial Institutions Reform, Recovery and Enforcement Act **(FIRREA)**
The Sales Comparison Approach	▪ Introduced licensure for appraisers in federally-related transactions
The Cost Approach	
The Income Capitalization Approach	▪ State-certified appraiser -- has passed the necessary examinations and competency standards set by each state
Regulation of Appraisal Practice	▪ Testing and certification conforms with Uniform Standards of Professional Appraisal Practice (USPAP)

Slide 4

# 16: Appraising & Estimating Market Value	Regulation of Appraisal Practice
	Professional standards
Real Estate Value	
Appraising Market Value	❑ Uniform Standards of Professional Appraisal Practice (USPAP) – principal concerns:
The Sales Comparison Approach	▪ Use recognized appraisal methods
The Cost Approach	▪ Exercise a defined due diligence
The Income Capitalization Approach	▪ Properly report results
Regulation of Appraisal Practice	▪ Proper disclosures and assumptions

Slide 5

Unit 17: REAL ESTATE FINANCE

- Anatomy of Mortgage Lending
- Initiating a Mortgage Loan
- Qualifying for a Mortgage Loan
- Closing a Loan
- Laws Affecting Mortgage Lending
- The Mortgage Market
- Types of Real Estate Loans

Slide 6

# 17: Real Estate Finance	Anatomy of Mortgage Lending
	Mechanics of a loan transaction
Anatomy of Mortgage Lending	
Initiating a Mortgage Loan	❑**Mortgage financing**: borrowed money secured by mortgage
Qualifying for a Mortgage Loan	❑**Instruments**: note & mortgage or trust deed
Closing a Loan	
Laws Affecting Mortgage Lending	❑**Mortgage process**: borrower gives lender note and mortgage; lender gives borrower funds and records a lien
The Mortgage Market	
Types of Real Estate Loans	❑**Trust deed process**: conveys title from borrower/trustor to third-party trustee who holds title for lender/beneficiary

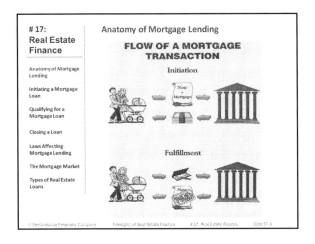

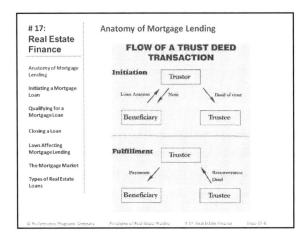

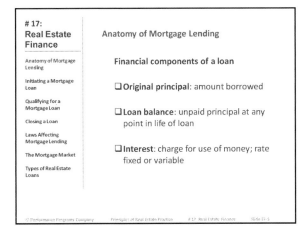

Anatomy of Mortgage Lending

Financial components of a loan

❑ **Original principal:** amount borrowed

❑ **Loan balance:** unpaid principal at any point in life of loan

❑ **Interest:** charge for use of money; rate fixed or variable

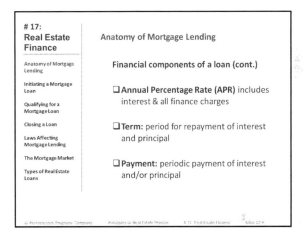

Anatomy of Mortgage Lending

Financial components of a loan (cont.)

❑ **Annual Percentage Rate (APR)** includes interest & all finance charges

❑ **Term:** period for repayment of interest and principal

❑ **Payment:** periodic payment of interest and/or principal

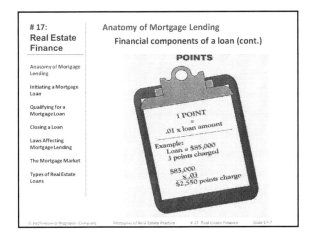

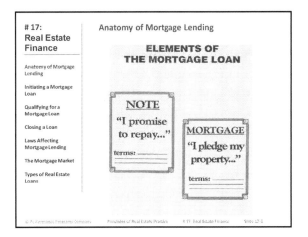

 # 17:
Real Estate Finance

Anatomy of Mortgage Lending

Initiating a Mortgage Loan

Qualifying for a Mortgage Loan

Closing a Loan

Laws Affecting Mortgage Lending

The Mortgage Market

Types of Real Estate Loans

Anatomy of Mortgage Lending

Promissory Note

❑ Legal instrument stating
- debt amount
- loan term
- method & timing of repayment
- interest rate
- promise to pay

❑ Negotiable instrument assignable to a third party

 # 17:
Real Estate Finance

Anatomy of Mortgage Lending

Initiating a Mortgage Loan

Qualifying for a Mortgage Loan

Closing a Loan

Laws Affecting Mortgage Lending

The Mortgage Market

Types of Real Estate Loans

Anatomy of Mortgage Lending

Mortgage document and trust deed

❑ Documents pledging property as collateral for loan
❑ May set forth terms covering
- principal & interest
- prepayment
- late charges
- T & I escrow
- liens
- insurance requirements
- occupancy
- maintenance
- lender's rights
- private mortgage insurance
- inspection
- other conditions

 # 17:
Real Estate Finance

Anatomy of Mortgage Lending

Initiating a Mortgage Loan

Qualifying for a Mortgage Loan

Closing a Loan

Laws Affecting Mortgage Lending

The Mortgage Market

Types of Real Estate Loans

Initiating a Mortgage Loan

The loan application

❑ Borrower provides
- personal and property data
- supporting documentation
- appraisal report
- credit report
- purchase contract
- income and/or employment verification

❑ Lenders' obligations
- must accept all completed applications
- notify applicants about disposition of application

 # 17:
Real Estate Finance

Anatomy of Mortgage Lending

Initiating a Mortgage Loan

Qualifying for a Mortgage Loan

Closing a Loan

Laws Affecting Mortgage Lending

The Mortgage Market

Types of Real Estate Loans

Initiating a Mortgage Loan

Mortgage loan underwriting

❑ Process of evaluating
- borrower's ability to repay
- value of the property

❑ Loan-to-value ratio (LTV)
- relationship of loan amount to property value
- expressed as a percentage
- 80% LTV = loan is 80% of property value

 # 17:
Real Estate Finance

Anatomy of Mortgage Lending

Initiating a Mortgage Loan

Qualifying for a Mortgage Loan

Closing a Loan

Laws Affecting Mortgage Lending

The Mortgage Market

Types of Real Estate Loans

Qualifying for a Mortgage Loan

Equal Credit Opportunity Act

❑ Lender must evaluate applicant's own income and credit information

❑ Lenders may not
- discount income from part-time work
- assume less income based on future family plans
- refuse loan solely due to location
- question age, sex, religion, race or national origin

 # 17:
Real Estate Finance

Anatomy of Mortgage Lending

Initiating a Mortgage Loan

Qualifying for a Mortgage Loan

Closing a Loan

Laws Affecting Mortgage Lending

The Mortgage Market

Types of Real Estate Loans

Qualifying for a Mortgage Loan

Income qualification

❑ Income ratio & debt ratio qualify borrower's income
- income ratio applied to gross income determines housing expense maximum
- debt ratio takes revolving debt into account

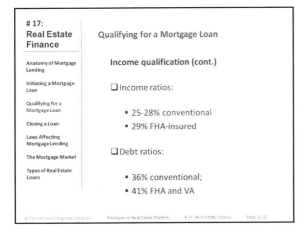

 # 17:
Real Estate Finance

Anatomy of Mortgage Lending

Initiating a Mortgage Loan

Qualifying for a Mortgage Loan

Closing a Loan

Laws Affecting Mortgage Lending

The Mortgage Market

Types of Real Estate Loans

Qualifying for a Mortgage Loan

Income qualification (cont.)

❏ Income ratios:

- 25-28% conventional
- 29% FHA-insured

❏ Debt ratios:

- 36% conventional;
- 41% FHA and VA

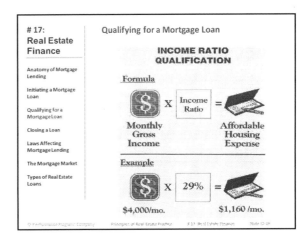

 # 17:
Real Estate Finance

Anatomy of Mortgage Lending

Initiating a Mortgage Loan

Qualifying for a Mortgage Loan

Closing a Loan

Laws Affecting Mortgage Lending

The Mortgage Market

Types of Real Estate Loans

Qualifying for a Mortgage Loan

INCOME RATIO QUALIFICATION

Formula

$ X Income Ratio = Affordable Housing Expense

Monthly Gross Income

Example

$ X 29% =

$4,000/mo. $1,160 /mo.

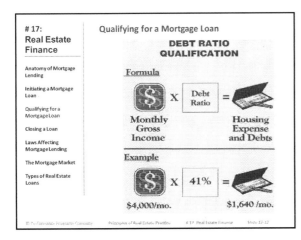

 # 17:
Real Estate Finance

Anatomy of Mortgage Lending

Initiating a Mortgage Loan

Qualifying for a Mortgage Loan

Closing a Loan

Laws Affecting Mortgage Lending

The Mortgage Market

Types of Real Estate Loans

Qualifying for a Mortgage Loan

DEBT RATIO QUALIFICATION

Formula

$ X Debt Ratio = Housing Expense and Debts

Monthly Gross Income

Example

$ X 41% =

$4,000/mo. $1,640 /mo.

 # 17:
Real Estate Finance

Anatomy of Mortgage Lending

Initiating a Mortgage Loan

Qualifying for a Mortgage Loan

Closing a Loan

Laws Affecting Mortgage Lending

The Mortgage Market

Types of Real Estate Loans

Qualifying for a Mortgage Loan

Cash qualification
❏ lender verifies applicant's sources of cash for down payment

Net worth
❏ extent to which applicant's assets exceed liabilities

Credit evaluation
❏ lender obtains credit reports to evaluate applicant's payment behavior

Loan commitment
❏ lender's written pledge to grant loan under certain terms
❏ commitment may be firm or conditional

 # 17:
Real Estate Finance

Anatomy of Mortgage Lending

Initiating a Mortgage Loan

Qualifying for a Mortgage Loan

Closing a Loan

Laws Affecting Mortgage Lending

The Mortgage Market

Types of Real Estate Loans

Closing a Loan

❏ Occurs at closing of the transaction

❏ Funds disbursed from escrow per instructions

❏ Buyer / borrower executes all documents and receives copies

❏ Title to mortgaged property transfers to borrower and is duly recorded

---

 # 17:
Real Estate Finance

Anatomy of Mortgage Lending

Initiating a Mortgage Loan

Qualifying for a Mortgage Loan

Closing a Loan

Laws Affecting Mortgage Lending

The Mortgage Market

Types of Real Estate Loans

Laws Affecting Mortgage Lending

MAJOR FINANCING LAWS

Truth in Lending / Regulation Z
- Disclosure   • Advertising
- Recission right

Equal Credit Opportunity Act
- No discrimination   • Evaluation rules
- Reason for denial

Real Estate Settlement Procedures Act
- Uniform Settlement Statement
- Information booklet
- Cost estimate and disclosure

National Flood Insurance Act
- Required for flood zone

 # 17:
Real Estate Finance

Anatomy of Mortgage Lending

Initiating a Mortgage Loan

Qualifying for a Mortgage Loan

Closing a Loan

Laws Affecting Mortgage Lending

The Mortgage Market

Types of Real Estate Loans

Laws Affecting Mortgage Lending

Truth-in-Lending and Regulation Z

❑ **Reg Z** implements **Truth-in-Lending Simplification and Reform Act** and **Consumer Credit Protection Act**

❑ Lender must **disclose finance charges** and APR prior to closing;

❑ Borrower has limited right of rescission, but excludes primary residence

❑ Lender must follow **advertising requirements** for full disclosure of costs, loan mechanics

---

 # 17:
Real Estate Finance

Anatomy of Mortgage Lending

Initiating a Mortgage Loan

Qualifying for a Mortgage Loan

Closing a Loan

Laws Affecting Mortgage Lending

The Mortgage Market

Types of Real Estate Loans

Laws Affecting Mortgage Lending

Equal Credit Opportunity Act (ECOA)

❑ Prohibits discrimination in lending based on
  - race or color
  - religion
  - national origin
  - sex
  - marital status
  - age
  - dependency upon public assistance

❑ Licensees assisting in qualifying must also comply

❑ Denied applicants must get notice within 30 days

 # 17:
Real Estate Finance

Anatomy of Mortgage Lending

Initiating a Mortgage Loan

Qualifying for a Mortgage Loan

Closing a Loan

Laws Affecting Mortgage Lending

The Mortgage Market

Types of Real Estate Loans

Laws Affecting Mortgage Lending

Real Estate Settlement Procedures Act (RESPA)

❑ Standardizes settlement practices & ensures buyers understand settlement costs

❑ Lender must:

  - provide CFPB booklet explaining loans, settlement costs and procedures

  - provide CFPB Loan Estimate of settlement costs within three days of application

  - provide CFPB Closing Disclosure three days before loan consummation

---

 # 17:
Real Estate Finance

Anatomy of Mortgage Lending

Initiating a Mortgage Loan

Qualifying for a Mortgage Loan

Closing a Loan

Laws Affecting Mortgage Lending

The Mortgage Market

Types of Real Estate Loans

Laws Affecting Mortgage Lending

National Flood Insurance Act

❑ Borrowers of "federally-related loans" must obtain flood insurance if property is in designated flood-hazard area

❑ Flood-zone maps indicate where homeowners must obtain insurance

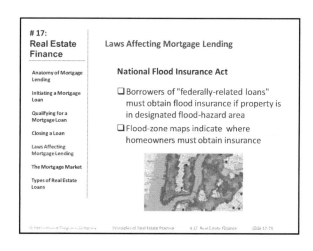

 # 17:
Real Estate Finance

Anatomy of Mortgage Lending

Initiating a Mortgage Loan

Qualifying for a Mortgage Loan

Closing a Loan

Laws Affecting Mortgage Lending

The Mortgage Market

Types of Real Estate Loans

The Mortgage Market

Supply and demand for money

❑ Money supply and demand forces affect interest rates, prices, availability of mortgage money

  - excess supply of money causes rates to fall and prices to rise

  - shortage of money increases interest rates and reduces prices

---

 # 17:
Real Estate Finance

Anatomy of Mortgage Lending

Initiating a Mortgage Loan

Qualifying for a Mortgage Loan

Closing a Loan

Laws Affecting Mortgage Lending

The Mortgage Market

Types of Real Estate Loans

The Mortgage Market

Supply and demand for money (cont.)

❑ Federal Reserve regulates money supply via

  - selling or buying **T-bills**;
    o sell = contract; buy = expand

  - raising/lowering **reserve requirement**
    o raise = contract; lower = expand

  - raising / lowering **discount rate**
    o raise = contract; lower = expand

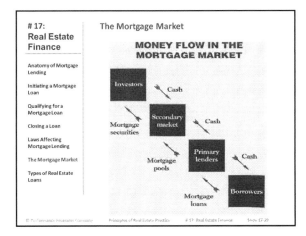

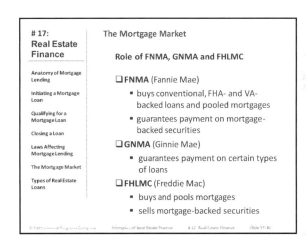

Slide 1

 # 17:
Real Estate Finance

Anatomy of Mortgage Lending

Initiating a Mortgage Loan

Qualifying for a Mortgage Loan

Closing a Loan

Laws Affecting Mortgage Lending

The Mortgage Market

Types of Real Estate Loans

Types of Real Estate Loans

Loan types by loan component (cont.)

❑ **Senior** – higher lien priority loan

❑ **Junior** – lower lien priority loan

❑ **Fixed or graduated payment**

❑ **Balloon** - lump sum principal payoff

❑ **Buydown** – prepaid interest up front; lowers rate over loan term

Slide 2

 # 17:
Real Estate Finance

Anatomy of Mortgage Lending

Initiating a Mortgage Loan

Qualifying for a Mortgage Loan

Closing a Loan

Laws Affecting Mortgage Lending

The Mortgage Market

Types of Real Estate Loans

Types of Real Estate Loans

Seller financing

❑ **Purchase money mortgages (PMMs)**
- Loans by seller to buyer for all or part of purchase price
- Subordinate lien to underlying mortgage
- Title transfers to buyer/borrower
- Wraparound: PMM where seller continues payment on underlying mortgage

Slide 3

 # 17:
Real Estate Finance

Anatomy of Mortgage Lending

Initiating a Mortgage Loan

Qualifying for a Mortgage Loan

Closing a Loan

Laws Affecting Mortgage Lending

The Mortgage Market

Types of Real Estate Loans

Types of Real Estate Loans

Seller financing (cont.)

❑ **Contracts for deed**
- Installment sale, i.e., periodic payments
- Seller finances buyer via contract
- Seller retains title until contract terms are fulfilled
- Any underlying mortgage stays in place

Slide 4

 # 17:
Real Estate Finance

Anatomy of Mortgage Lending

Initiating a Mortgage Loan

Qualifying for a Mortgage Loan

Closing a Loan

Laws Affecting Mortgage Lending

The Mortgage Market

Types of Real Estate Loans

Types of Real Estate Loans

Special-purpose loans

❑ **Home equity** – loan collateralized by equity

❑ **Package** – finances real and personal property

❑ **Construction**- temporary loan for construction

❑ **Bridge** – loan that 'bridges' time gap between short and long-term financing

Slide 5

 # 17:
Real Estate Finance

Anatomy of Mortgage Lending

Initiating a Mortgage Loan

Qualifying for a Mortgage Loan

Closing a Loan

Laws Affecting Mortgage Lending

The Mortgage Market

Types of Real Estate Loans

Types of Real Estate Loans

Special-purpose loans (cont.)

❑ **Equity participation** – non-occupying investor assists in down payment

❑ **Take-out / permanent loan** – long-term loan that retires construction loan

❑ **Reverse annuity** – secures equity for cash payments while occupying property

❑ **Blanket** – loan secured by more than one property

Slide 6

Unit 18: REAL ESTATE INVESTMENT

- Investment Fundamentals
- Real Estate as an Investment
- Real Estate Investment Entities
- Taxation of Real Estate Investments
- Investment Analysis of a Residence
- Investment Analysis of an Income Property

 # 18: Real Estate Investment

Investment Fundamentals

Real Estate as an Investment

Real Estate Investment Entities

Taxation of Real Estate Investments

Investment Analysis of a Residence

Investment Analysis of an Income Property

Slide 1

Investment Fundamentals

Real estate investment characteristics

❑ The greater the risk, the higher the return

❑ More management-intensive

❑ Income-producing investments relatively illiquid

Slide 2

Investment Fundamentals

Real estate investment rewards

❑ **Income**
  ▪ Rents may exceed expenses, generating profit

❑ **Appreciation**
  ▪ Demand spikes may increase value

❑ **Leverage**
  ▪ Use financing to control larger investment amounts

❑ **Tax benefits**
  ▪ Can deduct expenses and depreciation

Slide 3

Investment Fundamentals

Real estate investment risks

❑ **Market risk**
  ▪ Changes in supply & demand

❑ **Business risk**
  ▪ Fluctuations in businesses connected to the investment

❑ **Monetary & financial risk**
  ▪ Inflation
  ▪ Adverse interest rate movements

Slide 4

Investment Fundamentals

Types of investments

❑ **Four principal types of investment; money, equity, debt, real estate**

❑ **Money** – CDs; money market accounts

❑ **Equity** – stocks; equity mutual funds

❑ **Debt** – bonds, notes, mortgages

❑ **Real estate** – acquired for investment benefits as opposed to utility

---

Slide 5

Investment Fundamentals

Types of investments (cont.)

❑ **Two types of real estate investment**

  ▪ **Non-income: e.g., one's residence** – acquired for appreciation, tax benefits

  ▪ **Income-producing** – acquired for income, appreciation, tax benefits, leverage

---

Slide 6

Real Estate as an Investment

Risk and reward

❑ Risks and returns inherent in market variability

  ▪ Expected vs. real income

  ▪ Tax treatment of capital gains and income

  ▪ Opportunity cost of capital

  ▪ Illiquidity

  ▪ Management-intensive

Slide 1

 # 18:
Real Estate Investment

Investment Fundamentals

Real Estate as an Investment

Real Estate Investment Entities

Taxation of Real Estate Investments

Investment Analysis of a Residence

Investment Analysis of an Income Property

Real Estate Investment Entities

Direct
- ❑ Active investors buy and take direct responsibility for management and operation

Syndicate
- ❑ Group of investors who combine funds to buy, develop, and/or operate a property

General partnership
- ❑ Syndicate where all members participate equally

Slide 2

 # 18:
Real Estate Investment

Investment Fundamentals

Real Estate as an Investment

Real Estate Investment Entities

Taxation of Real Estate Investments

Investment Analysis of a Residence

Investment Analysis of an Income Property

Real Estate Investment Entities

Limited partnership
- ❑ General partner organizes, manages
- ❑ Passive investors invest but do not operate

Real Estate Investment Trust (REIT)
- ❑ Investors buy certificates in a trust
- ❑ Trust invests in mortgages or real estate

Real Estate Mortgage Investment Conduit (REMIC)
- ❑ Form of partnership which holds mortgages secured by real property

Slide 3

 # 18:
Real Estate Investment

Investment Fundamentals

Real Estate as an Investment

Real Estate Investment Entities

Taxation of Real Estate Investments

Investment Analysis of a Residence

Investment Analysis of an Income Property

Taxation of Real Estate Investments

- ❑ Income-producing investments are taxed on
  - the **annual income** they make, plus
  - on any **gain realized** when sold

Taxable income
- ❑ Gross income minus allowed expenses and deductions

- ❑ Net income from the investment is added to the investor's other ordinary taxable income

Slide 4

 # 18:
Real Estate Investment

Investment Fundamentals

Real Estate as an Investment

Real Estate Investment Entities

Taxation of Real Estate Investments

Investment Analysis of a Residence

Investment Analysis of an Income Property

Taxation of Real Estate Investments

Cost recovery, or depreciation
- ❑ Deduction of a portion of property's value from gross income each year over the depreciable life of asset
- ❑ Depreciable life defined by tax laws

Depreciable basis
- ❑ The non-land, or improvement portion of an income-producing property
- ❑ Cannot depreciate land value

Depreciation schedules / terms
- ❑ 27.5 years to 39 years

Slide 5

 # 18:
Real Estate Investment

Investment Fundamentals

Real Estate as an Investment

Real Estate Investment Entities

Taxation of Real Estate Investments

Investment Analysis of a Residence

Investment Analysis of an Income Property

Taxation of Real Estate Investments

Capital gain and loss

- ❑ The taxable gain (profit) or loss incurred when the income property is sold

- ❑ If sales proceeds exceed the current adjusted basis there is a gain; if less, then it is a loss (see analysis which follows)

Slide 6

 # 18:
Real Estate Investment

Investment Fundamentals

Real Estate as an Investment

Real Estate Investment Entities

Taxation of Real Estate Investments

Investment Analysis of a Residence

Investment Analysis of an Income Property

Taxation of Real Estate Investments

Adjusted basis
- ❑ The **cost** of the investment plus **capital improvements** less **depreciation**

Interest
- ❑ Deductible from income for tax purposes

- ❑ Cannot deduct principal

Slide 1

 # 18:
Real Estate Investment

Investment Fundamentals

Real Estate as an Investment

Real Estate Investment Entities

Taxation of Real Estate Investments

Investment Analysis of a Residence

Investment Analysis of an Income Property

Investment Analysis of a Residence

Appreciation

❑ Increase in value over time

❑ Stated as difference between original price and current market value, or

❑ Stated as a percentage increase over original price

Slide 2

 # 18:
Real Estate Investment

Investment Fundamentals

Real Estate as an Investment

Real Estate Investment Entities

Taxation of Real Estate Investments

Investment Analysis of a Residence

Investment Analysis of an Income Property

Investment Fundamentals
Calculating appreciation

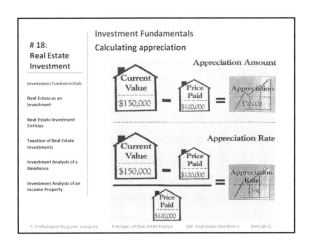

Slide 3

 # 18:
Real Estate Investment

Investment Fundamentals

Real Estate as an Investment

Real Estate Investment Entities

Taxation of Real Estate Investments

Investment Analysis of a Residence

Investment Analysis of an Income Property

Investment Analysis of a Residence

Non-income property tax deductions

❑ Mortgage interest
  ▪ Interest only – cannot deduct principal

❑ Property taxes and insurance
  ▪ Ad valorem taxes, hazard insurance

❑ Use of home office
  ▪ Based on square footage used for office

Slide 4

 # 18:
Real Estate Investment

Investment Fundamentals

Real Estate as an Investment

Real Estate Investment Entities

Taxation of Real Estate Investments

Investment Analysis of a Residence

Investment Analysis of an Income Property

Investment Analysis of a Residence

Tax liability on sale

❑ Seller of a principal residence owes tax on capital gain that results from sale unless excluded

❑ Capital gain is the amount realized minus the adjusted basis

❑ Gains tax exclusion
  ▪ up to $250,000 for a single seller and $500,000 for a married couple can be excluded from gains tax every two years

Slide 5

 # 18:
Real Estate Investment

Investment Fundamentals

Real Estate as an Investment

Real Estate Investment Entities

Taxation of Real Estate Investments

Investment Analysis of a Residence

Investment Analysis of an Income Property

Investment Analysis of a Residence

Gain on Sale

Selling price of old home	$350,000
- Selling costs	35,000
= Amount realized	315,000
Beginning basis of old home	200,000
+ Capital improvements	10,000
= Adjusted basis of old home	210,000
Amount realized	315,000
- Adjusted basis	210,000
= Gain on sale	105,000

Slide 6

 # 18:
Real Estate Investment

Investment Fundamentals

Real Estate as an Investment

Real Estate Investment Entities

Taxation of Real Estate Investments

Investment Analysis of a Residence

Investment Analysis of an Income Property

Investment Analysis of an Income Property

Pre-tax cash flow

❑ Pre-tax cash flow =

(net operating income (NOI) - debt service)

  ▪ **Debt service** = periodic principal and interest payments

# 18: **Real Estate Investment** Investment Fundamentals Real Estate as an Investment Real Estate Investment Entities Taxation of Real Estate Investments Investment Analysis of a Residence Investment Analysis of an Income Property	Investment Analysis of an Income Property
	Pre-tax Cash Flow

	potential rental income	$70,000	
−	vacancy and collection loss	4,200	
=	effective rental income	65,800	
+	other income 2,000		
=	**gross operating income**	**67,800**	
−	operating expenses	35,000	
−	reserves	3,500	
=	**net operating income**	**29,300**	
−	debt service	20,000	
=	**pre-tax cash flow**	**$9,300**	

# 18: **Real Estate Investment** Investment Fundamentals Real Estate as an Investment Real Estate Investment Entities Taxation of Real Estate Investments Investment Analysis of a Residence Investment Analysis of an Income Property	Investment Analysis of an Income Property

After-tax cash flow

❑ (Pre-tax cash flow − **tax liability**) = after tax cash flow

Tax liability

❑ Equals (taxable income x tax bracket)

Taxable income

❑ (NOI + reserves − interest − depreciation)

# 18: **Real Estate Investment** Investment Fundamentals Real Estate as an Investment Real Estate Investment Entities Taxation of Real Estate Investments Investment Analysis of a Residence Investment Analysis of an Income Property	Investment Analysis of an Income Property
	Tax Liability and After-tax cash flow

	net operating income (NOI)	29,300
+	reserves	3,500
−	interest expense	10,000
−	cost recovery expense	22,000
=	**taxable income**	**800**
x	tax rate (24%)	
=	**tax liability**	**192**
	------------------------------------	
	pre-tax cash flow	9,300
−	tax liability	192
=	after-tax cash flow	**$9,076**

# 18: **Real Estate Investment** Investment Fundamentals Real Estate as an Investment Real Estate Investment Entities Taxation of Real Estate Investments Investment Analysis of a Residence Investment Analysis of an Income Property	Investment Analysis of an Income Property

Investment performance

❑ **Return on investment**
- NOI ÷ Price = % return

❑ **Cash-on-cash return**
- Cash produced ÷ cash invested

❑ **Return on equity**
- Cash flow ÷ equity (current value − loan)

# 18: **Real Estate Investment** Investment Fundamentals Real Estate as an Investment Real Estate Investment Entities Taxation of Real Estate Investments Investment Analysis of a Residence Investment Analysis of an Income Property	Investment Analysis of an Income Property

Investment performance

❑ **Discounted cash flow analysis (DCF)**
- Sophisticated commercial financial analysis
- Takes into account the time value of money over a holding period

❑ **Internal rate of return (IRR)**
- Similarly sophisticated commercial financial analysis
- Identifies a rate of return using discount rates and present-value analysis

❑ DCF, IRR not generally used in residential brokerage

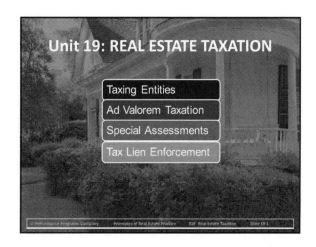

Unit 19: REAL ESTATE TAXATION

- Taxing Entities
- Ad Valorem Taxation
- Special Assessments
- Tax Lien Enforcement

 # 19:
Real Estate Taxation

Taxing Entities

Ad Valorem Taxation

Special Assessments

Tax Lien Enforcement

Taxing Entities

- ❑ Property tax, or ad valorem taxation -- not to be confused with an income-property's annual tax on taxable income

- ❑ No federal ad valorem taxation
  - ▪ can impose a tax lien, but not annual property tax

- ❑ States may levy property taxes
  - ▪ typically delegated to **county and local jurisdictions**
  - ▪ states may also impose tax liens

 # 19:
Real Estate Taxation

Taxing Entities

Ad Valorem Taxation

Special Assessments

Tax Lien Enforcement

Taxing Entities

Tax districts which levy property tax

- ❑ Counties
- ❑ Cities
- ❑ Municipalities
- ❑ Townships
- ❑ Special tax districts

- ❑ Established to collect funds for schools, fire protection, parks, community colleges, libraries, road maintenance, other public services

---

 # 19:
Real Estate Taxation

Taxing Entities

Ad Valorem Taxation

Special Assessments

Tax Lien Enforcement

Ad Valorem Taxation

Property tax

- ❑ **Ad valorem** tax levied annually on the taxable value of a property in order to help fund government and public services

- ❑ Taxable value is based on assessed value

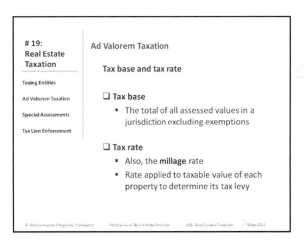

 # 19:
Real Estate Taxation

Taxing Entities

Ad Valorem Taxation

Special Assessments

Tax Lien Enforcement

Ad Valorem Taxation

Tax base and tax rate

- ❑ Tax base
  - ▪ The total of all assessed values in a jurisdiction excluding exemptions

- ❑ Tax rate
  - ▪ Also, the **millage** rate
  - ▪ Rate applied to taxable value of each property to determine its tax levy

---

 # 19:
Real Estate Taxation

Taxing Entities

Ad Valorem Taxation

Special Assessments

Tax Lien Enforcement

Ad Valorem Taxation

Tax base and tax rate (cont.)

- ❑ Assessed value
  - ▪ The valuation of properties for tax purposes, completed by **assessors**

- ❑ Equalization factors
  - ▪ Value-adjusting factors applied to assessed value to increase fairness, evenness of tax levies

---

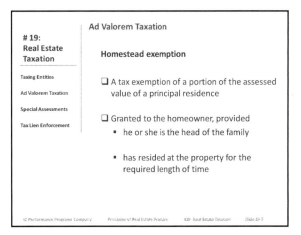

 # 19:
Real Estate Taxation

Taxing Entities

Ad Valorem Taxation

Special Assessments

Tax Lien Enforcement

Ad Valorem Taxation

Homestead exemption

- ❑ A tax exemption of a portion of the assessed value of a principal residence

- ❑ Granted to the homeowner, provided
  - ▪ he or she is the head of the family

  - ▪ has resided at the property for the required length of time

 # 19:
Real Estate Taxation

Taxing Entities

Ad Valorem Taxation

Special Assessments

Tax Lien Enforcement

Ad Valorem Taxation

Other exemptions

❑ Properties immune from ad valorem tax
  ▪ government-owned properties

❑ Exempt from taxes
  ▪ properties owned by non-profit-organizations

 # 19:
Real Estate Taxation

Taxing Entities

Ad Valorem Taxation

Special Assessments

Tax Lien Enforcement

Ad Valorem Taxation

Tax rate derivation

(1) taxing entity determines **budget requirements** to be met by ad valorem tax

(2) divide **tax requirement** by the **tax base**

 # 19:
Real Estate Taxation

Taxing Entities

Ad Valorem Taxation

Special Assessments

Tax Lien Enforcement

Ad Valorem Taxation

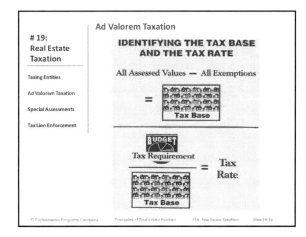

 # 19:
Real Estate Taxation

Taxing Entities

Ad Valorem Taxation

Special Assessments

Tax Lien Enforcement

Ad Valorem Taxation

Tax rate mills

❑ Tax rate stated as mills ($.001), or

❑ Dollars per $100 of assessed value, or

❑ Dollars per $1,000 of assessed value, or

❑ As a percentage of assessed value

 # 19:
Real Estate Taxation

Taxing Entities

Ad Valorem Taxation

Special Assessments

Tax Lien Enforcement

Ad Valorem Taxation

Tax billing and collection

❑ Individual tax bill

  ▪ (rate x taxable value)

❑ Taxable value

  ▪ (assessed value minus exemptions and adjustments)

 # 19:
Real Estate Taxation

Taxing Entities

Ad Valorem Taxation

Special Assessments

Tax Lien Enforcement

Ad Valorem Taxation

Tax bill calculation

I. Taxable Value

assessed value	$ 240,000
- homestead exemption	75,000
taxable value	$ 165,000

II. Tax Calculations

taxable value	$ 165,000
x 5 mills—school dist. .005	
= school tax	**$ 825**
taxable value $ 165,000	
x 2 mills—county .002	
= county tax	**$ 330**

III. Totaling

school tax	$ 825
+ county tax	330
= total tax bill	**$ 1,155**

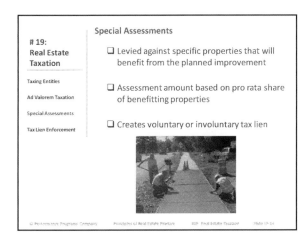

 # 19: Real Estate Taxation

Taxing Entities
Ad Valorem Taxation
Special Assessments
Tax Lien Enforcement

Special Assessments

❑ Levied against specific properties that will benefit from the planned improvement

❑ Assessment amount based on pro rata share of benefitting properties

❑ Creates voluntary or involuntary tax lien

 # 19: Real Estate Taxation

Taxing Entities
Ad Valorem Taxation
Special Assessments
Tax Lien Enforcement

Tax Lien Enforcement

❑ Tax lien enforcement & collection occurs via

▪ Tax certificate issuance

▪ Certificate buyer pays taxes due

▪ Application for a tax deed

▪ Tax sale and foreclosure initiation

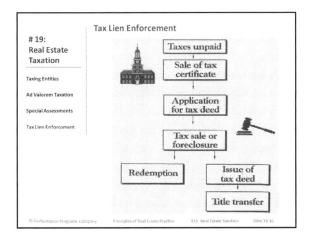

 # 19: Real Estate Taxation

Taxing Entities
Ad Valorem Taxation
Special Assessments
Tax Lien Enforcement

Tax Lien Enforcement

Taxes unpaid → Sale of tax certificate → Application for tax deed → Tax sale or foreclosure → Redemption / Issue of tax deed → Title transfer

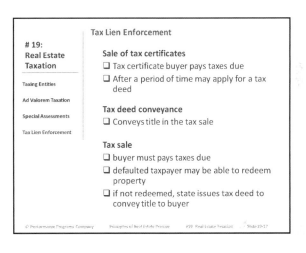

 # 19: Real Estate Taxation

Taxing Entities
Ad Valorem Taxation
Special Assessments
Tax Lien Enforcement

Tax Lien Enforcement

Sale of tax certificates
❑ Tax certificate buyer pays taxes due
❑ After a period of time may apply for a tax deed

Tax deed conveyance
❑ Conveys title in the tax sale

Tax sale
❑ buyer must pays taxes due
❑ defaulted taxpayer may be able to redeem property
❑ if not redeemed, state issues tax deed to convey title to buyer

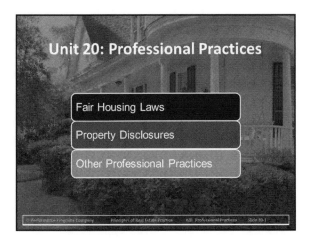

Unit 20: Professional Practices

Fair Housing Laws

Property Disclosures

Other Professional Practices

 # 20: Professional Practices

Fair Housing Laws
Property Disclosures
Other Professional Practices

Fair Housing Laws

❑ Anti-discrimination

▪ federal and state laws prohibit discrimination in housing

▪ citizens entitled to live wherever they wish without discrimination

▪ **State fair housing laws**
  o reflect national laws with certain differences

▪ **Fair housing and local zoning**
  o fair housing does not preempt local zoning, but zoning cannot be discriminatory against protected classes

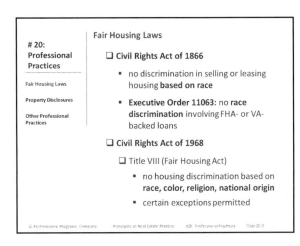

 # 20: Professional Practices

Fair Housing Laws

Property Disclosures

Other Professional Practices

Fair Housing Laws

❏ **Civil Rights Act of 1866**
- no discrimination in selling or leasing housing **based on race**
- **Executive Order 11063:** no **race discrimination** involving FHA- or VA-backed loans

❏ **Civil Rights Act of 1968**
  ❏ Title VIII (Fair Housing Act)
  - no housing discrimination based on **race, color, religion, national origin**
  - certain exceptions permitted

 # 20: Professional Practices

Fair Housing Laws

Property Disclosures

Other Professional Practices

Fair Housing Laws

❏ Forms of illegal discrimination
- discriminatory misrepresentation
- advertising
- unequal services
- steering
- blockbusting
- restricting access to market
- redlining

 # 20: Professional Practices

Fair Housing Laws

Property Disclosures

Other Professional Practices

Fair Housing Laws

PROHIBITED DISCRIMINATORY ACTS

Misrepresentation – "I guarantee you the house will appreciate."

Illegal Advertising – "Apartment for rent; Catholics only need apply."

Unequal Services – "I know I did that for them, but I'm way too busy now."

Steering – "You belong in this neighborhood."

Blockbusting – "The crime rate in your neighborhood is going to skyrocket soon."

MLS Restriction – "I'll have to see if it's OK to get you in the MLS."

Redlining – "We don't do loans over there."

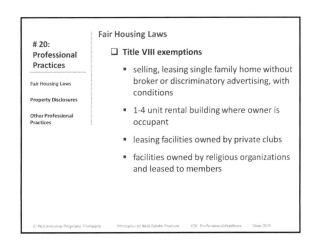

 # 20: Professional Practices

Fair Housing Laws

Property Disclosures

Other Professional Practices

Fair Housing Laws

❏ **Title VIII exemptions**
- selling, leasing single family home without broker or discriminatory advertising, with conditions
- 1-4 unit rental building where owner is occupant
- leasing facilities owned by private clubs
- facilities owned by religious organizations and leased to members

 # 20: Professional Practices

Fair Housing Laws

Property Disclosures

Other Professional Practices

Fair Housing Laws

❏ Jones v. Mayer
- discrimination in selling/renting residential housing based on race is prohibited without exception or exemption

❏ Equal Opportunity in Housing poster
- brokers must display
- affirms compliance with fair housing laws
- failure to display can be construed as discrimination
- see example on following slide

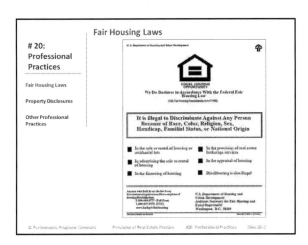

 # 20: Professional Practices

Fair Housing Laws

Property Disclosures

Other Professional Practices

Fair Housing Laws

Fair Housing Laws

20: Professional Practices

Fair Housing Laws
Property Disclosures
Other Professional Practices

❑ **Fair Housing Amendments Act of 1988**
- no discrimination based on
  - sex
  - against the handicapped
  - families with children
- **exemptions**
  - government-designated retirement housing
  - retirement community (62+ years of age)
  - retirement community if 80 % of dwellings have one person who is 55+
  - 1-4 unit dwellings where owners have no more than three houses

---

Fair Housing Laws

20: Professional Practices

Fair Housing Laws
Property Disclosures
Other Professional Practices

❑ Discrimination by the client
- laws apply to owners as well as agents
- agent liable if goes along with client discrimination
- agent should withdraw from relationship with discriminatory client

❑ Violations and enforcement
- file HUD complaint
- file suit in court
- may obtain injunction, damages
- violators subject to prosecution

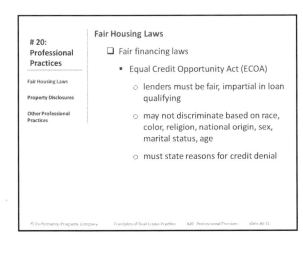

Fair Housing Laws

20: Professional Practices

Fair Housing Laws
Property Disclosures
Other Professional Practices

❑ Fair financing laws
- Equal Credit Opportunity Act (ECOA)
  - lenders must be fair, impartial in loan qualifying
  - may not discriminate based on race, color, religion, national origin, sex, marital status, age
  - must state reasons for credit denial

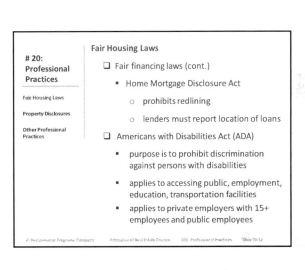

Fair Housing Laws

20: Professional Practices

Fair Housing Laws
Property Disclosures
Other Professional Practices

❑ Fair financing laws (cont.)
- Home Mortgage Disclosure Act
  - prohibits redlining
  - lenders must report location of loans

❑ Americans with Disabilities Act (ADA)
- purpose is to prohibit discrimination against persons with disabilities
- applies to accessing public, employment, education, transportation facilities
- applies to private employers with 15+ employees and public employees

---

Fair Housing Laws

20: Professional Practices

Fair Housing Laws
Property Disclosures
Other Professional Practices

❑ Americans with Disabilities Act (ADA)
- Title I: Employment
  - must have equal opportunity, enforced by ECOA
- Title II: State, local government
  - cannot discriminate in state and local services
- Title III: Public accommodations
  - cannot discriminate in public accommodations, commercial facilities

---

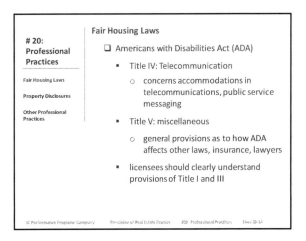

Fair Housing Laws

20: Professional Practices

Fair Housing Laws
Property Disclosures
Other Professional Practices

❑ Americans with Disabilities Act (ADA)
- Title IV: Telecommunication
  - concerns accommodations in telecommunications, public service messaging
- Title V: miscellaneous
  - general provisions as to how ADA affects other laws, insurance, lawyers
- licensees should clearly understand provisions of Title I and III

 # 20: Professional Practices

Fair Housing Laws

Property Disclosures

Other Professional Practices

Fair Housing Laws

❑ Americans with Disabilities Act (ADA)

- ADA requirements
    - landlords must modify housing to be accessible without hindrance
    - access must be equivalent to that provided for non-disabled persons
- penalties
    - violations can result in citations, license restrictions, fines, injunctions
    - owners can be liable for personal injury damages

 # 20: Professional Practices

Fair Housing Laws

Property Disclosures

Other Professional Practices

Property Disclosures

❑ Residential Property Condition

- Seller's Disclosure Form
    - sellers (not agents) must complete form in many states for prospective buyers
    - describes property condition at time of sale on state-approved forms
- owners role
    - seller's must affirm whether or not problems exist with property or it's systems
    - if unknown, seller must so state; if a defect is known, seller must disclose

---

 # 20: Professional Practices

Fair Housing Laws

Property Disclosures

Other Professional Practices

Property Disclosures

❑ Residential Property Condition

- owners role (cont.)
    - if seller is unaware of a problem, s/he can state "no representation" which removes liability for not disclosing
    - seller must sign, deliver to buyer and buyer must acknowledge receipt
- licensee's role
    - must disclose any material facts that are known or reasonably should have known

---

 # 20: Professional Practices

Fair Housing Laws

Property Disclosures

Other Professional Practices

Property Disclosures

❑ Residential Property Condition

- right of rescission
    - if seller does not complete and deliver form, buyer receives a right to rescind contract and reclaim deposit
    - right to cancel continues until closing or occupancy

 # 20: Professional Practices

Fair Housing Laws

Property Disclosures

Other Professional Practices

Property Disclosures

❑ Residential Property Condition

- property condition and material facts
    - material fact = a fact affecting the property's value or the prospect's decision to contract
    - property stigmas are not material facts (previous crime, suicide, disease, etc.)
    - no requirement to disclose non-material facts
    - material facts can include the surrounding area in addition to the immediate premises

---

 # 20: Professional Practices

Fair Housing Laws

Property Disclosures

Other Professional Practices

Property Disclosures

❑ Environmental issues

- licensees and principals are responsible for disclosing, remediating hazards
- lead-based paint
    - if property built before 1978, must disclose possible lead hazard
    - use form "Protect Your Family from Lead in Your Home"
    - buyers may want to conduct risk assessment prior to purchase

20: Professional Practices

Fair Housing Laws

Property Disclosures

Other Professional Practices

Property Disclosures

❑ Environmental issues

- mold
  - ○ must be disclosed if present in home
  - ○ must also disclose flooding and water damage that can cause mold
- Asbestos
  - ○ can cause lung cancer; must be removed by experts to prevent contamination
- air quality
  - ○ can/should test for carbon monoxide, radon, formaldehyde, other toxic chemicals prior to sale

---

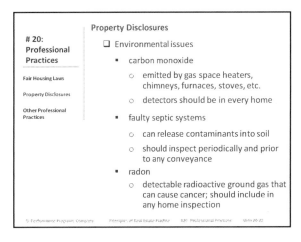

20: Professional Practices

Fair Housing Laws

Property Disclosures

Other Professional Practices

Property Disclosures

❑ Environmental issues

- carbon monoxide
  - ○ emitted by gas space heaters, chimneys, furnaces, stoves, etc.
  - ○ detectors should be in every home
- faulty septic systems
  - ○ can release contaminants into soil
  - ○ should inspect periodically and prior to any conveyance
- radon
  - ○ detectable radioactive ground gas that can cause cancer; should include in any home inspection

---

20: Professional Practices

Fair Housing Laws

Property Disclosures

Other Professional Practices

Property Disclosures

❑ Environmental issues

- urea formaldehyde
  - ○ hazard in foam insulation and pressed wood products, eg, particle board
  - ○ severity of hazard decreases over time
- underground storage tanks (UST)
  - ○ commercial hazard if leaking
  - ○ should disclose presence of any UST

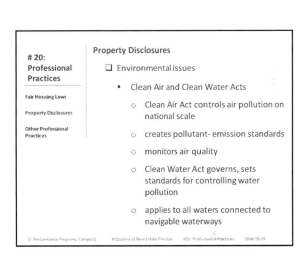

20: Professional Practices

Fair Housing Laws

Property Disclosures

Other Professional Practices

Property Disclosures

❑ Environmental issues

- Clean Air and Clean Water Acts
  - ○ Clean Air Act controls air pollution on national scale
  - ○ creates pollutant- emission standards
  - ○ monitors air quality
  - ○ Clean Water Act governs, sets standards for controlling water pollution
  - ○ applies to all waters connected to navigable waterways

20: Professional Practices

Fair Housing Laws

Property Disclosures

Other Professional Practices

Property Disclosures

❑ Environmental issues

- Safe Drinking Water Act
  - ○ regulates, protects public supply of drinking water
  - ○ sets protection standards, requires water suppliers to report discovered health risks
  - ○ sellers must disclose property's source of drinking water and proximity to septic systems
  - ○ should test any well system

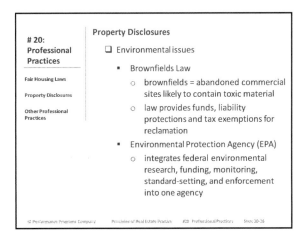

20: Professional Practices

Fair Housing Laws

Property Disclosures

Other Professional Practices

Property Disclosures

❑ Environmental issues

- Brownfields Law
  - ○ brownfields = abandoned commercial sites likely to contain toxic material
  - ○ law provides funds, liability protections and tax exemptions for reclamation
- Environmental Protection Agency (EPA)
  - ○ integrates federal environmental research, funding, monitoring, standard-setting, and enforcement into one agency

 # 20: Professional Practices

Fair Housing Laws

Property Disclosures

Other Professional Practices

Property Disclosures

❑ Environmental issues

- licensee disclosure obligations, liabilities
  o licensees should have general awareness and where to get expert help
  o not expected to have expert knowledge of law or physical condition
  o critical role is to
    • be aware of potential hazards
    • disclose material facts, have attorney draft disclosures
    • know where to find expert help

 # 20: Professional Practices

Fair Housing Laws

Property Disclosures

Other Professional Practices

Property Disclosures

❑ Warranties

- purpose and scope
  o aka, home service contracts, to cover service, repair of systems, appliances
  o typically annual contracts with costs depending on property size, location, type, degree of coverage
  o may be included in purchase price of a home
- limitations – warranties may exclude
  o pre-existing conditions, accidental breakages, poor installations, outdoor systems, certain appliances, etc.
  o homeowner must use warranty company to have services performed

---

 # 20: Professional Practices

Fair Housing Laws

Property Disclosures

Other Professional Practices

Property Disclosures

❑ Inspections

- process
  o inspections detect oversights or need for repairs
  o identify need for maintenance procedures
  o inspections uncover system, pest infestation, environmental issues
- termite inspections
  o not easily detectable by non-experts; should do annual inspections

---

 # 20: Professional Practices

Fair Housing Laws

Property Disclosures

Other Professional Practices

Property Disclosures

❑ Inspections

- environmental inspections, audits
  o home inspections should include environmental issues / hazards
  o can also conduct site assessments which examine possible impairments
- environmental impact statements (EIS)
  o performed for federally, some privately funded development projects
  o addresses air, water quality, noise, health, safety, wildlife, traffic, sewer impacts of project
  o culminates in permit or permit denial

 # 20: Professional Practices

Fair Housing Laws

Property Disclosures

Other Professional Practices

Property Disclosures

❑ Inspections

- licensee disclosure duties
  o in most states, licensees must disclose known, material facts on residential properties
  o must also disclose known results of any residential inspection
  o when not required, licensees should suggest professional inspections / audits

---

 # 20: Professional Practices

Fair Housing Laws

Property Disclosures

Other Professional Practices

Property Disclosures

❑ Homeowners' associations

- property disclosures include homeowners' associations
  o must disclose if subject to common interest plan
  o must disclose association's membership obligation, dues, restrictions
  o association must provide required disclosure documents, forms, timing requirements, etc.
  o seller responsible for disclosures, agent must ensure seller complies

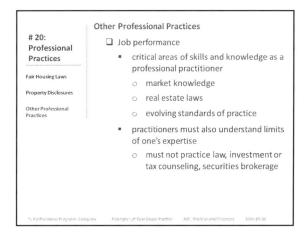

 # 20: Professional Practices

Fair Housing Laws

Property Disclosures

Other Professional Practices

Other Professional Practices

❑ Codes of ethics
- sources of practitioner ethics
  - ○ federal, state legislation
  - ○ state license regulation
  - ○ industry self-regulation via trade associations, institutes
- predominant influence in practitioner ethics is the Code of Ethics of the National Association of Realtors®
  - ○ covers all aspects of practice and transactions

 # 20: Professional Practices

Fair Housing Laws

Property Disclosures

Other Professional Practices

Other Professional Practices

❑ Job performance
- critical areas of skills and knowledge as a professional practitioner
  - ○ market knowledge
  - ○ real estate laws
  - ○ evolving standards of practice
- practitioners must also understand limits of one's expertise
  - ○ must not practice law, investment or tax counseling, securities brokerage

---

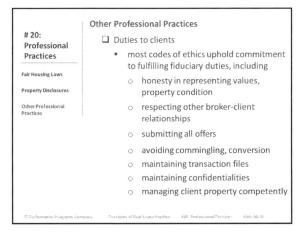

 # 20: Professional Practices

Fair Housing Laws

Property Disclosures

Other Professional Practices

Other Professional Practices

❑ Duties to clients
- most codes of ethics uphold commitment to fulfilling fiduciary duties, including
  - ○ honesty in representing values, property condition
  - ○ respecting other broker-client relationships
  - ○ submitting all offers
  - ○ avoiding commingling, conversion
  - ○ maintaining transaction files
  - ○ maintaining confidentialities
  - ○ managing client property competently

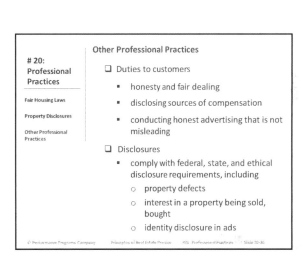

 # 20: Professional Practices

Fair Housing Laws

Property Disclosures

Other Professional Practices

Other Professional Practices

❑ Duties to customers
- honesty and fair dealing
- disclosing sources of compensation
- conducting honest advertising that is not misleading

❑ Disclosures
- comply with federal, state, and ethical disclosure requirements, including
  - ○ property defects
  - ○ interest in a property being sold, bought
  - ○ identity disclosure in ads

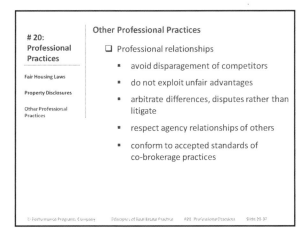

 # 20: Professional Practices

Fair Housing Laws

Property Disclosures

Other Professional Practices

Other Professional Practices

❑ Professional relationships
- avoid disparagement of competitors
- do not exploit unfair advantages
- arbitrate differences, disputes rather than litigate
- respect agency relationships of others
- conform to accepted standards of co-brokerage practices

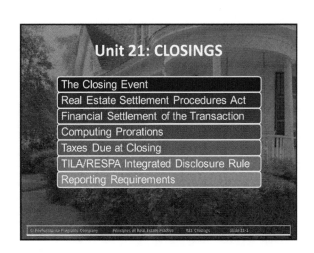

Unit 21: CLOSINGS

- The Closing Event
- Real Estate Settlement Procedures Act
- Financial Settlement of the Transaction
- Computing Prorations
- Taxes Due at Closing
- TILA/RESPA Integrated Disclosure Rule
- Reporting Requirements

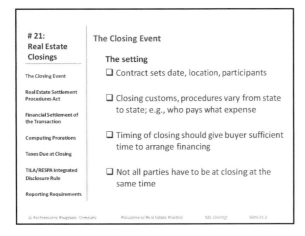

 # 21:
Real Estate Closings

The Closing Event

Real Estate Settlement Procedures Act

Financial Settlement of the Transaction

Computing Prorations

Taxes Due at Closing

TILA/RESPA Integrated Disclosure Rule

Reporting Requirements

The Closing Event

The setting

❑ Contract sets date, location, participants

❑ Closing customs, procedures vary from state to state; e.g., who pays what expense

❑ Timing of closing should give buyer sufficient time to arrange financing

❑ Not all parties have to be at closing at the same time

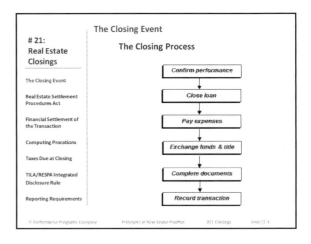

 # 21:
Real Estate Closings

The Closing Event

Real Estate Settlement Procedures Act

Financial Settlement of the Transaction

Computing Prorations

Taxes Due at Closing

TILA/RESPA Integrated Disclosure Rule

Reporting Requirements

The Closing Event

The Closing Process

- Confirm performance
- Close loan
- Pay expenses
- Exchange funds & title
- Complete documents
- Record transaction

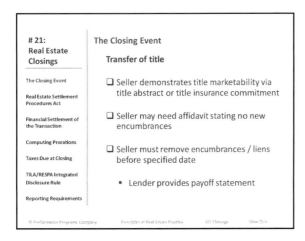

 # 21:
Real Estate Closings

The Closing Event

Real Estate Settlement Procedures Act

Financial Settlement of the Transaction

Computing Prorations

Taxes Due at Closing

TILA/RESPA Integrated Disclosure Rule

Reporting Requirements

The Closing Event

Transfer of title

❑ Seller demonstrates title marketability via title abstract or title insurance commitment

❑ Seller may need affidavit stating no new encumbrances

❑ Seller must remove encumbrances / liens before specified date

  ▪ Lender provides payoff statement

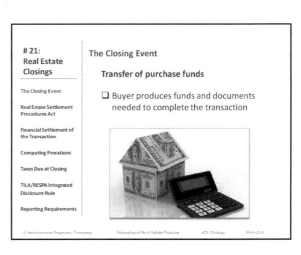

 # 21:
Real Estate Closings

The Closing Event

Real Estate Settlement Procedures Act

Financial Settlement of the Transaction

Computing Prorations

Taxes Due at Closing

TILA/RESPA Integrated Disclosure Rule

Reporting Requirements

The Closing Event

Transfer of purchase funds

❑ Buyer produces funds and documents needed to complete the transaction

 # 21:
Real Estate Closings

The Closing Event

Real Estate Settlement Procedures Act

Financial Settlement of the Transaction

Computing Prorations

Taxes Due at Closing

TILA/RESPA Integrated Disclosure Rule

Reporting Requirements

The Closing Event

Escrow procedures

❑ Escrow agent holds, disburses funds and releases documents when escrow conditions have been met

 # 21:
Real Estate Closings

The Closing Event

Real Estate Settlement Procedures Act

Financial Settlement of the Transaction

Computing Prorations

Taxes Due at Closing

TILA/RESPA Integrated Disclosure Rule

Reporting Requirements

The Closing Event

Lender closing requirements

❑ Primary lender concern: quality of the loan collateral

❑ Common requirements
  ▪ survey
  ▪ inspections
  ▪ hazard insurance
  ▪ title insurance
  ▪ certificate of occupancy
  ▪ reserves for taxes and insurance
  ▪ private mortgage insurance

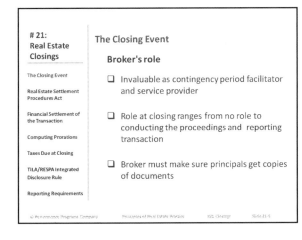

21:
Real Estate Closings

The Closing Event

Real Estate Settlement Procedures Act

Financial Settlement of the Transaction

Computing Prorations

Taxes Due at Closing

TILA/RESPA Integrated Disclosure Rule

Reporting Requirements

The Closing Event

Broker's role

❑ Invaluable as contingency period facilitator and service provider

❑ Role at closing ranges from no role to conducting the proceedings and reporting transaction

❑ Broker must make sure principals get copies of documents

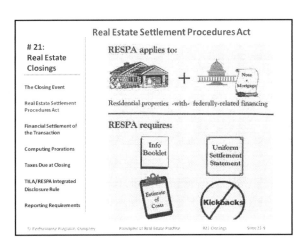

21:
Real Estate Closings

Real Estate Settlement Procedures Act

RESPA applies to:

Residential properties ~with~ federally-related financing

RESPA requires:

Info Booklet

Uniform Settlement Statement

Estimate of Costs

Kickbacks

21:
Real Estate Closings

Real Estate Settlement Procedures Act

❑ **Purposes**
  - clarify, disclose settlement costs
  - eliminate kickbacks and certain fees

❑ **Applies to**
  - residential property
  - must involve "federally-related" mortgage
  - includes VA and FHA loans

❑ **Regulated by**
  - Consumer Financial Protection Bureau (CFPB)

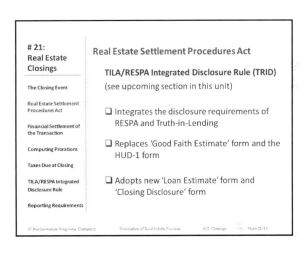

21:
Real Estate Closings

Real Estate Settlement Procedures Act

TILA/RESPA Integrated Disclosure Rule (TRID)
(see upcoming section in this unit)

❑ Integrates the disclosure requirements of RESPA and Truth-in-Lending

❑ Replaces 'Good Faith Estimate' form and the HUD-1 form

❑ Adopts new 'Loan Estimate' form and 'Closing Disclosure' form

21:
Real Estate Closings

Real Estate Settlement Procedures Act

RESPA Information booklet

❑ Lender must provide borrower with CFPB booklet, "Your Home Loan Toolkit"

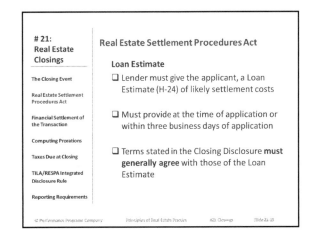

21:
Real Estate Closings

Real Estate Settlement Procedures Act

Loan Estimate

❑ Lender must give the applicant, a Loan Estimate (H-24) of likely settlement costs

❑ Must provide at the time of application or within three business days of application

❑ Terms stated in the Closing Disclosure **must generally agree** with those of the Loan Estimate

Slide 1

 # 21:
Real Estate Closings

The Closing Event

Real Estate Settlement Procedures Act

Financial Settlement of the Transaction

Computing Prorations

Taxes Due at Closing

TILA/RESPA Integrated Disclosure Rule

Reporting Requirements

Real Estate Settlement Procedures Act

Closing Disclosure (form H-24)

❑ Lender must use the Closing Disclosure form (H-25) to disclose settlement costs to the buyer

❑ Consumer must receive the completed form no later than three business days before closing

❑ Terms stated in the Closing Disclosure **must generally agree** with those of the Loan Estimate

Slide 2

 # 21:
Real Estate Closings

The Closing Event

Real Estate Settlement Procedures Act

Financial Settlement of the Transaction

Computing Prorations

Taxes Due at Closing

TILA/RESPA Integrated Disclosure Rule

Reporting Requirements

Real Estate Settlement Procedures Act

Referral fees and kickbacks

❑ RESPA prohibits payment of referral fees and kickbacks when in fact no services are rendered

❑ Prohibited fee-paid referrals include those for title searches, mortgage loans, appraisals, inspections, surveys, credit reports

❑ Business relationships between firms must be disclosed

Slide 3

 # 21:
Real Estate Closings

The Closing Event

Real Estate Settlement Procedures Act

Financial Settlement of the Transaction

Computing Prorations

Taxes Due at Closing

TILA/RESPA Integrated Disclosure Rule

Reporting Requirements

Financial Settlement of the Transaction

Settlement process

❑ Identify selling terms and closing costs

❑ Determine non-prorated debits and credits

❑ Determine prorated debits and credits

❑ Complete the closing statement

❑ Disburse funds

Slide 4

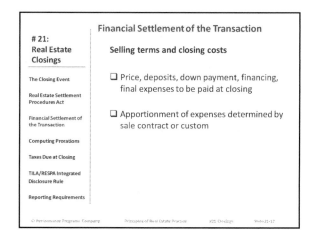

 # 21:
Real Estate Closings

The Closing Event

Real Estate Settlement Procedures Act

Financial Settlement of the Transaction

Computing Prorations

Taxes Due at Closing

TILA/RESPA Integrated Disclosure Rule

Reporting Requirements

Financial Settlement of the Transaction

Selling terms and closing costs

❑ Price, deposits, down payment, financing, final expenses to be paid at closing

❑ Apportionment of expenses determined by sale contract or custom

Slide 5

 # 21:
Real Estate Closings

The Closing Event

Real Estate Settlement Procedures Act

Financial Settlement of the Transaction

Computing Prorations

Taxes Due at Closing

TILA/RESPA Integrated Disclosure Rule

Reporting Requirements

Financial Settlement of the Transaction

Debits and credits

❑ Excess of buyer's debits over credits is amount **buyer must produce** at closing

❑ Excess of seller's credits over debits is amount **seller must receive**

Slide 6

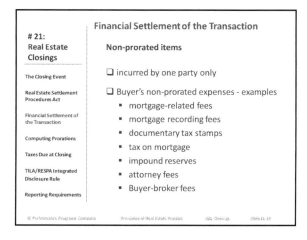

 # 21:
Real Estate Closings

The Closing Event

Real Estate Settlement Procedures Act

Financial Settlement of the Transaction

Computing Prorations

Taxes Due at Closing

TILA/RESPA Integrated Disclosure Rule

Reporting Requirements

Financial Settlement of the Transaction

Non-prorated items

❑ incurred by one party only

❑ Buyer's non-prorated expenses - examples
  - mortgage-related fees
  - mortgage recording fees
  - documentary tax stamps
  - tax on mortgage
  - impound reserves
  - attorney fees
  - Buyer-broker fees

 # 21:
Real Estate Closings

The Closing Event

Real Estate Settlement Procedures Act

Financial Settlement of the Transaction

Computing Prorations

Taxes Due at Closing

TILA/RESPA Integrated Disclosure Rule

Reporting Requirements

Financial Settlement of the Transaction

Non-prorated items (cont.)

❑ Seller's non-prorated expenses - examples
- stamp tax on deed
- title insurance
- inspection fees
- title-related expenses
- attorney expenses
- broker's fees

 # 21:
Real Estate Closings

The Closing Event

Real Estate Settlement Procedures Act

Financial Settlement of the Transaction

Computing Prorations

Taxes Due at Closing

TILA/RESPA Integrated Disclosure Rule

Reporting Requirements

Financial Settlement of the Transaction

Prorated items

❑ Incurred by buyer or seller in advance or arrears

❑ Shared by buyer and seller

❑ Typical prorations
- real estate taxes
- mortgage interest
- rents
- water, heating oil

 # 21:
Real Estate Closings

The Closing Event

Real Estate Settlement Procedures Act

Financial Settlement of the Transaction

Computing Prorations

Taxes Due at Closing

TILA/RESPA Integrated Disclosure Rule

Reporting Requirements

Computing Prorations

12-month/30-day method

❑ Finds average daily amount for 12-month year and 30-day month, or 360-day year

Procedure – prorating annual taxes (arrears)
1. Divide total amount by 360 = **daily amount**
2. Multiply seller's months times 30 (days)
3. Add to that the seller's days in month of closing = **total days seller owned**
4. Multiply total seller's days times daily amount = **seller's debit**
5. Debit seller that amount, credit buyer that amount (since buyer will pay total amount)

 # 21:
Real Estate Closings

The Closing Event

Real Estate Settlement Procedures Act

Financial Settlement of the Transaction

Computing Prorations

Taxes Due at Closing

TILA/RESPA Integrated Disclosure Rule

Reporting Requirements

Computing Prorations

Annual Tax Proration: 12-month/30-day method

(Closing: March 2; seller owns day of closing)

Total amount due:		=	$1,730.00
Monthly amount:	1,730 ÷ 12	=	$ 144.17
Daily amount:	144.17 ÷ 30	=	$ 4.81
Seller's share:	144.17 x 2 mo.	=	$ 288.34
	4.81 x 2 days	=	$ 9.62
Buyer's share	1,730 - 297.96	=	$ 1,432.04

 # 21:
Real Estate Closings

The Closing Event

Real Estate Settlement Procedures Act

Financial Settlement of the Transaction

Computing Prorations

Taxes Due at Closing

TILA/RESPA Integrated Disclosure Rule

Reporting Requirements

Computing Prorations

365-day method

❑ Uses total number of days in year (365)

Procedure – prorating annual taxes (arrears)
1. Divide total amount by 365 = **daily amount**
2. Add up total actual days seller owned
3. Multiply total seller's days times daily amount = **seller's debit**
4. Debit seller that amount, credit buyer that amount (since buyer will pay total amount)

 # 21:
Real Estate Closings

The Closing Event

Real Estate Settlement Procedures Act

Financial Settlement of the Transaction

Computing Prorations

Taxes Due at Closing

TILA/RESPA Integrated Disclosure Rule

Reporting Requirements

Computing Prorations

Annual Tax Proration: 365-day method

(Closing: March 2; seller owns day of closing)

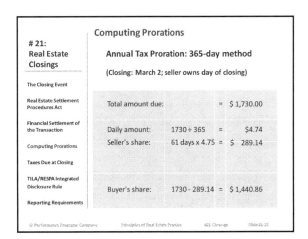

Total amount due:		=	$ 1,730.00
Daily amount:	1730 ÷ 365	=	$4.74
Seller's share:	61 days x 4.75	=	$ 289.14
Buyer's share:	1730 - 289.14	=	$ 1,440.86

Taxes Due at Closing

 # 21:
Real Estate Closings

The Closing Event

Real Estate Settlement Procedures Act

Financial Settlement of the Transaction

Computing Prorations

Taxes Due at Closing

TILA/RESPA Integrated Disclosure Rule

Reporting Requirements

State taxes on deed

❑ Also, transfer tax, documentary stamp tax

❑ Typically a state tax; county & municipality may also impose transfer taxes

❑ Actually paid when deed is recorded

❑ Quoted as dollar rate per $100.00 of selling price

❑ Fractions of $100.00 are rounded up

Taxes Due at Closing

 # 21:
Real Estate Closings

The Closing Event

Real Estate Settlement Procedures Act

Financial Settlement of the Transaction

Computing Prorations

Taxes Due at Closing

TILA/RESPA Integrated Disclosure Rule

Reporting Requirements

State taxes on mortgage

❑ State may impose taxes on mortgages, notes, contracts for deed

❑ Typically paid by buyer

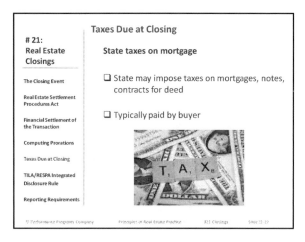

TILA/RESPA Integrated Disclosure Rule (TRID)

 # 21:
Real Estate Closings

The Closing Event

Real Estate Settlement Procedures Act

Financial Settlement of the Transaction

Computing Prorations

Taxes Due at Closing

TILA/RESPA Integrated Disclosure Rule

Reporting Requirements

Forms and Procedures

❑ effective October 3, 2015

❑ Mandatory provisions
  - Must hand out 'Your Home Loan Toolkit' booklet at time of loan application
  - Must deliver / mail 'Loan Estimate' form within 3 business days after loan application
  - 'Closing Disclosure' form 3 business days before consummation of loan

---

TILA/RESPA Integrated Disclosure Rule (TRID)

 # 21:
Real Estate Closings

The Closing Event

Real Estate Settlement Procedures Act

Financial Settlement of the Transaction

Computing Prorations

Taxes Due at Closing

TILA/RESPA Integrated Disclosure Rule

Reporting Requirements

Good faith

❑ Loan estimate costs based on best information available

❑ Good faith is where actual closing disclosure costs are equal to previously estimated costs within certain tolerances

❑ Some cost estimates have a 10% error tolerance; other costs have zero tolerance

---

TILA/RESPA Integrated Disclosure Rule (TRID)

 # 21:
Real Estate Closings

The Closing Event

Real Estate Settlement Procedures Act

Financial Settlement of the Transaction

Computing Prorations

Taxes Due at Closing

TILA/RESPA Integrated Disclosure Rule

Reporting Requirements

Applicable transactions for TRID

❑ Most closed-end consumer mortgages
  - construction loans
  - loans secured by land

❑ Not covered
  - home equity loans
  - reverse mortgages
  - loans on mobile homes
  - loans by small lenders

Reporting Requirements

 # 21:
Real Estate Closings

The Closing Event

Real Estate Settlement Procedures Act

Financial Settlement of the Transaction

Computing Prorations

Taxes Due at Closing

TILA/RESPA Integrated Disclosure Rule

Reporting Requirements

Who must report transactions closed

❑ "Real estate broker" as defined by the Tax Reform Act of 1986
  - Includes buyer's or seller's broker
  - settlement agent
  - mortgage lender
  - other IRS-designated party

What must be filed

❑ Form 1099-S information return
  - Includes identity of parties, sales proceeds
  - Tax reporting and withholding if FIRPTA applies (non-resident alien)

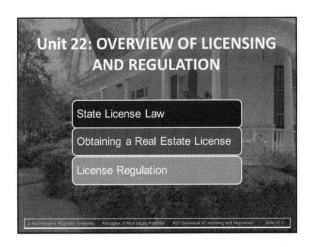

Unit 22: OVERVIEW OF LICENSING AND REGULATION

State License Law

Obtaining a Real Estate License

License Regulation

 # 22:
Real Estate Licensing and Regulation

State License Law

Obtaining a Real Estate License

License Regulation

State License Law

❑ **Note to students**: the following slides in this unit present an overview of license law fundamentals that apply generally to all states

❑ **Refer to laws of your state** to understand
  - how these basics apply to you in your state
  - what you will be tested on in your state to obtain your license

---

 # 22:
Real Estate Licensing and Regulation

State License Law

Obtaining a Real Estate License

License Regulation

State License Law

Purposes of state real estate legislation

❑ To protect the public and ensure professional competency of licensees

❑ To establish
  - requirements for licensure
  - guidelines of conduct for maintaining license
  - a real estate commission to administer and enforce the law

---

 # 22:
Real Estate Licensing and Regulation

State License Law

Obtaining a Real Estate License

License Regulation

Obtaining a Real Estate License

Services requiring licensure

❑ Generally, when parties perform a real estate service for another for consideration

❑ Specific services generally requiring license
  - brokerage
  - property management
  - appraising
  - counseling
  - syndicating
  - auctioning

 # 22:
Real Estate Licensing and Regulation

State License Law

Obtaining a Real Estate License

License Regulation

Obtaining a Real Estate License

❑ Parties exempted from licensure
  - wage-paid employees of property owners
  - transient facility (eg, hotel) employees
  - condo or cooperative managers
  - cemetery lot merchants
  - attorneys
  - court-appointed representatives

 # 22:
Real Estate Licensing and Regulation

State License Law

Obtaining a Real Estate License

License Regulation

Obtaining a Real Estate License

Types of license (see your state for specifics!)

❑ Broker / salesperson states
  - individual broker
  - salesperson
  - corporation
  - partnership
  - branch office
  - non-resident sales or broker

❑ Broker – only states
  - managing broker
  - broker
  - business entities (see above)

 # 22:
Real Estate Licensing and Regulation

State License Law

Obtaining a Real Estate License

License Regulation

Obtaining a Real Estate License

License status

❑ Active if practicing

❑ Inactive if not practicing

❑ Inactive or expired if renewal requirements not met

❑ **Voided** licenses
- by suspension
- by revocation
- by expiration

 # 22:
Real Estate Licensing and Regulation

State License Law

Obtaining a Real Estate License

License Regulation

Obtaining a Real Estate License

Licensing requirements

❑ **Personal**
- age, mental competence, general education, character

❑ **Specific education**
- completion of required real estate courses

❑ **Experience**
- may be required if applying for broker's license

 # 22:
Real Estate Licensing and Regulation

State License Law

Obtaining a Real Estate License

License Regulation

License Regulation

The Real Estate Commission

❑ State government entity that regulates and administers the license law

❑ Oversees licensing process

❑ Enforces license law provisions

❑ Handles consumer and licensee complaints

❑ Maintains education and research foundation

 # 22:
Real Estate Licensing and Regulation

State License Law

Obtaining a Real Estate License

License Regulation

License Regulation

Focuses of Commission regulation

❑ Licensing and license status

❑ Real estate schools and programs

❑ Practices of licensees

❑ Professional guidelines to protect public

❑ Disputes and complaints

❑ Issuance, suspension or revocation of licenses

 # 22:
Real Estate Licensing and Regulation

State License Law

Obtaining a Real Estate License

License Regulation

License Regulation

Bonds and recovery funds

❑ Ensure that the public will be able to collect on settlements for damages and money judgments against licensees

---

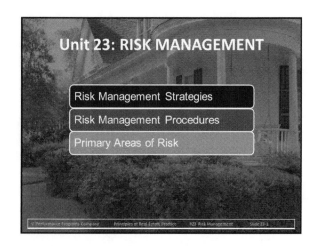

Unit 23: RISK MANAGEMENT

Risk Management Strategies

Risk Management Procedures

Primary Areas of Risk

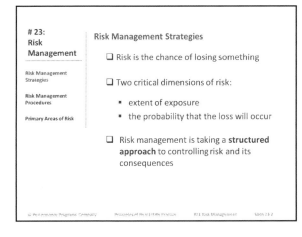

**# 23:
Risk
Management**

Risk Management
Strategies

Risk Management
Procedures

Primary Areas of Risk

Risk Management Strategies

❑ Risk is the chance of losing something

❑ Two critical dimensions of risk:

- extent of exposure
- the probability that the loss will occur

❑ Risk management is taking a **structured approach** to controlling risk and its consequences

**# 23:
Risk
Management**

Risk Management
Strategies

Risk Management
Procedures

Primary Areas of Risk

Risk Management Strategies

Four risk management strategies

❑ **Avoidance**
❑ **Reduction**
❑ **Transference**
❑ **Retention**

1) **Avoidance**
- refrain from risky activity
- eg, assuring buyers a property will appreciate

**# 23:
Risk
Management**

Risk Management
Strategies

Risk Management
Procedures

Primary Areas of Risk

Risk Management Strategies

Four risk management strategies (cont.)

2) **Reduction**
- reduce probability of loss
- reduce severity of loss
- share responsibility for a decision

3) **Transference**
- pass risk to another party
- get E & O insurance
- by contract; insurance

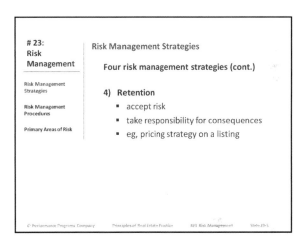

**# 23:
Risk
Management**

Risk Management
Strategies

Risk Management
Procedures

Primary Areas of Risk

Risk Management Strategies

Four risk management strategies (cont.)

4) **Retention**
- accept risk
- take responsibility for consequences
- eg, pricing strategy on a listing

**# 23:
Risk
Management**

Risk Management
Strategies

Risk Management
Procedures

Primary Areas of Risk

Risk Management Procedures

❑ Education
❑ Disclosure
❑ Documentation
❑ Insurance

Education

❑ Knowledge and skill reduce risk
❑ Understand forms and contracts
❑ Get job training

**# 23:
Risk
Management**

Risk Management
Strategies

Risk Management
Procedures

Primary Areas of Risk

Risk Management Procedures

Disclosure

❑ Provide information to reduce misunderstanding & lawsuits

Disclosure areas

❑ Agency
❑ Property condition
❑ Fiduciary / statutory duties
❑ Personal interest in selling a property

Slide 1 (top left):

 # 23:
Risk Management

Risk Management Strategies

Risk Management Procedures

Primary Areas of Risk

Risk Management Procedures

Documentation and record keeping

❑ Maintain evidence of compliance

❑ Elements of a paper trail
- manuals
- forms
- records
- contracts
- accounting
- other documents

Slide 2 (top right):

 # 23:
Risk Management

Risk Management Strategies

Risk Management Procedures

Primary Areas of Risk

Risk Management Procedures

Insurance – types of insurance to manage risk

❑ General liability
❑ E & O
❑ Fire and hazard
❑ Flood
❑ Casualty
❑ Workers
❑ Personal property
❑ Consequential loss
❑ Surety bond

Slide 3 (middle left):

Primary Areas of Risk

 # 23:
Risk Management

Risk Management Strategies

Risk Management Procedures

Primary Areas of Risk

❑ **Agency**
❑ **Property disclosures**
❑ **Listing and selling process**
❑ **Contracting process**
❑ **Fair Housing**
❑ **Antitrust**
❑ **Rules and regulations**
❑ **Misrepresentation**
❑ **Recommending providers**
❑ **Financing and closing**
❑ **Trust fund handling**
❑ **Safety and security**
❑ **Management Procedures**

Slide 4 (middle right):

Primary Areas Of Risk

 # 23:
Risk Management

Risk Management Strategies

Risk Management Procedures

Primary Areas of Risk

Agency
❑ Fulfill agency disclosure requirements
❑ Discharge fiduciary duties and duties to customers
❑ Avoid conflicts of interest
❑ Uphold legal confidentialities

Property disclosures
❑ Seller's property condition disclosure
❑ Material facts disclosure
❑ Lead paint, infestations, mold, radon

Slide 5 (bottom left):

Primary Areas of Risk

 # 23:
Risk Management

Risk Management Strategies

Risk Management Procedures

Primary Areas of Risk

Listing and selling risk areas

❑ Listing agreement accuracy

❑ Comparative market analysis results

❑ Closing cost estimates

❑ Advertising

❑ Authorizations and permissions

❑ Exceeding expertise

Slide 6 (bottom right):

Primary Areas of Risk

 # 23:
Risk Management

Risk Management Strategies

Risk Management Procedures

Primary Areas of Risk

Risk management in the contracting process

❑ Contracts for real estate must be in writing

❑ Inaccuracy endangers contract

❑ Avoid unauthorized practice of law
- may fill in blanks on standard contract forms;
- do not give legal advice to public

❑ Other risks in completing contracts
- illegal forms, omitted elements, lapsed contingencies, wrong data

**# 23:
Risk
Management**

Risk Management
Strategies

Risk Management
Procedures

Primary Areas of Risk

Primary Areas of Risk

Fair Housing

❑ Advertising may not state preference,
limitation or discrimination based on
race, color, religion, national origin, sex,
handicap, familial status

❑ Licensee must not be involved with
discriminatory actions of a client or
customer

**# 23:
Risk
Management**

Risk Management
Strategies

Risk Management
Procedures

Primary Areas of Risk

Primary Areas of Risk

Fair Housing

❑ Advertising may not state preference,
limitation or discrimination based on race,
color, religion, national origin, sex, handicap,
familial status

❑ Licensee must not be involved with
discriminatory actions of a client or
customer

❑ Make sure listing and purchase contracts are
in compliance

**# 23:
Risk
Management**

Risk Management
Strategies

Risk Management
Procedures

Primary Areas of Risk

Primary Areas of Risk

Antitrust – measures to avoid risk

❑ Cannot collude on prices; fix prices

❑ Cannot conspire with other companies to
restrict trade or unjustly impair a competitor

❑ Cannot create monopolies

❑ Cannot allocate markets among competitors

**# 23:
Risk
Management**

Risk Management
Strategies

Risk Management
Procedures

Primary Areas of Risk

Primary Areas of Risk

Rules and regulations

❑ **Prime causes of discipline**
  ▪ commission of prohibited acts
  ▪ practicing with an expired license
  ▪ disclosure failures
  ▪ earnest money mishandling

Primary Areas of Risk

**# 23:
Risk
Management**

Risk Management
Strategies

Risk Management
Procedures

Primary Areas of Risk

Misrepresentation

❑ **Unintentional**
  ▪ inaccurate information conveyed
    unknowingly
  ▪ occurs most often in measurements,
    property characterizations

❑ **Intentional**
  ▪ fraud
  ▪ knowingly conveying false information

Primary Areas of Risk

**# 23:
Risk
Management**

Risk Management
Strategies

Risk Management
Procedures

Primary Areas of Risk

Misrepresentation (cont.)

❑ **Ways to reduce risks in misrepresentation**

  ▪ measure and calculate areas accurately

  ▪ do not over-rely on measurements by
    others

  ▪ refrain from exaggeration

  ▪ avoid stating opinions a consumer might
    take for expertise

 # 23:
Risk
Management

Risk Management
Strategies

Risk Management
Procedures

Primary Areas of Risk

Primary Areas of Risk

Recommending providers

❑ Risks include
- consumer dissatisfaction
- possible liability for undisclosed business relationship

❑ Best practices
- do not recommend vendors
- provide a list of trusted vendors with a disclaimer and no recommendation

---

 # 23:
Risk
Management

Risk Management
Strategies

Risk Management
Procedures

Primary Areas of Risk

Primary Areas of Risk

Financing and closing – risk areas

❑ ECOA violations

❑ failed transactions due to lack of contingency–period diligence

❑ failure to ensure proper disclosure of closing costs

❑ RESPA violations

 # 23:
Risk
Management

Risk Management
Strategies

Risk Management
Procedures

Primary Areas of Risk

Primary Areas of Risk

Trust fund handling risk areas

❑ Mishandling of earnest money deposits

❑ Commingling trust funds

❑ Conversion of trust funds

❑ Errors in use of trust accounts

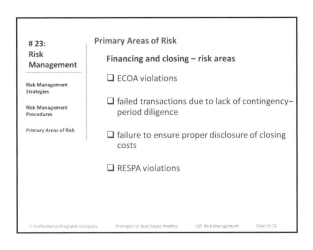

Unit 24: PROPERTY MANAGEMENT

Management Functions
The Management Agreement
Leasing Considerations
The Management Business

 # 24:
Property
Management

Management Functions

The Management
Agreement

Leasing Considerations

The Management
Business

Management Functions

❑ Three main types of manager

- individual broker or firm managing properties for multiple owners

- building manager employed by an owner to manage a single property

- resident manager, employed by owner, broker, or management firm to live and manage on site

---

 # 24:
Property
Management

Management Functions

The Management
Agreement

Leasing Considerations

The Management
Business

Management Functions

Manager's duties and activities
❑ Manager is a fiduciary of the principal
❑ Duty to act in principal's best interests
❑ May specialize in a property type

❑ Manager needs skills in
- marketing
- accounting
- finance
- construction

 # 24: Property Management

Management Functions
- The Management Agreement
- Leasing Considerations
- The Management Business

Management Functions

Principal management functions

- ❑ Reporting
- ❑ Budgeting
- ❑ Renting
- ❑ Property maintenance
- ❑ Construction
- ❑ Risk management

 # 24: Property Management

Management Functions
- The Management Agreement
- Leasing Considerations
- The Management Business

Management Functions

Reporting

- ❑ May be required monthly, quarterly, annually

- ❑ Reports include
  - annual operating budget
  - cash flow reports
  - profit and loss statements
  - budget comparison statements

 # 24: Property Management

Management Functions
- The Management Agreement
- Leasing Considerations
- The Management Business

Management Functions

Budgeting

- ❑ Operating budget based on expected expenses and revenues

- ❑ Determines key financial requirements
  - needed rental rates
  - capital expenditures
  - reserves
  - salaries and wages

- ❑ Projects income based on past performance and current market

---

 # 24: Property Management

Management Functions
- The Management Agreement
- Leasing Considerations
- The Management Business

Management Functions

Budgeting (cont.)

- ❑ **Potential gross income =**
  (scheduled rents + revenue from other sources)

- ❑ **Effective gross income =**
  (total gross - vacancies, bad debt)

- ❑ **Net operating income =**
  (gross - operating expenses)

- ❑ **Cash flow =**
  (net operating income - debt service, reserves)

 # 24: Property Management

Management Functions
- The Management Agreement
- Leasing Considerations
- The Management Business

Management Functions

Renting Responsibility

- ❑ Manager must keep property properly rented

- ❑ Vacancies minimization
  - proper rent levels
  - sufficient marketing
  - good tenant relations

- ❑ Select compatible tenants

- ❑ Collect rents

- ❑ Comply with fair housing laws, ADA, ECOA

 # 24: Property Management

Management Functions
- The Management Agreement
- Leasing Considerations
- The Management Business

Management Functions

Property maintenance

- ❑ Attain best balance between costs of services, owner financial objectives, and tenant needs

- ❑ Maintenance types
  - routine everyday
  - preventive, or corrective
  - staffed in-house vs. contracted out

 # 24: Property Management

Management Functions

The Management Agreement

Leasing Considerations

The Management Business

Management Functions

Construction

❑ **Improvements**: tenant alterations, renovations, and expansion

❑ **Site**: environmental remediation

❑ **ADA concerns**:
  ▪ feasibility of restructuring, retrofitting, new construction to achieve compliance

---

 # 24: Property Management

Management Functions

The Management Agreement

Leasing Considerations

The Management Business

Management Functions

Risk management

❑ Risks to manage
  ▪ natural disaster
  ▪ personal injury
  ▪ terrorism
  ▪ employee malfeasance

❑ Management strategy
  ▪ avoid / remove the source
  ▪ installing protective systems
  ▪ buy insurance

 # 24: Property Management

Management Functions

The Management Agreement

Leasing Considerations

The Management Business

Management Functions

Risk management (cont.)

❑ Life safety systems
  ▪ sprinklers
  ▪ fire doors
  ▪ smoke alarms
  ▪ fire escapes
  ▪ monitoring systems

 # 24: Property Management

Management Functions

The Management Agreement

Leasing Considerations

The Management Business

Management Functions

Risk management (cont.)

❑ **Types of insurance for rented properties**
  ▪ Casualty
  ▪ Liability
  ▪ Workers compensation
  ▪ Fire and hazard
  ▪ Flood
  ▪ Contents
  ▪ Consequential loss
  ▪ Surety bonds
  ▪ Multi-peril

 # 24: Property Management

Management Functions

The Management Agreement

Leasing Considerations

The Management Business

The Management Agreement

Components

❑ Names of parties
❑ Property description
❑ Agreement term
❑ Owner's purpose
❑ Responsibilities
❑ Authority
❑ Budget
❑ Allocation of costs
❑ Reporting
❑ Compensation
❑ Equal opportunity statement

 # 24: Property Management

Management Functions

The Management Agreement

Leasing Considerations

The Management Business

The Management Agreement

Landlord rights, duties and liabilities

❑ Receive rent
❑ Maintain premises in specified condition
❑ Enter and inspect units
❑ Examine books
❑ Enter into contracts
❑ Hire vendors
❑ Set rents
❑ Pay management fees
❑ Comply with environmental laws and fair housing

The Management Agreement

24:
Property Management

Management Functions

The Management Agreement

Leasing Considerations

The Management Business

Manager's rights, duties and liabilities

- ❑ Hire and fire
- ❑ Enter into contracts
- ❑ Perform management tasks
- ❑ Maintain financial records
- ❑ Make reports
- ❑ Budget, collect rent
- ❑ Find tenants
- ❑ Maintain the property
- ❑ Meet owner goals
- ❑ Liability for trust funds
- ❑ Comply with fair housing laws, credit laws, employment

Leasing Considerations

24:
Property Management

Management Functions

The Management Agreement

Leasing Considerations

The Management Business

Lease types in review

- ❑ **For years** – specific lease term
- ❑ **Periodic** – term automatically renews
- ❑ **At will** – no specified lease term
- ❑ **At sufferance** – tenancy without consent
- ❑ **Gross** – landlord pays expenses
- ❑ **Net** – tenant pays expenses
- ❑ **Percentage** – tenant pays % of sales

Leasing Considerations

24:
Property Management

Management Functions

The Management Agreement

Leasing Considerations

The Management Business

Inclusions and exclusions
- ❑ Lease sets forth what is included, excluded in lease
  - ▪ Delineates what landlord must maintain, insure, replace
  - ▪ E.g., appliances, furniture

Alterations
- ❑ What is permitted, permission process
- ❑ What must be returned to original condition

Leasing Considerations

24:
Property Management

Management Functions

The Management Agreement

Leasing Considerations

The Management Business

Landlord rights and responsibilities

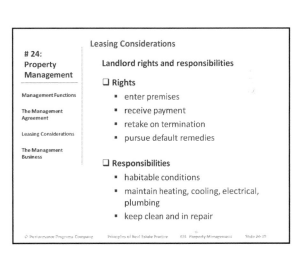

- ❑ **Rights**
  - ▪ enter premises
  - ▪ receive payment
  - ▪ retake on termination
  - ▪ pursue default remedies

- ❑ **Responsibilities**
  - ▪ habitable conditions
  - ▪ maintain heating, cooling, electrical, plumbing
  - ▪ keep clean and in repair

Leasing Considerations

24:
Property Management

Management Functions

The Management Agreement

Leasing Considerations

The Management Business

Tenant rights and responsibilities

- ❑ **Rights**
  - ▪ quiet enjoyment
  - ▪ habitable conditions
  - ▪ right to take action for default

- ❑ **Responsibilities**
  - ▪ pay rent
  - ▪ obey rules
  - ▪ give proper notice
  - ▪ return property in prescribed condition
  - ▪ use only for intended purpose

Leasing Considerations

24:
Property Management

Management Functions

The Management Agreement

Leasing Considerations

The Management Business

Evictions

- ❑ Actual → prescribed legal procedure
  - ▪ serve notice
  - ▪ initiate suit
  - ▪ obtain judgment
  - ▪ re-take premises

- ❑ Constructive → tenant vacates on account of landlord failure to maintain premises

 # 24: Property Management

Management Functions

The Management Agreement

Leasing Considerations

The Management Business

Leasing Considerations

Causes for termination of a lease

❑ Expiration
❑ Performance
❑ Agreement
❑ Abandonment
❑ Breach
❑ Notice
❑ Destruction of premises
❑ Condemnation
❑ Foreclosure
❑ Death of either party

 # 24: Property Management

Management Functions

The Management Agreement

Leasing Considerations

The Management Business

Leasing Considerations

Security deposit management procedures

❑ Handling deposits determined by
  ▪ state law
  ▪ regulations
  ▪ agreement

❑ Funds held in trust

❑ Return of funds prescribed by law

 # 24: Property Management

Management Functions

The Management Agreement

Leasing Considerations

The Management Business

The Management Business

Management specializations

❑ Leasing
❑ Asset management
❑ Corporate properties
❑ Resorts
❑ Association management
❑ Housing programs
❑ Mobile home parks
❑ Office buildings

 # 24: Property Management

Management Functions

The Management Agreement

Leasing Considerations

The Management Business

The Management Business

Securing business

❑ Develop reputation and competence

❑ Obtain training

❑ Use effective advertising

❑ Develop management plan in accordance with owner objectives

---

 # 24: Property Management

Management Functions

The Management Agreement

Leasing Considerations

The Management Business

The Management Business

Professional development

❑ Training, designations, certifications increase and demonstrate competence

❑ Professional organizations
  ▪ Institute of Real Estate Management
  ▪ Building Owners and Mgrs. Association
  ▪ National Apartment Association
  ▪ Nat. Assoc. of Residential Property Mgrs.
  ▪ Nat. Assoc. of Condominium Mgrs.
  ▪ Int'l Council of Shopping Centers
  ▪ Int'l Facilities Management Association

Unit 25: GEORGIA LICENSING REGULATION & ENFORCEMENT

Definitions
The Real Estate Commission
Licensing Regulations
Disciplinary Actions
Violations and Unfair Trade Practices

 # 25:

GA Licensing Regulation & Enforcement

Definitions

The Real Estate Commission

Licensing Regulations

Disciplinary Actions

Violations and Unfair Trade Practices

Definitions

❑ **Agency**
- Where broker represents a client with client's permission

❑ **Broker**
- The party representing another with the intent of being paid
- May be client in agency relationship or a consumer if acting as a transaction broker

❑ **Brokerage agreement**
- Broker enters into express written contract to perform service for compensation

❑ **Brokerage relationship**
- Includes agency and non-agency relationships

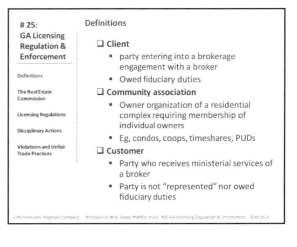

 # 25:

GA Licensing Regulation & Enforcement

Definitions

The Real Estate Commission

Licensing Regulations

Disciplinary Actions

Violations and Unfair Trade Practices

Definitions

❑ **Client**
- party entering into a brokerage engagement with a broker
- Owed fiduciary duties

❑ **Community association**
- Owner organization of a residential complex requiring membership of individual owners
- Eg, condos, coops, timeshares, PUDs

❑ **Customer**
- Party who receives ministerial services of a broker
- Party is not "represented" nor owed fiduciary duties

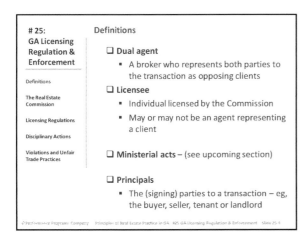

 # 25:

GA Licensing Regulation & Enforcement

Definitions

The Real Estate Commission

Licensing Regulations

Disciplinary Actions

Violations and Unfair Trade Practices

Definitions

❑ **Dual agent**
- A broker who represents both parties to the transaction as opposing clients

❑ **Licensee**
- Individual licensed by the Commission
- May or may not be an agent representing a client

❑ **Ministerial acts** – (see upcoming section)

❑ **Principals**
- The (signing) parties to a transaction – eg, the buyer, seller, tenant or landlord

---

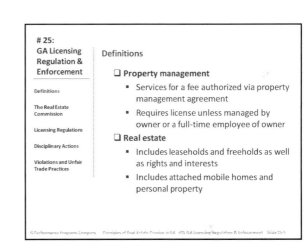

 # 25:

GA Licensing Regulation & Enforcement

Definitions

The Real Estate Commission

Licensing Regulations

Disciplinary Actions

Violations and Unfair Trade Practices

Definitions

❑ **Property management**
- Services for a fee authorized via property management agreement
- Requires license unless managed by owner or a full-time employee of owner

❑ **Real estate**
- Includes leaseholds and freeholds as well as rights and interests
- Includes attached mobile homes and personal property

 # 25:

GA Licensing Regulation & Enforcement

Definitions

The Real Estate Commission

Licensing Regulations

Disciplinary Actions

Violations and Unfair Trade Practices

Definitions

❑ **Salesperson**
- Individual other than associate broker who acts on behalf of the broker in performing services

❑ **Timely**
- Phrase used in contracts to mean certain things must be completed diligently, as soon as possible, or worst case, 'in a reasonable time'

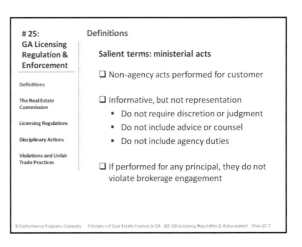

 # 25:

GA Licensing Regulation & Enforcement

Definitions

The Real Estate Commission

Licensing Regulations

Disciplinary Actions

Violations and Unfair Trade Practices

Definitions

Salient terms: ministerial acts

❑ Non-agency acts performed for customer

❑ Informative, but not representation
- Do not require discretion or judgment
- Do not include advice or counsel
- Do not include agency duties

❑ If performed for any principal, they do not violate brokerage engagement

Slide 1

 # 25:
GA Licensing Regulation & Enforcement

Definitions

The Real Estate Commission

Licensing Regulations

Disciplinary Actions

Violations and Unfair Trade Practices

Definitions

Salient terms: ministerial acts (cont.)

❑ Examples of ministerial acts
- Completing contract forms as directed by customer
- Identifying transaction-related professional to perform services
- Identifying neighborhood features for principals to a transaction

Slide 2

 # 25:
GA Licensing Regulation & Enforcement

Definitions

The Real Estate Commission

Licensing Regulations

Disciplinary Actions

Violations and Unfair Trade Practices

The Real Estate Commission

❑ The governing body regulating GA licensing activity and licensees

Purpose

❑ To protect the public interest by regulating the real estate brokerage industry

Members

❑ Six members appointed by Governor
- five are brokers
- one is unlicensed to represent the pubic

Slide 3

 # 25:
GA Licensing Regulation & Enforcement

Definitions

The Real Estate Commission

Licensing Regulations

Disciplinary Actions

Violations and Unfair Trade Practices

The Real Estate Commission

Scope of authority

❑ Derived from statutory law

❑ Establishes fees

❑ Adopts, promulgates rules and regulations

❑ Maintains records, licensee history

❑ Regulates licensure and licensing activities
- can revoke, suspend or deny a license
- can discipline licensees
- duty to appoint Commissioner

Slide 4

 # 25:
GA Licensing Regulation & Enforcement

Definitions

The Real Estate Commission

Licensing Regulations

Disciplinary Actions

Violations and Unfair Trade Practices

The Real Estate Commission

Declaratory rulings

❑ Given by Commission re: applicability of statutes or rules

❑ Furnished within 60 days of receiving a signed, notarized request.

Rule change request

❑ Anyone can petition the Commission re: promulgating or changing a rule

❑ Petition must be in writing and notarized

❑ Commission provides a denial with reason, or adopts changes

Slide 5

 # 25:
GA Licensing Regulation & Enforcement

Definitions

The Real Estate Commission

Licensing Regulations

Disciplinary Actions

Violations and Unfair Trade Practices

Licensing Regulations

Licensed activities requiring licensure

❑ Listing or selling other's real estate
❑ Lease and manage real estate, with exceptions
❑ Negotiating
❑ Exchanging
❑ Prospecting
❑ Counseling in real estate
❑ Selling timeshares
❑ Auctioning real estate

Slide 6

 # 25:
GA Licensing Regulation & Enforcement

Definitions

The Real Estate Commission

Licensing Regulations

Disciplinary Actions

Violations and Unfair Trade Practices

Licensing Regulations

Exemptions to licensure

❑ Owners and their employees

❑ Attorneys and CPAs who are practicing such

❑ A receiver, administrator, executor, guardian, trustee in bankruptcy, or party acting under court order

❑ Government and utility employees

 # 25:
GA Licensing Regulation & Enforcement

Definitions

The Real Estate Commission

Licensing Regulations

Disciplinary Actions

Violations and Unfair Trade Practices

Licensing Regulations

Exemptions to licensure (cont.)

❏ Certain referral agents if not paid

❏ Broker's property management assistant performing certain limited activities

❏ Community association manager if member

❏ **"Innkeeper's exemption"**
  ▪ manage properties with temporary tenants (< 90 days)

 # 25:
GA Licensing Regulation & Enforcement

Definitions

The Real Estate Commission

Licensing Regulations

Disciplinary Actions

Violations and Unfair Trade Practices

Licensing Regulations

Licensing qualifications

❏ Four license categories
  ▪ Broker
  ▪ Broker associate
  ▪ Salesperson
  ▪ Community association manager

 # 25:
GA Licensing Regulation & Enforcement

Definitions

The Real Estate Commission

Licensing Regulations

Disciplinary Actions

Violations and Unfair Trade Practices

Licensing Regulations

Licensing qualifications (cont.)

❏ **Broker** and **associate broker**
  ▪ 21 years old
  ▪ GA resident or resident of state with reciprocity
  ▪ high school diploma or equivalent
  ▪ active license for three of preceding five years
  ▪ acceptable criminal history report
  ▪ 60-hr broker course
  ▪ fidelity bond

 # 25:
GA Licensing Regulation & Enforcement

Definitions

The Real Estate Commission

Licensing Regulations

Disciplinary Actions

Violations and Unfair Trade Practices

Licensing Regulations

Licensing qualifications (cont.)

❏ **Salesperson**
  ▪ 18 years old
  ▪ Georgia resident or resident of state with reciprocity
  ▪ high school diploma or equivalent
  ▪ criminal history report
  ▪ 75-hr pre-license course or equivalent
  ▪ pass licensing exam
  ▪ complete 25-hr post-license course within one year

 # 25:
GA Licensing Regulation & Enforcement

Definitions

The Real Estate Commission

Licensing Regulations

Disciplinary Actions

Violations and Unfair Trade Practices

Licensing Regulations

Licensing qualifications (cont.)

❏ **Community association manager**
  ▪ 18 years old
  ▪ resident of Georgia or state with reciprocity
  ▪ high school diploma or equivalent
  ▪ criminal history report
  ▪ 25-hr community association manager course or equivalent
  ▪ pass licensing exam

 # 25:
GA Licensing Regulation & Enforcement

Definitions

The Real Estate Commission

Licensing Regulations

Disciplinary Actions

Violations and Unfair Trade Practices

Licensing Regulations

Licensing qualifications (cont.)

❏ Licensees other than brokers
  ▪ must be under a single Georgia broker except for reciprocity

❏ Firm license
  ▪ must designate qualifying broker
  ▪ each type of firm has specific requirements for qualifying broker

 # 25:

GA Licensing Regulation & Enforcement

Definitions

The Real Estate Commission

Licensing Regulations

Disciplinary Actions

Violations and Unfair Trade Practices

Licensing Regulations

Licensing qualifications (cont.)

❑ **Sole proprietorship** license
  ▪ Must be owned solely by licensed broker

❑ **Corporation** license
  ▪ Must have corporate officer as broker

❑ **Partnership** license
  ▪ Qualifying broker must be a partner

❑ **LLC** license
  ▪ Qualifying broker must be a member or manager

 # 25:

GA Licensing Regulation & Enforcement

Definitions

The Real Estate Commission

Licensing Regulations

Disciplinary Actions

Violations and Unfair Trade Practices

Licensing Regulations

Licensing qualifications (cont.)

❑ **Business entity ethics qualifications**
  ▪ Applicants must be honest, trustworthy, have good reputation and be competent
  ▪ Evidenced by clean criminal record, disciplinary actions

❑ **Criminal history**
  ▪ Applies to all applicants
  ▪ Due 60 days preceding application
  ▪ Applicant may be denied license if there are convictions or discipline

---

 # 25:

GA Licensing Regulation & Enforcement

Definitions

The Real Estate Commission

Licensing Regulations

Disciplinary Actions

Violations and Unfair Trade Practices

Licensing Regulations

Licensing qualifications (cont.)

❑ **Application deadline**
  ▪ must apply for active or inactive license within 3 months of passing exam

❑ **Child support**
  ▪ license may be suspended for non-payment of child support

❑ **Disabled veterans**
  ▪ May receive up to ten points credit on license exam

 # 25:

GA Licensing Regulation & Enforcement

Definitions

The Real Estate Commission

Licensing Regulations

Disciplinary Actions

Violations and Unfair Trade Practices

Licensing Regulations

Licensing reciprocity

❑ New resident with non-Georgia license / non-resident licensee – may get GA license without exam or education provided:
  ▪ state must have equivalent education and exam
  ▪ license must have been issued within 12 months of application
  ▪ license must be in good standing
  ▪ applicant must appoint Commissioner as agent for any litigation / discipline

---

 # 25:

GA Licensing Regulation & Enforcement

Definitions

The Real Estate Commission

Licensing Regulations

Disciplinary Actions

Violations and Unfair Trade Practices

Licensing Regulations

Expired and inactive licenses

❑ **Expiration**
  ▪ License expires if not renewed by expiration date
  ▪ If expired for non-payment, one may reinstate within 2 years if pay all fees
  ▪ If lapse is 2-5 years, may renew by paying fees and completing CE
  ▪ If lapse 5+ years, applicant must get education, pass test, get new license

---

 # 25:

GA Licensing Regulation & Enforcement

Definitions

The Real Estate Commission

Licensing Regulations

Disciplinary Actions

Violations and Unfair Trade Practices

Licensing Regulations

Expired and inactive licenses

❑ **Inactive licenses**
  ▪ Licensees may de-activate by converting to inactive status
  ▪ Inactive licensees may not practice real estate
  ▪ Request to Commission must be within 30 days of ceasing activity
  ▪ Must still pay renewal fees

 # 25:

GA Licensing Regulation & Enforcement

Definitions

The Real Estate Commission

Licensing Regulations

Disciplinary Actions

Violations and Unfair Trade Practices

Licensing Regulations

License renewal

❑ Nine hours CE required for each year of 4-year renewal period (total 36 hours)

❑ 3 of 4 hours for each year **must be license law** content

❑ **Salesperson's 1ˢᵗ renewal**: 25-hour post license course earns 9 hours credit for 36-hour requirement, thus must take 27 more hours before renewal

---

 # 25:

GA Licensing Regulation & Enforcement

Definitions

The Real Estate Commission

Licensing Regulations

Disciplinary Actions

Violations and Unfair Trade Practices

Licensing Regulations

License renewal (cont.)

❑ Inactive licensees must complete CE to reactivate

❑ Licensees exempt from CE if licensed prior to 1980.

❑ Must renew every four years on last day of month of birth

Auctioneering

❑ Must obtain individual / company auctioneer license to auction real property

---

 # 25:

GA Licensing Regulation & Enforcement

Definitions

The Real Estate Commission

Licensing Regulations

Disciplinary Actions

Violations and Unfair Trade Practices

Disciplinary Actions

Initiation of actions

❑ Commission may investigate actions of licensees, firms

❑ If on its own motion, Commission must investigate within three years of the possible violation

❑ Investigation determines whether a violation occurred – if not, the case is closed

❑ If violation did occur, hearings are conducted and disciplinary actions taken

---

 # 25:

GA Licensing Regulation & Enforcement

Definitions

The Real Estate Commission

Licensing Regulations

Disciplinary Actions

Violations and Unfair Trade Practices

Disciplinary Actions

Hearings, revocation, suspension, censure

❑ Cannot take disciplinary action without a hearing

❑ If guilty, penalty can be
  ▪ revocation, suspension, censure, reprimand
  ▪ fine
  ▪ downgrade of broker license to salesperson
  ▪ required completion of course in brokerage
  ▪ citation and letter of finding if no one harmed by violation

---

 # 25:

GA Licensing Regulation & Enforcement

Definitions

The Real Estate Commission

Licensing Regulations

Disciplinary Actions

Violations and Unfair Trade Practices

Disciplinary Actions

Post-hearing procedures

❑ The violating party may request a review of the decision within 30 days

❑ All motions must be filed 7 days prior to the hearing date

❑ Licensees must notify the Commission of the final disposition of any action or conviction within ten days of conclusion of the proceedings

---

 # 25:

GA Licensing Regulation & Enforcement

Definitions

The Real Estate Commission

Licensing Regulations

Disciplinary Actions

Violations and Unfair Trade Practices

Disciplinary Actions

Surrendering license

❑ On notice of suspension or revocation, licensee must surrender his/her license

❑ If a broker, must forward all affiliated licensees' licenses in addition to the broker's license

License reinstatement

❑ Licensee must apply for licensure as an original applicant

❑ When a broker's or associate broker's license is revoked or surrendered, licensee must wait 10 years before reapplying for licensure

 # 25:

GA Licensing Regulation & Enforcement

Definitions

The Real Estate Commission

Licensing Regulations

Disciplinary Actions

Violations and Unfair Trade Practices

Disciplinary Actions

Retention of records on hearings

❑ Commission retains records of investigations that did not result in disciplinary action for 15 years.

❑ Records of hearings resulting in disciplinary action Recovery Fund are retained for 40 years.

 # 25:

GA Licensing Regulation & Enforcement

Definitions

The Real Estate Commission

Licensing Regulations

Disciplinary Actions

Violations and Unfair Trade Practices

Disciplinary Actions

Education, Research and Recovery Fund

❑ Purpose of fund to compensate consumers who suffer losses due to licensees' violations

❑ Source of funds
  ▪ Accrues from license application fees and possible annual licensee renewal assessments

❑ Who can collect
  ▪ Parties aggrieved by licensee's violations of law, if uncollectable from licensee

---

 # 25:

GA Licensing Regulation & Enforcement

Definitions

The Real Estate Commission

Licensing Regulations

Disciplinary Actions

Violations and Unfair Trade Practices

Disciplinary Actions

Education, Research & Recovery Fund (cont.)

❑ Effect on licensee
  ▪ license is automatically revoked

  ▪ If judgment is against the firm, the qualifying broker's license is revoked

  ▪ Licensee may not be relicensed until the payment is repaid in full, plus interest

---

 # 25:

GA Licensing Regulation & Enforcement

Definitions

The Real Estate Commission

Licensing Regulations

Disciplinary Actions

Violations and Unfair Trade Practices

Violations and Unfair Trade Practices

❑ The following are unfair trade practices and other violations that can result in disciplinary actions and license revocation

Discrimination

❑ **Fair housing violations** based on family status, race, sex, color, disability, religion, or national origin
  ▪ Refusing to rent, lease or sell or deny real estate to any person
  ▪ Discriminatory advertising
  ▪ Blockbusting

 # 25:

GA Licensing Regulation & Enforcement

Definitions

The Real Estate Commission

Licensing Regulations

Disciplinary Actions

Violations and Unfair Trade Practices

Violations and Unfair Trade Practices

❑ **Deceptive advertising**
  ▪ Using misleading or inaccurate terms, values, services in consummating transactions

❑ **Accounting negligence**
  ▪ Trust fund mismanagement
  ▪ Co-mingling funds
  ▪ Conversion of funds

❑ **Failure to disclose**
  ▪ Receipts and expenditures of client
  ▪ Referrals

 # 25:

GA Licensing Regulation & Enforcement

Definitions

The Real Estate Commission

Licensing Regulations

Disciplinary Actions

Violations and Unfair Trade Practices

Violations and Unfair Trade Practices

❑ **Representing another broker**
  ▪ Accepting commissions from other brokers

❑ **Undisclosed interest**
  ▪ Acting as agent and principal without disclosure

❑ **Guaranteeing profits**
  ▪ Cannot 'guarantee' appreciation

❑ **Unauthorized representation**
  ▪ Cannot sell or lease without owner consent or on unapproved terms

 # 25:

GA Licensing Regulation & Enforcement

Definitions

The Real Estate Commission

Licensing Regulations

Disciplinary Actions

Violations and Unfair Trade Practices

Violations and Unfair Trade Practices

- ❑ **Agency interference**
    - ▪ Cannot interfere or try to get listing while property is listed by someone else
- ❑ **Out-of-jurisdiction practice**
- ❑ **Compensating non-licensees**
    - ▪ Cannot pay non-licensee for performing licensed activities, with some exceptions
- ❑ **Listing non-compliance**
    - ▪ Failing to include listing termination date
    - ▪ Cannot have automatic extensions

 # 25:

GA Licensing Regulation & Enforcement

Definitions

The Real Estate Commission

Licensing Regulations

Disciplinary Actions

Violations and Unfair Trade Practices

Violations and Unfair Trade Practices

- ❑ **Document delivery**
    - ▪ Must provide copies of transaction docs to all signing parties
    - ▪ Must deliver closing statements to principals
- ❑ **Material misrepresentation**
    - ▪ Advertising, written & oral communications
- ❑ **Representing value opinion as an appraisal**
- ❑ **Undisclosed dual agency**
    - ▪ Must get written consent of both parties

 # 25:

GA Licensing Regulation & Enforcement

Definitions

The Real Estate Commission

Licensing Regulations

Disciplinary Actions

Violations and Unfair Trade Practices

Violations and Unfair Trade Practices

- ❑ **Creating liens**
    - ▪ Cannot lien if no basis for claim in listing
- ❑ **Dishonesty or incompetence**
    - ▪ Must safeguard interests of public
- ❑ **Failing to retain records**
    - ▪ Three years for transaction and trust fund records
    - ▪ Failure to produce records for Commission

 # 25:

GA Licensing Regulation & Enforcement

Definitions

The Real Estate Commission

Licensing Regulations

Disciplinary Actions

Violations and Unfair Trade Practices

Violations and Unfair Trade Practices

- ❑ **Community association violations**
    - ▪ Cannot conduct any act which is to be performed only by a broker, associate broker, or salesperson
    - ▪ Licensee must have written consent to sell, lease, or exchange property of a member of the community association
    - ▪ Upon agreement termination, failing to deliver complete and accurate records of all transactions and funds

---

 # 25:

GA Licensing Regulation & Enforcement

Definitions

The Real Estate Commission

Licensing Regulations

Disciplinary Actions

Violations and Unfair Trade Practices

Violations and Unfair Trade Practices

- ❑ **Altering commissions**
    - ▪ Cannot try to alter a licensee's commission without the licensee's permission
- ❑ **Referrals in violation**
    - ▪ Failing to obtain a written agreement to refer a person to another licensee
    - ▪ Failing to inform the person who is being referred whether licensee will receive anything of value for making the referral
    - ▪ Paying a referral fee to someone who is unlicensed is prohibited

---

 # 25:

GA Licensing Regulation & Enforcement

Definitions

The Real Estate Commission

Licensing Regulations

Disciplinary Actions

Violations and Unfair Trade Practices

Violations and Unfair Trade Practices

- ❑ **Financing disclosure**
    - ▪ Must include terms in financing contingencies
    - ▪ Must include correct money amounts in contracts
- ❑ **Business name differs from registered name**
- ❑ **Undisclosed real estate activities**
    - ▪ Must inform broker of personal real estate activities performed

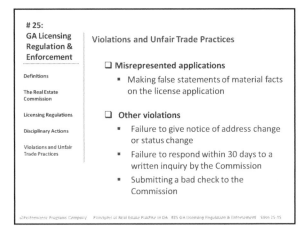

#25: GA Licensing Regulation & Enforcement

Definitions

The Real Estate Commission

Licensing Regulations

Disciplinary Actions

Violations and Unfair Trade Practices

Violations and Unfair Trade Practices

❑ **Trust fund violations**

- Failure to register trust fund-designated accounts
- Failure to conduct proper reconciliations
- Failure to make proper disbursals

❑ **Broker activity with lapsed license**

❑ **Commission notifications**

- failing to notify final disposition of any administrative, civil, or criminal action within ten days of the conclusion of the court action

---

#25: GA Licensing Regulation & Enforcement

Definitions

The Real Estate Commission

Licensing Regulations

Disciplinary Actions

Violations and Unfair Trade Practices

Violations and Unfair Trade Practices

❑ **Misrepresented applications**

- Making false statements of material facts on the license application

❑ **Other violations**

- Failure to give notice of address change or status change
- Failure to respond within 30 days to a written inquiry by the Commission
- Submitting a bad check to the Commission

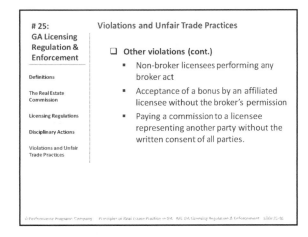

#25: GA Licensing Regulation & Enforcement

Definitions

The Real Estate Commission

Licensing Regulations

Disciplinary Actions

Violations and Unfair Trade Practices

Violations and Unfair Trade Practices

❑ **Other violations (cont.)**

- Non-broker licensees performing any broker act
- Acceptance of a bonus by an affiliated licensee without the broker's permission
- Paying a commission to a licensee representing another party without the written consent of all parties.

Unit 26: GEORGIA BROKERAGE REGULATION

- Brokerage Relationships in Real Estate Transactions Act
- Management Responsibilities of Real Estate Firms
- Managing Trust Accounts
- Advertising
- Handling Transactions

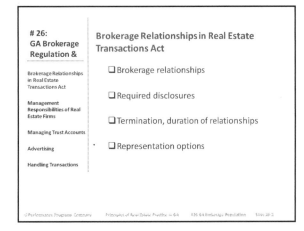

#26: GA Brokerage Regulation &

Brokerage Relationships in Real Estate Transactions Act

Management Responsibilities of Real Estate Firms

Managing Trust Accounts

Advertising

Handling Transactions

Brokerage Relationships in Real Estate Transactions Act

❑ Brokerage relationships

❑ Required disclosures

❑ Termination, duration of relationships

❑ Representation options

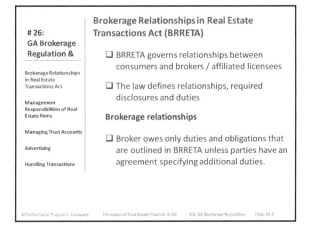

#26: GA Brokerage Regulation &

Brokerage Relationships in Real Estate Transactions Act

Management Responsibilities of Real Estate Firms

Managing Trust Accounts

Advertising

Handling Transactions

Brokerage Relationships in Real Estate Transactions Act (BRRETA)

❑ BRRETA governs relationships between consumers and brokers / affiliated licensees

❑ The law defines relationships, required disclosures and duties

Brokerage relationships

❑ Broker owes only duties and obligations that are outlined in BRRETA unless parties have an agreement specifying additional duties.

 # 26:
GA Brokerage Regulation &

Brokerage Relationships in Real Estate Transactions Act

Management Responsibilities of Real Estate Firms

Managing Trust Accounts

Advertising

Handling Transactions

Brokerage Relationships in Real Estate Transactions Act (BRRETA)

Brokerage relationships

❏ Per BRRETA, broker is **NOT considered to have a fiduciary relationship** with any party

❏ Broker is responsible only for
  ❏ exercising **reasonable care** in carrying out **duties** specified **in BRRETA**
  ❏ Discharging duties for the client as delineated in the **brokerage engagement**

 # 26:
GA Brokerage Regulation &

Brokerage Relationships in Real Estate Transactions Act

Management Responsibilities of Real Estate Firms

Managing Trust Accounts

Advertising

Handling Transactions

Brokerage Relationships in Real Estate Transactions Act (BRRETA)

Brokerage relationships

❏ Agency disclosures
  - Must be made in writing, in a timely manner
  - Made no later than when any party first makes an offer
  - Must disclose to both parties in writing who licensee is working for
  - If the firm is not an agent of either party, must disclose who will pay commission

---

 # 26:
GA Brokerage Regulation &

Brokerage Relationships in Real Estate Transactions Act

Management Responsibilities of Real Estate Firms

Managing Trust Accounts

Advertising

Handling Transactions

Brokerage Relationships in Real Estate Transactions Act (BRRETA)

Brokerage relationships

❏ **Duties prior to entering relationship**
  - Must inform what types of agency are available
  - Must include broker's compensation and whether shared by other brokers
  - Must disclose that client information will be confidential during and beyond engagement

---

 # 26:
GA Brokerage Regulation &

Brokerage Relationships in Real Estate Transactions Act

Management Responsibilities of Real Estate Firms

Managing Trust Accounts

Advertising

Handling Transactions

Brokerage Relationships in Real Estate Transactions Act (BRRETA)

Brokerage relationships

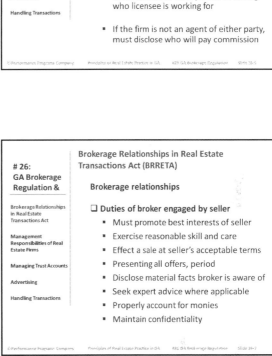

❏ **Duties of broker engaged by seller**
  - Must promote best interests of seller
  - Exercise reasonable skill and care
  - Effect a sale at seller's acceptable terms
  - Presenting all offers, period
  - Disclose material facts broker is aware of
  - Seek expert advice where applicable
  - Properly account for monies
  - Maintain confidentiality

 # 26:
GA Brokerage Regulation &

Brokerage Relationships in Real Estate Transactions Act

Management Responsibilities of Real Estate Firms

Managing Trust Accounts

Advertising

Handling Transactions

Brokerage Relationships in Real Estate Transactions Act (BRRETA)

Brokerage relationships

❏ **Duties of broker engaged by landlord (LL)**
  - Must promote best interests of LL
  - Exercise reasonable skill and care
  - Procure a tenant under acceptable terms
  - Disclose material facts broker is aware of
  - Seek expert advice where applicable
  - Properly account for monies
  - Maintain confidentiality

 # 26:
GA Brokerage Regulation &

Brokerage Relationships in Real Estate Transactions Act

Management Responsibilities of Real Estate Firms

Managing Trust Accounts

Advertising

Handling Transactions

Brokerage Relationships in Real Estate Transactions Act (BRRETA)

Required disclosures

❏ **Material facts: broker engaged by seller / LL**
  - All material facts relating to property
  - Adverse conditions within one mile of property otherwise undiscoverable by a drive-by or review of public documents
  - Broker does not have to seek out adverse material facts
  - Broker not liable for wrong disclosures if passing along info with disclosed source

 # 26:

GA Brokerage Regulation &

Brokerage Relationships in Real Estate Transactions Act

Management Responsibilities of Real Estate Firms

Managing Trust Accounts

Advertising

Handling Transactions

Brokerage Relationships in Real Estate Transactions Act (BRRETA)

Required disclosures

❑ **Material facts: broker engaged by buyer/tenant**
- Must disclose all known facts to seller regarding buyer's financial ability to perform
- Must disclose whether buyer will occupy the property
- Broker not liable for unintentionally mistaken disclosures if passing along info with disclosed source
- Buyer must disclose adverse material facts to seller regarding financial performance

---

 # 26:

GA Brokerage Regulation &

Brokerage Relationships in Real Estate Transactions Act

Management Responsibilities of Real Estate Firms

Managing Trust Accounts

Advertising

Handling Transactions

Brokerage Relationships in Real Estate Transactions Act (BRRETA)

Termination, duration of relationships

❑ **Relationship term**
- Period from starting date to the earlier of successful performance or expiration
- If no stated expiration or performance, relationship ends **one year** after initiation

❑ **Duties after termination**
- Accounting for monies
- Maintaining confidentiality unless required by law, given permission, or the info became public by another source

---

 # 26:

GA Brokerage Regulation &

Brokerage Relationships in Real Estate Transactions Act

Management Responsibilities of Real Estate Firms

Managing Trust Accounts

Advertising

Handling Transactions

Brokerage Relationships in Real Estate Transactions Act (BRRETA)

Designated agency

❑ The assigning by broker of different licensees to exclusively represent opposing clients in the same transaction

❑ Must comply with BRRETA requirements

❑ If in compliance, neither broker nor affiliated licensees will be deemed to be dual agents

---

 # 26:

GA Brokerage Regulation &

Brokerage Relationships in Real Estate Transactions Act

Management Responsibilities of Real Estate Firms

Managing Trust Accounts

Advertising

Handling Transactions

Brokerage Relationships in Real Estate Transactions Act (BRRETA)

Designated agency confidentiality restrictions

❑ May not disclose confidential info except to broker
- Includes info that client has not consented be disclosed
- Must disclose if required by law
- Other agents in firm may not have access to confidential information

---

 # 26:

GA Brokerage Regulation &

Brokerage Relationships in Real Estate Transactions Act

Management Responsibilities of Real Estate Firms

Managing Trust Accounts

Advertising

Handling Transactions

Brokerage Relationships in Real Estate Transactions Act (BRRETA)

Dual agency consent requirements

❑ Dual agent is agent representing both parties in a transaction

❑ Must get written consent
- Must disclose that opposing interests are adverse
- Must include that agent will disclose adverse material facts to both parties
- Must include that client is giving consent voluntarily

 # 26:

GA Brokerage Regulation &

Brokerage Relationships in Real Estate Transactions Act

Management Responsibilities of Real Estate Firms

Managing Trust Accounts

Advertising

Handling Transactions

Brokerage Relationships in Real Estate Transactions Act (BRRETA)

Other dual agency requirements

❑ Broker must maintain, enforce an office brokerage relationship policy
- Policy must permit or reject disclosed dual agency

❑ Written disclosure for dual agency
- Must be made to both parties
- Must disclose who pays commission
- Must be made prior to any offer
- Undisclosed dual agency violates law

Slide 1

 # 26:

GA Brokerage Regulation &

Brokerage Relationships in Real Estate Transactions Act

Management Responsibilities of Real Estate Firms

Managing Trust Accounts

Advertising

Handling Transactions

Brokerage Relationships in Real Estate Transactions Act (BRRETA)

Transaction broker / facilitator

❑ A licensee who represents neither party
❑ May perform ministerial acts for consumers
❑ Permitted acts include
  ▪ Identifying property
  ▪ Providing information, statistics
  ▪ Providing pre-printed forms, documents
  ▪ Identifying transaction services specialists

Slide 2

 # 26:

GA Brokerage Regulation &

Brokerage Relationships in Real Estate Transactions Act

Management Responsibilities of Real Estate Firms

Managing Trust Accounts

Advertising

Handling Transactions

Brokerage Relationships in Real Estate Transactions Act (BRRETA)

Transaction broker required actions

❑ Must disclose adverse material facts regarding property and neighborhood within one mile
❑ Must present all offers
❑ Must account for entrusted funds
❑ May not knowingly give false information
❑ Sellers must still disclose material property facts
❑ Buyers must still inspect property and neighborhood

Slide 3

 # 26:

GA Brokerage Regulation &

Brokerage Relationships in Real Estate Transactions Act

Management Responsibilities of Real Estate Firms

Managing Trust Accounts

Advertising

Handling Transactions

Brokerage Relationships in Real Estate Transactions Act (BRRETA)

Stigmatized property disclosures

❑ Not required to disclose
  ▪ If previously occupied by person with non-communicable disease, AIDS, HIV-positive
  ▪ If property was site of homicide, felony, suicide, other death
❑ Disclosing stigmatizing information where disclosure is not mandated requires seller's permission
❑ Consult attorney on disclosures that may stigmatize a property

Slide 4

 # 26:

GA Brokerage Regulation &

Brokerage Relationships in Real Estate Transactions Act

Management Responsibilities of Real Estate Firms

Managing Trust Accounts

Advertising

Handling Transactions

Management Responsibilities of Real Estate Firms

Brokerage operations - license requirements

❑ **Sole proprietor**
  ▪ broker is accountable to Commission for all acts of subordinates
❑ **Partnership**
  ▪ one partner must be accountable qualifying broker
❑ **Limited partnership**
  ▪ Qualifying broker must be the general partner
❑ **LLC**
  ▪ Qualifying broker must be member or manager

Slide 5

 # 26:

GA Brokerage Regulation &

Brokerage Relationships in Real Estate Transactions Act

Management Responsibilities of Real Estate Firms

Managing Trust Accounts

Advertising

Handling Transactions

Management Responsibilities of Real Estate Firms

Brokerage operations requirements

❑ **Death, resignation, termination of qualifying broker**

  ▪ Must get new qualifying broker in 60 days or cease operations until one is found

  ▪ Must designate party to sign docs and required applications

Slide 6

 # 26:

GA Brokerage Regulation &

Brokerage Relationships in Real Estate Transactions Act

Management Responsibilities of Real Estate Firms

Managing Trust Accounts

Advertising

Handling Transactions

Management Responsibilities of Real Estate Firms

Brokerage operations requirements

❑ **Employee vs. independent contractor**
  ▪ Affiliates may have either status
  ▪ Function of broker's choice, what is agreed to

❑ **Change of address**
  ▪ Must notify Commission within 30 days

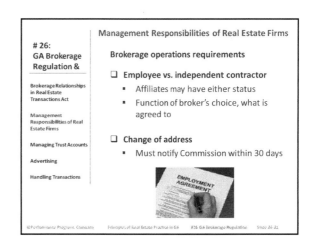

Slide 1

26:
GA Brokerage Regulation &

Brokerage Relationships in Real Estate Transactions Act

Management Responsibilities of Real Estate Firms

Managing Trust Accounts

Advertising

Handling Transactions

Management Responsibilities of Real Estate Firms

Broker & qualifying broker requirements

❑ **Name of firm**
- Can only conduct business under registered name

❑ **Brokerage activities supervision**
- Brokerage activities must be under the direct supervision of broker or qualifying broker
- Responsible for any violations of License Law (§ 43-40), and the Rules and Regulations
- Broker or qualifying broker responsible unless able to demonstrate that procedures were in place for affiliates' supervision

Slide 2

26:
GA Brokerage Regulation &

Brokerage Relationships in Real Estate Transactions Act

Management Responsibilities of Real Estate Firms

Managing Trust Accounts

Advertising

Handling Transactions

Management Responsibilities of Real Estate Firms

Broker & qualifying broker requirements

❑ **Training responsibility**
- Must provide training in rules and laws
- Include training in fair housing, contract law, financing and brokerage trends

❑ **Violation notifications**
- Must notify Commission of any license law violations

❑ **Advertising compliance**
- Broker must review ads, comply with laws

Slide 3

26:
GA Brokerage Regulation &

Brokerage Relationships in Real Estate Transactions Act

Management Responsibilities of Real Estate Firms

Managing Trust Accounts

Advertising

Handling Transactions

Management Responsibilities of Real Estate Firms

Broker & qualifying broker requirements

❑ **Contract review**
- Broker must review all contracts obtained by affiliates within 30 days of contract date

❑ **Records maintenance**
- Broker responsible for safekeeping all transaction and relationship records

Slide 4

26:
GA Brokerage Regulation &

Brokerage Relationships in Real Estate Transactions Act

Management Responsibilities of Real Estate Firms

Managing Trust Accounts

Advertising

Handling Transactions

Management Responsibilities of Real Estate Firms

Broker & qualifying broker requirements

❑ **Affiliate compensation agreements**
- Affiliates must have a written agreement specifying compensation terms
- Agreement must specify how paid for work-in-progress prior to the termination
- Commission does not regulate or enforce the content of the agreements
- Broker responsible for complying with requirement to have an agreement

Slide 5

26:
GA Brokerage Regulation &

Brokerage Relationships in Real Estate Transactions Act

Management Responsibilities of Real Estate Firms

Managing Trust Accounts

Advertising

Handling Transactions

Management Responsibilities of Real Estate Firms

Broker & qualifying broker requirements

❑ **Transaction compliance**
- An individual must be reasonably available to assist licensees in transactions
- Broker is still responsible despite delegations
- Qualifying broker must ensure that any licensing activity is done only by licensees
- Broker responsible for implementing compliance procedures for these areas

Slide 6

26:
GA Brokerage Regulation &

Brokerage Relationships in Real Estate Transactions Act

Management Responsibilities of Real Estate Firms

Managing Trust Accounts

Advertising

Handling Transactions

Management Responsibilities of Real Estate Firms

Broker & qualifying broker requirements

❑ **Licensee transferring brokers**
- Broker must forward affiliate's license to Commission or new broker
- Licensee cannot practice until s/he delivers approved application to transfer the license to the Commission
- May complete unfinished business with former broker if both brokers agree
- Cannot work on any listing unless authorized

Management Responsibilities of Real Estate Firms

26:
GA Brokerage
Regulation &

Brokerage Relationships
in Real Estate
Transactions Act

Management
Responsibilities of Real
Estate Firms

Managing Trust Accounts

Advertising

Handling Transactions

Support personnel, ministerial activities

❑ The firm and affiliated licensee are responsible for acts of support personnel and for their compliance with license law

❑ Support personnel may only perform ministerial activities

❑ Must have written agreements with all staff support personnel
- must specify duties
- must include prohibited activities
- Must include broker's approval of compensation

Management Responsibilities of Real Estate Firms

26:
GA Brokerage
Regulation &

Brokerage Relationships
in Real Estate
Transactions Act

Management
Responsibilities of Real
Estate Firms

Managing Trust Accounts

Advertising

Handling Transactions

Support personnel, ministerial activities

❑ **Permitted ministerial activities**
- schedule appointments to show listed property
- schedule inspections, closings, open houses
- answer phone calls and emails
- submit change data to MLS
- assemble documents for closings
- compute commission checks
- verify the status of a loan commitment
- have keys made for listings

Management Responsibilities of Real Estate Firms

26:
GA Brokerage
Regulation &

Brokerage Relationships
in Real Estate
Transactions Act

Management
Responsibilities of Real
Estate Firms

Managing Trust Accounts

Advertising

Handling Transactions

Support personnel, ministerial activities

❑ **Permitted ministerial activities   (cont.)**
- install or remove lock boxes
- place and remove signs
- type contract forms as directed
- write, place ads, promo materials
- record and deposit earnest money
- manage documents and records
- obtain or deliver keys
- monitor personnel files and commission reports
- order routine repair items
- perform physical maintenance tasks

Management Responsibilities of Real Estate Firms

26:
GA Brokerage
Regulation &

Brokerage Relationships
in Real Estate
Transactions Act

Management
Responsibilities of Real
Estate Firms

Managing Trust Accounts

Advertising

Handling Transactions

Support personnel, ministerial activities

❑ **Prohibited activities for support personnel**
- answer property, contract questions at an open house
- prospect or make cold calls
- create or place ads without approval
- show property
- answer property / client questions not in the listing material
- discuss or advise regarding terms of the sale
- explain contracts or other documents
- negotiate agent's compensation
- represent he or she is licensed

Managing Trust Accounts

26:
GA Brokerage
Regulation &

Brokerage Relationships
in Real Estate
Transactions Act

Management
Responsibilities of Real
Estate Firms

Managing Trust Accounts

Advertising

Handling Transactions

Basic provisions

❑ Trust funds must be deposited in separate, federally insured trust-designated account
❑ Must be registered with Commission which must be authorized to examine the account
❑ Cannot be subject to attachment or garnishment
❑ Affiliates must give earnest monies, deposits to broker ASAP
❑ Broker note entitled to any trust funds prior to closing

Managing Trust Accounts

26:
GA Brokerage
Regulation &

Brokerage Relationships
in Real Estate
Transactions Act

Management
Responsibilities of Real
Estate Firms

Managing Trust Accounts

Advertising

Handling Transactions

Basic provisions (cont.)

❑ Broker must promptly deposit escrow monies

❑ Worst case, funds must be deposited within 3 business days of contract acceptance

❑ Licensee selling his/her owned property must deposit all monies **into his/her broker's trust account** within 3 days of contract acceptance

Slide 1

26:
GA Brokerage
Regulation &

Brokerage Relationships
in Real Estate
Transactions Act

Management
Responsibilities of Real
Estate Firms

Managing Trust Accounts

Advertising

Handling Transactions

Managing Trust Accounts

Nonresident broker trust account

❑ Nonresident brokers may maintain trust funds in the broker's state of residence if Commission is authorized to audit

Affiliated Licensees Receiving Funds

❑ With broker approval, affiliate licensee may own, operate trust-designated account

❑ Must register account with Commission

❑ Must reconcile periodically for broker

Slide 2

26:
GA Brokerage
Regulation &

Brokerage Relationships
in Real Estate
Transactions Act

Management
Responsibilities of Real
Estate Firms

Managing Trust Accounts

Advertising

Handling Transactions

Managing Trust Accounts

Broker's funds in trust account

❑ May maintain own funds if clearly identified as such and used to keep account open
  ▪ Service charges
  ▪ Minimum balances
  ▪ Costs for checks, fees, etc.

❑ Broker must remove any excess funds from the account on a monthly basis

---

Slide 3

26:
GA Brokerage
Regulation &

Brokerage Relationships
in Real Estate
Transactions Act

Management
Responsibilities of Real
Estate Firms

Managing Trust Accounts

Advertising

Handling Transactions

Managing Trust Accounts

Accounting requirements for trust account

❑ Must account for details of each deposit
  ▪ parties
  ▪ Deposit amounts
  ▪ Property identification
  ▪ Disbursement details

❑ May be manual or electronic
❑ Must be accessible and available to Commission

Slide 4

26:
GA Brokerage
Regulation &

Brokerage Relationships
in Real Estate
Transactions Act

Management
Responsibilities of Real
Estate Firms

Managing Trust Accounts

Advertising

Handling Transactions

Managing Trust Accounts

Disbursements

❑ Must abide by terms of transaction contract

❑ May disburse at closing or upon receipt of authorization signed by all parties

❑ May also be disbursed via court order, interpleader

Slide 5

26:
GA Brokerage
Regulation &

Brokerage Relationships
in Real Estate
Transactions Act

Management
Responsibilities of Real
Estate Firms

Managing Trust Accounts

Advertising

Handling Transactions

Managing Trust Accounts

Trust accounts in property / association management

❑ Brokers managing properties or community associations may maintain separate rental or assessment trust accounts

❑ Account balance must always at least equal the total of all security deposits

❑ A managing licensee must deposit all trust funds in the account – may not post a bond in lieu of deposits

---

Slide 6

26:
GA Brokerage
Regulation &

Brokerage Relationships
in Real Estate
Transactions Act

Management
Responsibilities of Real
Estate Firms

Managing Trust Accounts

Advertising

Handling Transactions

Managing Trust Accounts

Trust account examination by Commission

❑ Brokers must authorize Commission audits of trust accounts during each renewal period

❑ Broker may provide a CPA's report in lieu of examination in Commission's format

❑ All records supporting the account must be made available to the Commission

Slide 1

 # 26:
GA Brokerage Regulation &

Brokerage Relationships in Real Estate Transactions Act

Management Responsibilities of Real Estate Firms

Managing Trust Accounts

Advertising

Handling Transactions

Managing Trust Accounts

Trust account reconciliation

❑ Brokers must prepare monthly, written reconciliations with the bank's balance

❑ Items to be included in reconciliation
- the date performed and date of reconciliation
- account identifications and balance
- outstanding deposits and checks
- list of the broker's outstanding trust liability showing the amount and source of funds received and not disbursed

❑ Must retain records for at least 3 years

Slide 2

 # 26:
GA Brokerage Regulation &

Brokerage Relationships in Real Estate Transactions Act

Management Responsibilities of Real Estate Firms

Managing Trust Accounts

Advertising

Handling Transactions

Managing Trust Accounts

Abandoned funds in a trust account

❑ If principal abandons trust funds given to the broker, the broker may not disburse unless authorized in the trust agreement.

❑ Must comply with the requirements of the Disposition of Unclaimed Property Act or other requirements

❑ **Disputed disbursements**
- Broker must immediately notify all parties in writing
- All refunds must be paid by check or credited at the closing of transaction

Slide 3

 # 26:
GA Brokerage Regulation &

Brokerage Relationships in Real Estate Transactions Act

Management Responsibilities of Real Estate Firms

Managing Trust Accounts

Advertising

Handling Transactions

Advertising

❑ Advertising defined as use of any media to inform the general public of real estate for sale, lease, rent or exchange

Misleading advertising

❑ Ads must not be misleading, inaccurate or misrepresent material facts

❑ If principal does not comply, licensee must take corrective steps

❑ **Key issues not to misrepresent**
- Property
- Values
- Policies or services

Slide 4

 # 26:
GA Brokerage Regulation &

Brokerage Relationships in Real Estate Transactions Act

Management Responsibilities of Real Estate Firms

Managing Trust Accounts

Advertising

Handling Transactions

Advertising

Advertising requirements

❑ Advertising must be supervised by broker

❑ Must include the name of the firm; no blind ads

❑ Must have owner's authorization to advertise his/her property

❑ Signs must be removed within 10 days after listing expiration

❑ Discriminatory advertising is prohibited

Slide 5

 # 26:
GA Brokerage Regulation &

Brokerage Relationships in Real Estate Transactions Act

Management Responsibilities of Real Estate Firms

Managing Trust Accounts

Advertising

Handling Transactions

Advertising

Internet advertising requirements

❑ Must disclose name and phone number of firm on every webpage

❑ If website not owned by the licensee or firm, advertising must provide a direct link on every viewable webpage

Updating the site

❑ Site info must be within 30 of being current

❑ If managed by a 3rd party, must give proper notice to update

Slide 6

 # 26:
GA Brokerage Regulation &

Brokerage Relationships in Real Estate Transactions Act

Management Responsibilities of Real Estate Firms

Managing Trust Accounts

Advertising

Handling Transactions

Advertising

Trade names and franchise names

❑ Firms using a trade name, or any franchisee, must clearly and unmistakably include the firm's name as registered with the Commission

❑ Firm's name must appear adjacent to any real estate so the public can identify the firm that has the real estate listed

❑ Firm must use registered name on contracts and office signs

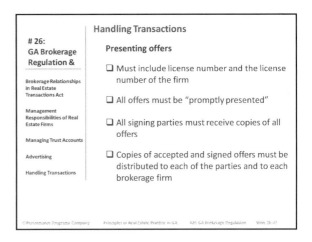

 # 26:

GA Brokerage Regulation &

Brokerage Relationships in Real Estate Transactions Act

Management Responsibilities of Real Estate Firms

Managing Trust Accounts

Advertising

Handling Transactions

Advertising

Firm names and telephone numbers

❑ Firms must include name of firm and telephone number in ads

❑ Phone number must reach a broker or manager

Licensees advertising as principals

❑ Ads must be transparent that owner is a licensee

❑ Ads must be under the direct supervision of the broker and in the name of the firm

---

 # 26:

GA Brokerage Regulation &

Brokerage Relationships in Real Estate Transactions Act

Management Responsibilities of Real Estate Firms

Managing Trust Accounts

Advertising

Handling Transactions

Handling Transactions

Presenting offers

❑ Must include license number and the license number of the firm

❑ All offers must be "promptly presented"

❑ All signing parties must receive copies of all offers

❑ Copies of accepted and signed offers must be distributed to each of the parties and to each brokerage firm

---

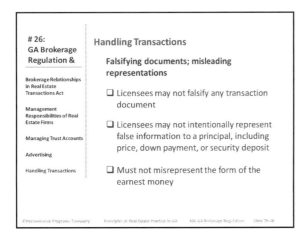

 # 26:

GA Brokerage Regulation &

Brokerage Relationships in Real Estate Transactions Act

Management Responsibilities of Real Estate Firms

Managing Trust Accounts

Advertising

Handling Transactions

Handling Transactions

Falsifying documents; misleading representations

❑ Licensees may not falsify any transaction document

❑ Licensees may not intentionally represent false information to a principal, including price, down payment, or security deposit

❑ Must not misrepresent the form of the earnest money

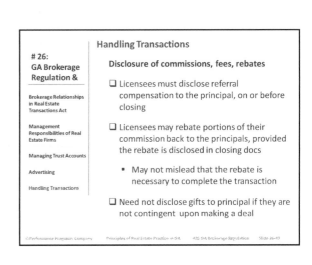

 # 26:

GA Brokerage Regulation &

Brokerage Relationships in Real Estate Transactions Act

Management Responsibilities of Real Estate Firms

Managing Trust Accounts

Advertising

Handling Transactions

Handling Transactions

Disclosure of commissions, fees, rebates

❑ Licensees must disclose referral compensation to the principal, on or before closing

❑ Licensees may rebate portions of their commission back to the principals, provided the rebate is disclosed in closing docs

▪ May not mislead that the rebate is necessary to complete the transaction

❑ Need not disclose gifts to principal if they are not contingent upon making a deal

---

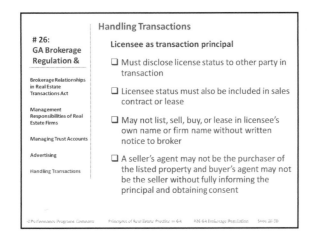

 # 26:

GA Brokerage Regulation &

Brokerage Relationships in Real Estate Transactions Act

Management Responsibilities of Real Estate Firms

Managing Trust Accounts

Advertising

Handling Transactions

Handling Transactions

Licensee as transaction principal

❑ Must disclose license status to other party in transaction

❑ Licensee status must also be included in sales contract or lease

❑ May not list, sell, buy, or lease in licensee's own name or firm name without written notice to broker

❑ A seller's agent may not be the purchaser of the listed property and buyer's agent may not be the seller without fully informing the principal and obtaining consent

---

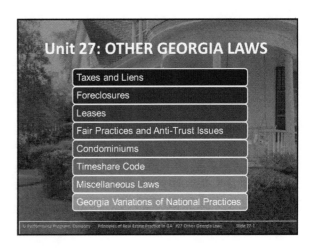

Unit 27: OTHER GEORGIA LAWS

- Taxes and Liens
- Foreclosures
- Leases
- Fair Practices and Anti-Trust Issues
- Condominiums
- Timeshare Code
- Miscellaneous Laws
- Georgia Variations of National Practices

Slide 27-2

 # 27: Other Georgia Laws

Taxes and Liens
Foreclosures
Leases
Fair Practices and Anti-Trust Issues
Condominiums
Timeshare Code
Miscellaneous Laws
Georgia Variations of National Practices

Taxes and Liens

Taxes

❑ **Georgia ad valorem tax**
- GA real property generally assessed at 40% market value
- Ag property assessed generally at 75% market value

❑ **Millage rates**
- Mills equal one-tenth of a cent
- X number of mills applied to the assessed value to determine a particular tax owed, eg, school tax

❑ **Occupational tax**
- May be imposed on gross receipts of brokers for transactions

Slide 27-3

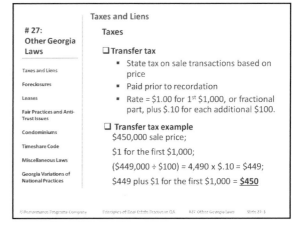

 # 27: Other Georgia Laws

Taxes and Liens
Foreclosures
Leases
Fair Practices and Anti-Trust Issues
Condominiums
Timeshare Code
Miscellaneous Laws
Georgia Variations of National Practices

Taxes and Liens

Taxes

❑ **Transfer tax**
- State tax on sale transactions based on price
- Paid prior to recordation
- Rate = $1.00 for 1st $1,000, or fractional part, plus $.10 for each additional $100.

❑ **Transfer tax example**
$450,000 sale price;
$1 for the first $1,000;
($449,000 ÷ $100) = 4,490 x $.10 = $449;
$449 plus $1 for the first $1,000 = **$450**

Slide 27-4

 # 27: Other Georgia Laws

Taxes and Liens
Foreclosures
Leases
Fair Practices and Anti-Trust Issues
Condominiums
Timeshare Code
Miscellaneous Laws
Georgia Variations of National Practices

Taxes and Liens

Taxes

❑ **Intangible tax**
- Tax on amount of mortgage note
- Must record in county within 90 days
- Paid by borrower
- Rate = $1.50 per $500, or fractional part

❑ **Intangible tax example**
$250,000 loan amount;
($250,000 ÷ $500) = 500 x $1.50 = **$750**

Slide 27-5

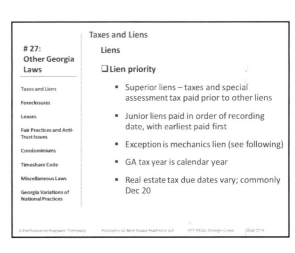

 # 27: Other Georgia Laws

Taxes and Liens
Foreclosures
Leases
Fair Practices and Anti-Trust Issues
Condominiums
Timeshare Code
Miscellaneous Laws
Georgia Variations of National Practices

Taxes and Liens

Liens

❑ **Lien priority**
- Superior liens – taxes and special assessment tax paid prior to other liens
- Junior liens paid in order of recording date, with earliest paid first
- Exception is mechanics lien (see following)
- GA tax year is calendar year
- Real estate tax due dates vary; commonly Dec 20

Slide 27-6

 # 27: Other Georgia Laws

Taxes and Liens
Foreclosures
Leases
Fair Practices and Anti-Trust Issues
Condominiums
Timeshare Code
Miscellaneous Laws
Georgia Variations of National Practices

Taxes and Liens

Liens

❑ **Mechanic's (or materialman's) liens**
- Lien on unpaid charges for construction and / or materials
- Priority determined by when work commenced or materials delivered
- Expires within 12 months if no court action is taken
- Must advise owner that lien is contestable
- Must give owner notice of filing within two days

Slide 27-7

 # 27: Other Georgia Laws

Taxes and Liens
Foreclosures
Leases
Fair Practices and Anti-Trust Issues
Condominiums
Timeshare Code
Miscellaneous Laws
Georgia Variations of National Practices

Foreclosures

Owner's rights

❑ **GA allows equitable right of redemption**
- GA owner has a right to redeem the mortgaged property prior to the foreclosure sale
- No statutory right of redemption after sale in GA

❑ **Mortgage instruments**
- GA property finance instrument called **security deed**
- Less risky; allows for non-judicial foreclosure via 'power of sale' clause
- Lender holds legal title

Slide 1

 # 27:
Other Georgia Laws

Taxes and Liens

Foreclosures

Leases

Fair Practices and Anti-Trust Issues

Condominiums

Timeshare Code

Miscellaneous Laws

Georgia Variations of National Practices

Leases

Basic requirements

❑ GA recognizes
- estate for years
- estate from period to period
- tenancy at will

❑ Leases exceeding one year must be in writing to be enforceable

❑ Lease must conform to contract validity requirements

Slide 2

 # 27:
Other Georgia Laws

Taxes and Liens

Foreclosures

Leases

Fair Practices and Anti-Trust Issues

Condominiums

Timeshare Code

Miscellaneous Laws

Georgia Variations of National Practices

Leases

Rights and duties

❑ Tenants
- Right to use
- Must not damage property
- Must maintain property and pay rent
- May remove trade fixtures

❑ Landlord
- Must keep premises in good repair
- Must safeguard and return deposit
- May not suspend utilities during any eviction proceeding

Slide 3

 # 27:
Other Georgia Laws

Taxes and Liens

Foreclosures

Leases

Fair Practices and Anti-Trust Issues

Condominiums

Timeshare Code

Miscellaneous Laws

Georgia Variations of National Practices

Leases

Security deposits

❑ Must be deposited in trust account

❑ Bank and account number must be disclosed to tenant

❑ Landlord must give tenant list of existing damages, if any

❑ Tenant may inspect prior to occupancy

❑ Landlord must inspect premises 3 days prior to expiration, list any damages

❑ Tenant can inspect, dispute damages list

Slide 4

 # 27:
Other Georgia Laws

Taxes and Liens

Foreclosures

Leases

Fair Practices and Anti-Trust Issues

Condominiums

Timeshare Code

Miscellaneous Laws

Georgia Variations of National Practices

Leases

Security deposits (cont.)

❑ Landlord must return deposit within one month

❑ Landlord cannot deduct for ordinary wear and tear

❑ Landlord may retain deposit for tenant's
- Failure to pay rent / utilities
- Abandonment
- Needed repairs for damages
- Unpaid pet fees

Slide 5

 # 27:
Other Georgia Laws

Taxes and Liens

Foreclosures

Leases

Fair Practices and Anti-Trust Issues

Condominiums

Timeshare Code

Miscellaneous Laws

Georgia Variations of National Practices

Leases

Termination

❑ Tenancy at will requires 60 days notice from landlord, 30 days from tenant

Eviction

❑ Landlord must give notice, reasonable time to respond
❑ If tenant does not vacate, landlord files dispossessory affidavit in court
❑ Tenant must respond in 7 days
❑ If no response, landlord gets a writ of possession
❑ Sheriff then removes tenant

Slide 6

 # 27:
Other Georgia Laws

Taxes and Liens

Foreclosures

Leases

Fair Practices and Anti-Trust Issues

Condominiums

Timeshare Code

Miscellaneous Laws

Georgia Variations of National Practices

Fair Practices and Anti-Trust Issues

GA Fair Business Practices Act

❑ Prohibits unfair / deceptive acts in sale, lease of goods, services or property for personal, family or household purposes

❑ Prohibits misrepresentation regarding another business or its services / products

❑ Prohibits advertising where intent is to sell on different terms

 # 27:
Other Georgia Laws

Taxes and Liens

Foreclosures

Leases

Fair Practices and Anti-Trust Issues

Condominiums

Timeshare Code

Miscellaneous Laws

Georgia Variations of National Practices

Fair Practices and Anti-Trust Issues

GA Uniform Deceptive Trade Practices Act

❑ Prohibits deceptive acts or omissions

❑ Permits an injured party to take legal action

❑ Prohibits disparaging the goods, services, or business of another by false or misleading representation

---

 # 27:
Other Georgia Laws

Taxes and Liens

Foreclosures

Leases

Fair Practices and Anti-Trust Issues

Condominiums

Timeshare Code

Miscellaneous Laws

Georgia Variations of National Practices

Condominiums

Condominium Acts

❑ Georgia Apartment Ownership Act regulates pre-1975 condos

❑ Replaced by GA Condominium Act

❑ Condos created by developer's recorded Declaration of Condominium

❑ GA 'leasehold condominium'
  ▪ Each unit owner owns an estate for years leasehold estate in the unit

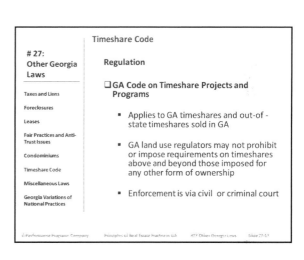

 # 27:
Other Georgia Laws

Taxes and Liens

Foreclosures

Leases

Fair Practices and Anti-Trust Issues

Condominiums

Timeshare Code

Miscellaneous Laws

Georgia Variations of National Practices

Condominiums

Rights and duties

❑ Rescission of sales contract
  ▪ Buyer has 7 days after receiving disclosure package to rescind an offer

❑ Duties of associations
  ▪ Must keep property insured
  ▪ Must manage finances and records
  ▪ Must ensure property is maintained

❑ Disclosure package
  ▪ Must contain plats, floor plans, common elements, critical legal information

---

 # 27:
Other Georgia Laws

Taxes and Liens

Foreclosures

Leases

Fair Practices and Anti-Trust Issues

Condominiums

Timeshare Code

Miscellaneous Laws

Georgia Variations of National Practices

Timeshare Code

Regulation

❑ GA Code on Timeshare Projects and Programs
  ▪ Applies to GA timeshares and out-of-state timeshares sold in GA
  ▪ GA land use regulators may not prohibit or impose requirements on timeshares above and beyond those imposed for any other form of ownership
  ▪ Enforcement is via civil or criminal court

 # 27:
Other Georgia Laws

Taxes and Liens

Foreclosures

Leases

Fair Practices and Anti-Trust Issues

Condominiums

Timeshare Code

Miscellaneous Laws

Georgia Variations of National Practices

Timeshare Code

Definitions

❑ Developer
  ▪ Party creating timeshare program

❑ Timeshare agent
  ▪ Party authorized to sell or manage timeshares

❑ Escrow agent
  ▪ Party entrusted with deposits and duty to administer terms of contract

---

 # 27:
Other Georgia Laws

Taxes and Liens

Foreclosures

Leases

Fair Practices and Anti-Trust Issues

Condominiums

Timeshare Code

Miscellaneous Laws

Georgia Variations of National Practices

Timeshare Code

Definitions (cont.)

❑ Timeshare exchange program
  ▪ Where owners exchange occupancy rights with other timeshare owners

❑ Multi-location developer
  ▪ Developer selling his/her timeshare intervals in a multi-location plan

❑ Timeshare estates
  ▪ Includes owned or leased interest divided into certain time periods

Slide 1

 # 27:
Other Georgia Laws

Taxes and Liens

Foreclosures

Leases

Fair Practices and Anti-Trust Issues

Condominiums

Timeshare Code

Miscellaneous Laws

Georgia Variations of National Practices

Timeshare Code

Types of GA timeshares

❑ **Timeshare estates**
- Includes owned or leased interest divided into certain time periods

❑ **Timeshare use**
- Where party contracts for right to occupy the property exclusively
- Eg, vacation license; prepaid hotel reservation; club memberships, etc.

Slide 2

 # 27:
Other Georgia Laws

Taxes and Liens

Foreclosures

Leases

Fair Practices and Anti-Trust Issues

Condominiums

Timeshare Code

Miscellaneous Laws

Georgia Variations of National Practices

Timeshare Code

Features and requirements

❑ **Recording**
- Transfer docs, liens may be recorded

❑ **Valuation**
- Timeshare estates valued as if owned by a sole owner
- Constitutes a separate estate in real property

❑ **Public offering statement**
- Must contain consumer protection disclosures required by Code
- Given out prior to sales agreement

Slide 3

 # 27:
Other Georgia Laws

Taxes and Liens

Foreclosures

Leases

Fair Practices and Anti-Trust Issues

Condominiums

Timeshare Code

Miscellaneous Laws

Georgia Variations of National Practices

Timeshare Code

Features and requirements (cont.)

❑ **Rescission**
- Buyer or developer may cancel sales agreement for seven days following contracting, Sundays and holidays excepted, without penalty
- If canceled, developer must return all buyer payments within 30 days

❑ **Licensed activity**
- Selling GA timeshares requires a GA real estate license

Slide 4

 # 27:
Other Georgia Laws

Taxes and Liens

Foreclosures

Leases

Fair Practices and Anti-Trust Issues

Condominiums

Timeshare Code

Miscellaneous Laws

Georgia Variations of National Practices

Miscellaneous Laws

❑ **Uniform Electronic Transactions Act**
- Electronic signatures are enforceable
- Electronic contracts are valid and enforceable
- Electronic records are a valid form of written records

❑ **Georgia Property Owners Association Act**
- Creates automatic statutory liens for unpaid POA fees
- If unpaid POA fees survive a conveyance, buyer is liable

Slide 5

 # 27:
Other Georgia Laws

Taxes and Liens

Foreclosures

Leases

Fair Practices and Anti-Trust Issues

Condominiums

Timeshare Code

Miscellaneous Laws

Georgia Variations of National Practices

Miscellaneous Laws

❑ **GA Land Sales Act**
- Applies to land subdivided into more than 150 lots of less than 5 acres each
- Gives 7-day rescission right to buyer if certain documents are not transmitted at least 48 hours prior to contracting

❑ **GA Land Conservation Program**
- Funds GA Conservation Tax Credit Program
- Offers tax benefits, special financing for conservation donations
- Funds conservation projects

Slide 6

 # 27:
Other Georgia Laws

Taxes and Liens

Foreclosures

Leases

Fair Practices and Anti-Trust Issues

Condominiums

Timeshare Code

Miscellaneous Laws

Georgia Variations of National Practices

Miscellaneous Laws

❑ **GA Joint Tenancy Act of 1976**
- Recognizes joint tenancy and tenancy in common
- Joint tenancy has right of survivorship
- Trusts are also a recognized form of ownership
- GA does not recognize tenancy by the entirety
- GA is not a community property state; all property acquired during marriage is divided equitably

Slide 1

27:
Other Georgia Laws

Taxes and Liens

Foreclosures

Leases

Fair Practices and Anti-Trust Issues

Condominiums

Timeshare Code

Miscellaneous Laws

Georgia Variations of National Practices

Miscellaneous Laws

❏ **GA Residential Mortgage Fraud Act**
- Applies to GA-only residential property of 1-4 units
- Illegal to make misrepresentations or omissions
- Focus is in areas of appraisals, loan apps, closing statements, qualifying docs, and other loan docs

❏ **GA Lead Paint Protection Act of 1994**
- Requires disclosure of known lead-based paint hazards to buyers, renters

Slide 2

27:
Other Georgia Laws

Taxes and Liens

Foreclosures

Leases

Fair Practices and Anti-Trust Issues

Condominiums

Timeshare Code

Miscellaneous Laws

Georgia Variations of National Practices

Georgia Variations of National Practices

❏ **Property condition disclosure**
- Georgia does not require sellers to give buyers written disclosure of property condition
- Seller and agent must disclose known adverse material facts and defects
- Agent's disclosures include physical conditions, environmental contamination, and known adverse neighborhood conditions in a one-mile radius not reasonably discoverable by a buyer

Slide 3

27:
Other Georgia Laws

Taxes and Liens

Foreclosures

Leases

Fair Practices and Anti-Trust Issues

Condominiums

Timeshare Code

Miscellaneous Laws

Georgia Variations of National Practices

Georgia Variations of National Practices

❏ **Legal descriptions**
- Must be included in sales contracts and leases; address is not sufficient for enforceability
- GA descriptions include county, district, land lot, then metes and bounds or lot and block

❏ **Compensation**
- Must be licensed to be able to sue for providing real estate services for a party or to take action against another broker for collection of compensation

Slide 4

27:
Other Georgia Laws

Taxes and Liens

Foreclosures

Leases

Fair Practices and Anti-Trust Issues

Condominiums

Timeshare Code

Miscellaneous Laws

Georgia Variations of National Practices

Georgia Variations of National Practices

❏ **Net Listings**
- Net listings are illegal
- Brokers must tell sellers the selling price and broker's fee

❏ **Practice of law**
- Only licensed attorneys may practice law
- Illegal practice includes
  ➢ Closing a transaction
  ➢ Preparing legal documents
  ➢ Charging a fee for doc completion
  ➢ Providing a legal opinion

Slide 5

27:
Other Georgia Laws

Taxes and Liens

Foreclosures

Leases

Fair Practices and Anti-Trust Issues

Condominiums

Timeshare Code

Miscellaneous Laws

Georgia Variations of National Practices

Georgia Variations of National Practices

❏ **Statute of limitations**
- Written contracts not under seal: 6 years
- Written, under seal: 20 years

❏ **General warranty deeds**
- Covenant of title
- Covenant of quiet enjoyment
- Covenant against encumbrances

❏ GA also uses **special warranty** and **quit claim deeds**

Slide 6

27:
Other Georgia Laws

Taxes and Liens

Foreclosures

Leases

Fair Practices and Anti-Trust Issues

Condominiums

Timeshare Code

Miscellaneous Laws

Georgia Variations of National Practices

Georgia Variations of National Practices

❏ **Wills in GA**
- Cannot be oral or in testator's handwriting
- Must have two witnesses
- Can be superseded by GA law requiring surviving spouse to receive one year's support

❏ **Adverse possession**
- Must be accompanied by claim of right
- Prescriptive period; good title = 20 years
- Prescriptive period with color of title = 7 years

 # 27:
Other Georgia Laws

Taxes and Liens

Foreclosures

Leases

Fair Practices and Anti-Trust Issues

Condominiums

Timeshare Code

Miscellaneous Laws

Georgia Variations of National Practices

Georgia Variations of National Practices

❑ Estate on condition
- Ownership limited by some condition requiring performance before or after owner gets full ownership
- Similar to fee simple defeasible

❑ Title search
- Normal title search spans 50 years

Georgia Variations of National Practices

 # 27:
Other Georgia Laws

Taxes and Liens

Foreclosures

Leases

Fair Practices and Anti-Trust Issues

Condominiums

Timeshare Code

Miscellaneous Laws

Georgia Variations of National Practices

Appraisal licensure

❑ **State Trainee Appraiser**
- Entry level; may perform only under direct control of superior

❑ **State Registered Appraiser**
- May perform on any property **not** subject to federally-related financing

❑ **State Licensed Appraiser**
- May perform any appraisal with value limitations

Georgia Variations of National Practices

 # 27:
Other Georgia Laws

Taxes and Liens

Foreclosures

Leases

Fair Practices and Anti-Trust Issues

Condominiums

Timeshare Code

Miscellaneous Laws

Georgia Variations of National Practices

Appraisal licensure

❑ **State Certified Residential Appraiser**
- May perform on any property **not** subject to federally-related financing and properties with such financing up to a value of $250,000

❑ **State Certified General Appraiser**
- May perform any appraisal for any purpose without limitation

---

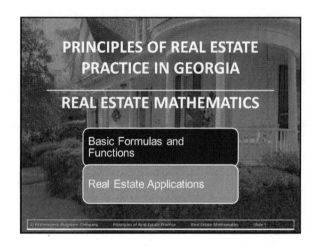

PRINCIPLES OF REAL ESTATE PRACTICE IN GEORGIA

REAL ESTATE MATHEMATICS

Basic Formulas and Functions

Real Estate Applications

Real Estate Mathematics

Basic Formulas and Functions

Real Estate Applications
Legal descriptions
Listing agreements
Brokerage business
Contracts for sale
Appraisal
Finance
Investment
Taxation
Closings

Basic Formulas and Functions

Adding and multiplying fractions

❑ Adding fractions
- Formulas
  - same denominator

    $(a/c) + (b/c) = (a + b)/c$

  - different denominator

    $(a/c) + (b/d) = (ad + bc)/cd$

Real Estate Mathematics

Basic Formulas and Functions

Real Estate Applications
Legal descriptions
Listing agreements
Brokerage business
Contracts for sale
Appraisal
Finance
Investment
Taxation
Closings

Basic Formulas and Functions

Adding and multiplying fractions

❑ Adding fractions (cont.)
- Examples
  - same denominator:

    $(2/5) + (6/5) = (2 + 6)/5 = 8/5$

  - different denominator:

    $(3/4) + (4/7) = (3x7 + 4x4)/4x7$

    $= (21 + 16)/ 28$

    $= 37/ 28$

Slide 4

Real Estate Mathematics

Basic Formulas and Functions

Legal descriptions
Listing agreements
Brokerage business
Contracts for sale
Appraisal
Finance
Investment
Taxation
Closings

Basic Formulas and Functions

Adding and multiplying fractions

❑ Multiplying fractions

- **Formula**
  - $(a/c) \times (b/d) = (a \times b) / (c \times d)$

- **Example**
  - $(4/9) \times (2/3) = (4 \times 2) / (9 \times 3) = 8/27$

Slide 5

Real Estate Mathematics

Basic Formulas and Functions

Real Estate Applications
Legal descriptions
Listing agreements
Brokerage business
Contracts for sale
Appraisal
Finance
Investment
Taxation
Closings

Basic Formulas and Functions

Converting decimals and percentages

❑ Converting a decimal to a percent

- **Formula**
  - (decimal number) x 100 = (% number)

- **Examples**
  - $.473 \times 100 = 47.3\%$
  - $3.456 \times 100 = 345.6\%$
  - $.0042 \times 100 = .42\%$

Slide 6

Real Estate Mathematics

Basic Formulas and Functions

Real Estate Applications
Legal descriptions
Listing agreements
Brokerage business
Contracts for sale
Appraisal
Finance
Investment
Taxation
Closings

Basic Formulas and Functions

Converting decimals and percentages

❑ Converting a percent to a decimal

- **Formula**
  - (% number) / 100 = (decimal number)

- **Examples**
  - $47.3\% / 100 = .473$
  - $345.6\% / 100 = 3.456$

Slide 7

Real Estate Mathematics

Basic Formulas and Functions

Real Estate Applications
Legal descriptions
Listing agreements
Brokerage business
Contracts for sale
Appraisal
Finance
Investment
Taxation
Closings

Basic Formulas and Functions

Converting fractions and percentages

❑ Converting a fraction to a percent

- **Formula**
  1) a/b = a divided by b = decimal number
  2) decimal number x 100 = % number

- **Example**
  - $4/5 = 4$ divided by $5 = 0.8$
  - $.8 \times 100 = 80\%$

Slide 8

Real Estate Mathematics

Basic Formulas and Functions

Real Estate Applications
Legal descriptions
Listing agreements
Brokerage business
Contracts for sale
Appraisal
Finance
Investment
Taxation
Closings

Basic Formulas and Functions

Converting fractions and percentages

❑ Converting a % to a fraction and reducing it

- **Formula**
  1) X% = X / 100
  2) (x ÷ a) / (100 ÷ a)

     where "a" is the largest number that divides <u>evenly</u> into the numerator and denominator

- **Example**
  - $45\% = 45/100$
  - $(45 ÷ 5) / (100 ÷ 5) = 9/20$

Slide 9

Real Estate Mathematics

Basic Formulas and Functions

Real Estate Applications
Legal descriptions
Listing agreements
Brokerage business
Contracts for sale
Appraisal
Finance
Investment
Taxation
Closings

Basic Formulas and Functions

Multiplying with percentages

- **Formula**
  1) Convert % to decimal by dividing by 100
  2) Multiply whole amount x decimal

- **Example:** what is 33% of 400?
  - $33\% = 33/100 = .33$
  - $400 \times .33 = 132$

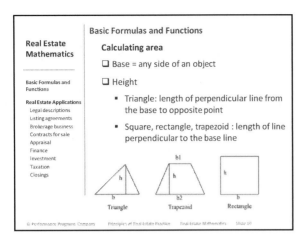

Real Estate Mathematics

Basic Formulas and Functions

Real Estate Applications
Legal descriptions
Listing agreements
Brokerage business
Contracts for sale
Appraisal
Finance
Investment
Taxation
Closings

Basic Formulas and Functions

Calculating area

❑ Base = any side of an object

❑ Height

- Triangle: length of perpendicular line from the base to opposite point

- Square, rectangle, trapezoid : length of line perpendicular to the base line

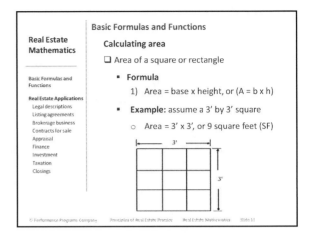

Real Estate Mathematics

Basic Formulas and Functions

Real Estate Applications
Legal descriptions
Listing agreements
Brokerage business
Contracts for sale
Appraisal
Finance
Investment
Taxation
Closings

Basic Formulas and Functions

Calculating area

❑ Area of a square or rectangle

- **Formula**
  1) Area = base x height, or (A = b x h)

- **Example:** assume a 3' by 3' square

  o Area = 3' x 3', or 9 square feet (SF)

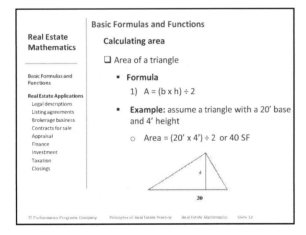

Real Estate Mathematics

Basic Formulas and Functions

Real Estate Applications
Legal descriptions
Listing agreements
Brokerage business
Contracts for sale
Appraisal
Finance
Investment
Taxation
Closings

Basic Formulas and Functions

Calculating area

❑ Area of a triangle

- **Formula**
  1) A = (b x h) ÷ 2

- **Example:** assume a triangle with a 20' base and 4' height

  o Area = (20' x 4') ÷ 2 or 40 SF

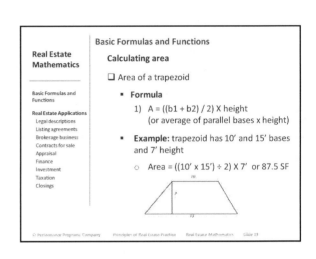

Real Estate Mathematics

Basic Formulas and Functions

Real Estate Applications
Legal descriptions
Listing agreements
Brokerage business
Contracts for sale
Appraisal
Finance
Investment
Taxation
Closings

Basic Formulas and Functions

Calculating area

❑ Area of a trapezoid

- **Formula**
  1) A = ((b1 + b2) / 2) X height
     (or average of parallel bases x height)

- **Example:** trapezoid has 10' and 15' bases and 7' height

  o Area = ((10' x 15') ÷ 2) X 7' or 87.5 SF

Real Estate Mathematics

Basic Formulas and Functions

Real Estate Applications
Legal descriptions
Listing agreements
Brokerage business
Contracts for sale
Appraisal
Finance
Investment
Taxation
Closings

Real Estate Applications

Legal descriptions

❑ Linear measures
  1 inch = 1/12 foot = 1/36 yard
  1 foot = 12 inches = 1/3 yard
  1 yard = 36 inches = 3 feet
  1 mile = 5280 feet = 1,760 yards

❑ Area measures
  1 square inch = 1/144th square foot
  1 square foot = 1/9th square yard
  1 square yard = 9 square feet

  1 acre = 43,560 SF
  1 square mile = 640 acres
  1 section = 1 mile x 1 mile = 640 acres
  1 township = 6 mi x 6 mi = 36 sq. miles

Real Estate Mathematics

Basic Formulas and Functions

Real Estate Applications
Legal descriptions
Listing agreements
Brokerage business
Contracts for sale
Appraisal
Finance
Investment
Taxation
Closings

Real Estate Applications

Legal descriptions

❑ Fractions of sections

Fraction	# acres
1 section	= 640 acres
1/2 section	= 320 acres
1/4 section	= 160 acres
1/8 section	= 80 acres
1/16 section	= 40 acres
1/32 section	= 20 acres
1/64 section	= 10 acres

Real Estate Mathematics

Basic Formulas and Functions

Real Estate Applications
Legal descriptions
Listing agreements
Brokerage business
Contracts for sale
Appraisal
Finance
Investment
Taxation
Closings

Real Estate Applications

Legal descriptions

❑ Calculating area from the legal description

- **Formula**
  1) Multiply all <u>denominators</u> of the fractions together in the description
  2) Divide the resulting product into <u>640</u> (acres)

- Example: calculate area of the N ½ of SW ¼ of NE ¼ of section 8
  - 2 x 4 x 4 = 32
  - 640 ÷ 32 = 20 acres

Real Estate Mathematics

Basic Formulas and Functions

Real Estate Applications
Legal descriptions
Listing agreements
Brokerage business
Contracts for sale
Appraisal
Finance
Investment
Taxation
Closings

Real Estate Applications

Listing agreements

❑ **Co-brokerage commission**

- **Formula**
  1) sale price x commission rate = total commission
  2) total commission x split rate = co-brokerage commission

- **Example**: $600,000 house; 6% commission; 50-50 co-brokerage split
  - $600,000 x .06 = $36,000 tot. comm.
  - $30,000 x .50 = $18,000 split comm.

Real Estate Mathematics

Basic Formulas and Functions

Real Estate Applications
Legal descriptions
Listing agreements
Brokerage business
Contracts for sale
Appraisal
Finance
Investment
Taxation
Closings

Real Estate Applications

Listing agreements

❑ **Agent's commission**

- **Formula**
  - Broker commission x split rate = agent's commission

- **Example**: $18,000 commission; 60-40 split-agent-to-broker
  - $18,000 x .6 = $10,800 total agent commission ($7,200 to broker)

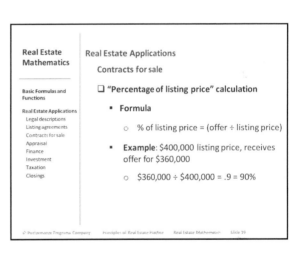

Real Estate Mathematics

Basic Formulas and Functions

Real Estate Applications
Legal descriptions
Listing agreements
Contracts for sale
Appraisal
Finance
Investment
Taxation
Closings

Real Estate Applications

Contracts for sale

❑ **"Percentage of listing price" calculation**

- **Formula**
  - % of listing price = (offer ÷ listing price)

- **Example**: $400,000 listing price, receives offer for $360,000
  - $360,000 ÷ $400,000 = .9 = 90%

Real Estate Mathematics

Basic Formulas and Functions

Real Estate Applications
Legal descriptions
Listing agreements
Contracts for sale
Appraisal
Finance
Investment
Taxation
Closings

Real Estate Applications

Contracts for sale

❑ **Earnest money deposit calculation**

- **Formula**
  - Deposit = price x required percentage

- **Example**: seller wants 2% deposit on $320,000 property
  - $320,000 x 2% = $6,400 deposit required

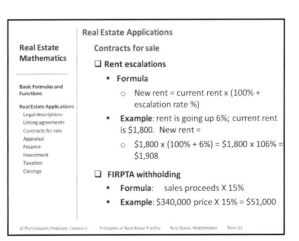

Real Estate Mathematics

Basic Formulas and Functions

Real Estate Applications
Legal descriptions
Listing agreements
Contracts for sale
Appraisal
Finance
Investment
Taxation
Closings

Real Estate Applications

Contracts for sale

❑ **Rent escalations**
- **Formula**
  - New rent = current rent x (100% + escalation rate %)
- **Example**: rent is going up 6%; current rent is $1,800. New rent =
  - $1,800 x (100% + 6%) = $1,800 x 106% = $1,908

❑ **FIRPTA withholding**
- **Formula**:   sales proceeds X 15%
- **Example**: $340,000 price X 15% = $51,000

Slide 1

Real Estate Mathematics

Basic Formulas and Functions

Real Estate Applications
Legal descriptions
Listing agreements
Contracts for sale
Appraisal
Finance
Investment
Taxation
Closings

Real Estate Applications

Appraisal

❑ **Adjusting comparables**

- **Rules**

1) NEVER adjust the subject!

2) If comparable is <u>better</u> than the subject, <u>subtract</u> value from the comparable

3) If the comparable is <u>worse</u> than the subject, <u>add</u> value to the comparable

- **Example**: comp has pool, subject does not; value adjust = $25,000

   o <u>Subtract $25,000 from comp</u> for pool

Slide 2

Real Estate Mathematics

Basic Formulas and Functions

Real Estate Applications
Legal descriptions
Listing agreements
Contracts for sale
Appraisal
Finance
Investment
Taxation
Closings

Real Estate Applications

Appraisal

❑ **Income capitalization: Gross Rent Multiplier (GRM)**

- **Formulas**

   o Monthly rent x GRM = value

   o Price ÷ monthly rent = GRM

- **Example**: rent/mo. = $20,000; GRM = 90; Value = $1,800,000

   o $20,000 x 90 = $1,800,000 value

   o $1,800,000 ÷ $20,000 = 90 GRM

Slide 3

Real Estate Mathematics

Basic Formulas and Functions

Real Estate Applications
Legal descriptions
Listing agreements
Contracts for sale
Appraisal
Finance
Investment
Taxation
Closings

Real Estate Applications

Appraisal

❑ **Income capitalization: capitalizing net income**

- **Formulas**

   o NOI ÷ cap rate = value

   o NOI ÷ value = cap rate

   o Value x cap rate = NOI

- **Examples**: NOI = $50,000; cap rate =10%; Value = $500,000

   o $50,000 NOI ÷ 10% = $500,000 value

   o $50,000 NOI ÷ $500,000 = 10% cap rate

   o $500,000 Value x 10% = $50,000 NOI

Slide 4

Real Estate Mathematics

Basic Formulas and Functions

Real Estate Applications
Legal descriptions
Listing agreements
Contracts for sale
Appraisal
Finance
Investment
Taxation
Closings

Real Estate Applications

Finance

❑ **Calculating loan amounts, rates, payments: interest only loans**

- **Formulas**

Where **I = interest amount**; **P = principal**; **R = interest rate**:

   o I = P x R where I = annual interest

   o R = I ÷ P where I = annual interest

   o P = I ÷ R where I = annual interest

Slide 5

Real Estate Mathematics

Basic Formulas and Functions

Real Estate Applications
Legal descriptions
Listing agreements
Contracts for sale
Appraisal
Finance
Investment
Taxation
Closings

Real Estate Applications

Finance

❑ **Calculating loan amounts, rates, payments: interest only loans (cont.)**

- **Examples**: Assume $300,000 interest-only loan; 10% interest; $2,500/mo. payments

   o **Payment/mo** = ($300,000 loan amount x 10% interest rate) ÷ 12 = $2,500/mo

   o **Interest rate** = ($2,500 x 12) = $30,000 annual interest; $30,000 ÷ $300,000 = 10%

   o **Loan amount** = $30,000 annual interest ÷ 10% rate = $300,000

Slide 6

Real Estate Mathematics

Basic Formulas and Functions

Real Estate Applications
Legal descriptions
Listing agreements
Contracts for sale
Appraisal
Finance
Investment
Taxation
Closings

Real Estate Applications

Finance

❑ **Loan-to-value ratio (LTV) calculation**

- **Formula**

   o **Loan amount** = market value x LTV

   o **LTV** = loan amount ÷ market value

   o **Market value** = loan amount ÷ LTV

- **Examples**: Bank requires 75% LTV, property value is $200,000

   o **Loan amount** = ($200,000 x 80%) = $160 K

   o **LTV** = ($160 K ÷ $200 K) = 80%

   o **Market value** = ($160 K ÷ 80%) = $200 K

Real Estate Mathematics

Basic Formulas and Functions

Real Estate Applications
Legal descriptions
Listing agreements
Contracts for sale
Appraisal
Finance
Investment
Taxation
Closings

Real Estate Applications

Finance

❑ Underwriting: income ratio calculation

- Formula: conventional loan
  - PITI/mo = 25-28% x monthly income
- Formula: FHA loan
  - PITI/mo = 31% x monthly gross income
- **Examples**: Borrower income = $4,000; borrower can afford PITI/mo. payments of:
  - **Conventional**: ($4,000 x 28%) = $1,200
  - **FHA**: ($4,000 x 31%) = $1,240

Performance Programs Company   Principles of Real Estate Practice   Real Estate Mathematics   Slide 28

Real Estate Mathematics

Basic Formulas and Functions

Real Estate Applications
Legal descriptions
Listing agreements
Contracts for sale
Appraisal
Finance
Investment
Taxation
Closings

Real Estate Applications

Finance

❑ Underwriting: debt ratio calculation

- **Formula: conventional loan**
  - (36% x income/mo) – monthly debt
- **Formula: FHA loan**
  - (43% x income/mo) – monthly debt
- **Examples**: Borrower income = $4,000; debt of $600/mo. Borrower can afford:
  - **Conventional**: (36% x 4,000) – 600 = $840/mo
  - **FHA**: (43% x 4,000) – 600 = $1,120

Performance Programs Company   Principles of Real Estate Practice   Real Estate Mathematics   Slide 29

Real Estate Mathematics

Basic Formulas and Functions

Real Estate Applications
Legal descriptions
Listing agreements
Contracts for sale
Appraisal
Finance
Investment
Taxation
Closings

Real Estate Applications

Finance

❑ Points

- **Formula:**
  - 1 point = 1%, or (.01) of loan amount
- **Example:** Lender charges 3 points on $350,000 loan. Points charges are:
  - 3 points = 3% or .03 loan amount
  - .03 x $350,000 = $10,500

Performance Programs Company   Principles of Real Estate Practice   Real Estate Mathematics   Slide 30

Real Estate Mathematics

Basic Formulas and Functions

Real Estate Applications
Legal descriptions
Listing agreements
Contracts for sale
Appraisal
Finance
Investment
Taxation
Closings

Real Estate Applications

Investment

❑ Appreciation

- **Formulas:**
  - Total appreciation = (current value - original price)
  - Appreciation rate = (total appreciation ÷ original price)
  - Appreciation rate/year = (one-year increase ÷ prior year value)

Performance Programs Company   Principles of Real Estate Practice   Real Estate Mathematics   Slide 31

Real Estate Mathematics

Basic Formulas and Functions

Real Estate Applications
Legal descriptions
Listing agreements
Contracts for sale
Appraisal
Finance
Investment
Taxation
Closings

Real Estate Applications

Investment

❑ Appreciation

- **Examples**: Home bought for $500,000 appreciates $50,000/yr for 3 years. (note: figures are not compounded!)
  - Total appreciation = ($650,000 – 500,000) = $150,000
  - Appreciation rate = ($150,000 ÷ $500,000) = 30%
  - Annual appreciation rate = ($50,000 ÷ $500,000) = .01 or 10%

Performance Programs Company   Principles of Real Estate Practice   Real Estate Mathematics   Slide 32

Real Estate Mathematics

Basic Formulas and Functions

Real Estate Applications
Legal descriptions
Listing agreements
Contracts for sale
Appraisal
Finance
Investment
Taxation
Closings

Real Estate Applications

Investment

❑ Equity

- **Formula**
  - Equity = (current value – current loan balance)
- **Example**: home bought for $600,000 with a loan of $450,000. Appreciation = $60,000; original loan paid down by $30,000. Current equity is:
  - ($600K + 60K) - ($450,000 - 30,000) = ($660K – 420K) = $240,000 equity

Performance Programs Company   Principles of Real Estate Practice   Real Estate Mathematics   Slide 33

121

Real Estate Mathematics

Basic Formulas and Functions

Real Estate Applications
Legal descriptions
Listing agreements
Contracts for sale
Appraisal
Finance
Investment
Taxation
Closings

Real Estate Applications

Investment

❏ Pre-tax cash flow

potential rental income	$50,000
- vacancy and collection loss	3,000
= effective rental income	47,000
+ other income	2,000
= gross operating income (GOI)	49,000
- operating expenses	20,000
- reserves	3,000
= net operating income (NOI)	26,000
- debt service	15,000
= pre-tax cash flow	11,000

Real Estate Mathematics

Basic Formulas and Functions

Real Estate Applications
Legal descriptions
Listing agreements
Contracts for sale
Appraisal
Finance
Investment
Taxation
Closings

Real Estate Applications

Investment

❏ Tax Liability

Formula and example

net operating income (NOI)	26,000
+ reserves	3,000
- interest expense	15,000
- cost recovery expense	5,000
= taxable income	9,000
x tax rate (28%)	
= tax liability	2,520

Real Estate Mathematics

Basic Formulas and Functions

Real Estate Applications
Legal descriptions
Listing agreements
Contracts for sale
Appraisal
Finance
Investment
Taxation
Closings

Real Estate Applications

Investment

❏ Annual depreciation calculation

Calculation steps:

(1) identify improvements-to-land ratio

(2) identify value of improvements:

(ratio x property price)

(3) Identify annual depreciation:

(value of improvements ÷ total depreciation term)

Real Estate Mathematics

Basic Formulas and Functions

Real Estate Applications
Legal descriptions
Listing agreements
Contracts for sale
Appraisal
Finance
Investment
Taxation
Closings

Real Estate Applications

Investment

❏ Annual depreciation calculation

Calculation example: property value = $400,000; 75% of value is improvements; depreciation term = 39 years

(1) improvements-to-land ratio: 75% - 25%

(2 value of improvements:

(75% x $400,000) = $300,000

(3) annual depreciation:

($300,000 ÷ 39) = $1,923

Real Estate Mathematics

Basic Formulas and Functions

Real Estate Applications
Legal descriptions
Listing agreements
Contracts for sale
Appraisal
Finance
Investment
Taxation
Closings

Real Estate Applications

Investment

❏ Capital gain formula and example

Selling price of property	$300,000
- Selling costs	24,000
= Amount realized (ending basis)	$276,000
Beginning basis of property	$250,000
+ Capital improvements	10,000
- Total depreciation expense	0
= Adjusted basis of property	260,000
Amount realized (ending basis)	$276,000
- Adjusted basis of property	260,000
= Capital gain	$ 16,000

Real Estate Mathematics

Basic Formulas and Functions

Real Estate Applications
Legal descriptions
Listing agreements
Contracts for sale
Appraisal
Finance
Investment
Taxation
Closings

Real Estate Applications

Investment

❏ Investment return ratios: assume $200,000 property; $50 K down; $150K interest-only loan; $8,000 cash flow; $30,000 appreciation

- **Return on investment**
  - NOI ÷ price
  - $20,000 ÷ $200,000 = 10%
- **Cash-on-Cash return**
  - Cash flow ÷ cash invested
  - $8,000 ÷ $50, 000 = 16%
- **Return on equity**
  - Cash flow ÷ equity
  - $8,000 ÷ $80,000 = 10%

Slide 1

Real Estate Mathematics

Basic Formulas and Functions

Real Estate Applications
Legal descriptions
Listing agreements
Contracts for sale
Appraisal
Finance
Investment
Taxation
Closings

Real Estate Applications

Taxation

❑ Tax rate calculation

- Formula
    o Tax rate (millage) =
       (tax requirement ÷ tax base)

- **Example:** tax required from municipal budget: $10 M; tax base after exemptions = $300 M
    o Tax rate (millage) =
       $10M ÷ $300M = .0333, or 33.33 mils

Slide 2

Real Estate Mathematics

Basic Formulas and Functions

Real Estate Applications
Legal descriptions
Listing agreements
Contracts for sale
Appraisal
Finance
Investment
Taxation
Closings

Real Estate Applications

Taxation

❑ Homestead exemption calculation

- **Formula and example**

assessed value	$360,000
- homestead exemption	50,000
= taxable value	$310,000

Slide 3

Real Estate Mathematics

Basic Formulas and Functions

Real Estate Applications
Legal descriptions
Listing agreements
Contracts for sale
Appraisal
Finance
Investment
Taxation
Closings

Real Estate Applications

Taxation

❑ Property tax calculation

- Formula
    (1) taxable value of property x tax rate (mill rate) for each taxing authority
    (2) total tax = sum of all taxes
- **Example:** taxable value after exemptions = $400 K; rates as shown; property tax is:

School tax:	$400,000 x 10 mills	= $4,000
City tax:	400,000 x 4 mills	= 1,600
County tax:	400,000 x 3 mills	= 1,200
Total tax:		= $6,800

Slide 4

Real Estate Mathematics

Basic Formulas and Functions

Real Estate Applications
Legal descriptions
Listing agreements
Contracts for sale
Appraisal
Finance
Investment
Taxation
Closings

Real Estate Applications: Closings

❑ Prorations: 12-month/ 30-day method and 365-day method

- **Formulas and rules: both methods**
    (1) Identify daily amount of proration:
       12-month/ 30-day method: divide total proration amount by 12 for monthly; 360 or 30 for daily amounts
       365-day method: divide total by 365 or # days in month for monthly proration
    (2) Identify seller's # days
    (3) Seller's days x daily amt. = seller's share
    (4) (Total proration – seller's share) = buyer's share
    (5) Credit/debit buyer/seller accordingly

Slide 5

Real Estate Mathematics

Basic Formulas and Functions

Real Estate Applications
Legal descriptions
Listing agreements
Contracts for sale
Appraisal
Finance
Investment
Taxation
Closings

Real Estate Applications: Closings

❑ Prorations

- **Example data:** Closing is January 25; belongs to seller; monthly rent received = $2,400; taxes = $4,000, paid in arrears.
- **Rent proration: 365-day method**
    (1) Daily amount: $2,400/mo ÷ 31 days = $77.42 daily amt.
    (2) # Seller's days = 25
    (3) Seller's share = 25 x $77.42 = $1,935.50
    (5) Buyer's share = (2,400 – 1,935.50) = $464.50
    (6) Credit buyer, debit seller $464.50

Slide 6

Real Estate Mathematics

Basic Formulas and Functions

Real Estate Applications
Legal descriptions
Listing agreements
Contracts for sale
Appraisal
Finance
Investment
Taxation
Closings

Real Estate Applications: Closings

❑ Prorations

- **Example data:** Closing is Jan 25; belongs to seller; taxes = $2,000, paid in arrears.
- **Tax proration: 365-day method**
    (1) $4,000 ÷ 365 days = $10.96 daily amt.
    (2) Seller's days = 25
    (3) Seller's share = 25 x $10.96 = $274
    (5) Buyer's share = ($4,000 – 274) = $3,726
    (6) Credit buyer, debit seller $274